Third
Edition

COMPUTER
ETHICS

Deborah G. Johnson

Georgia Institute of Technology

PEARSON
Prentice
Hall

Pearson Education International

Once again for two people who make me smile,

Jesse E. Johnson

Rose M. Johnson

Editorial Director: Charlyse Jones-Owens
Senior Acquisition Editor: Ross Miller
Managing Editor: Jan Stephan
Project Liaison: Fran Russello
Project Manager: Publications Development Company of Texas
Prepress and Manufacturing Buyer: Sherry Lewis
Cover Art Director: Jayne Conte
Cover Designer: Bruce Kenselaar
Marketing Manager: Don Allmon

This book was set in 9.5/12 New Baskerville by Publications Development Company of
Texas and was printed and bound by R. R. Donnelley & Sons Company.

The cover was printed by Phoenix Color Corp.

© 2001, 1994, 1985 by Prentice-Hall, Inc.
A Division of Pearson Education
Upper Saddle River, New Jersey 07458

Printed in the United States of America

10 9 8 7 6 5 4 3 2 1

ISBN 0-13-124788-3

Pearson Education LTD.
Pearson Education Australia PTY, Limited
Pearson Education Singapore, Pte. Ltd
Pearson Education North Asia Ltd
Pearson Education Canada, Ltd.
Pearson Educación de Mexico, S.A. de C.V.
Pearson Education -- Japan
Pearson Education Malaysia, Pte. Ltd
Pearson Education, Upper Saddle River, New Jersey

CONTENTS

PREFACE

With the publication of the third edition of *Computer Ethics*, I am reminded of the day in 1984 when I received the page-proofs of the first edition. I had just returned home from the hospital after having given birth to my daughter. I had composed the book on an Osborne computer using a word processor—I think it was called WordStar—that has been obsolete for more than 10 years now. Today my daughter, now a teenager, is more comfortable with computers than I am. She spends a good deal of her day sitting in front of a computer screen chatting with friends, doing schoolwork, and exploring the Web. I composed this edition of the book on a laptop computer using a version of MS Word that automatically corrected my misspellings and grammar. And, of course, in writing this edition of the book, I frequently went to the Web to look for resources and check references. While I continue to be cautious in making grand pronouncements about the significance of these technological changes for the quality and character of human lives, the changes that have taken place in these 16 years are awe-inspiring.

As I began writing this edition, it was strikingly clear that my primary task was to address the technological changes that have occurred since the second edition, especially the growth and penetration of the Internet into so many domains of life. What are we to make of Web sites, cookies, data mining tools, customized online services, and e-commerce? I have addressed many of these new issues while at the same time holding on to what I continue to believe are the core issues in computer ethics: professional ethics, privacy, property, accountability, and social implications and values. Indeed, you will see that in Chapter 1, I continue to struggle with the question at the heart of the field, what is computer ethics? Are the ethical issues surrounding computers unique? What is the connection between ethics and technology?

Contemplating the connection between technology and ethics raises an interesting and important question: Does the field of computer ethics simply follow the development of computer technology? Should computer ethicists simply react to technological developments? Wouldn't it be better if the sequence were reversed so that technological development followed ethics? Historically, the field of computer ethics has been reactive to the technology. As I explain in Chapter 1, new technological developments create new possibilities and the new possibilities need to be evaluated. As in the last edition, I build on the idea in Jim Moor's seminal piece "What Is Computer Ethics?" (1985) that new technologies create policy vacuums. The task of computer ethics, he argues, is to fill these policy vacuums. In a sense, the ethical issues *are* the policy vacuums, and policy vacuums are created when there is a new development or use of computer technology.

On the other hand, I want to suggest that it would be better if at least some of the movement were in the other direction—technology following ethics. Suppose, that is, we lived in a world where ethicists (or anyone, for that matter) identified potentially unethical situations or arrangements or ethically better possibilities, and engineers and computer scientists went to work designing technologies to change or remedy or improve the situation. I can think of a few examples when this has occurred, but only a few. Arguably, privacy-enhancing technologies and anonymous re-mailers are cases in point. Perhaps freeware and shareware are also examples. For the most part, however, the ethical issues have followed, rather than led, the technology. Here in very broad brush-strokes is my understanding of the evolution of the field of computer ethics, especially in the United States.

HISTORICAL OVERVIEW

In the decades immediately following World War II, ethical concerns were raised about computers, though these concerns were only vaguely expressed and articulated. One of the most salient concerns was that computers threatened our notion of what it means to be human because computers could do the very thing that was considered unique to humans, rational thinking. There was much discussion of *artificial intelligence.* There was some fear (and fascination with the idea) that computers might take over decision making from humans. I am thinking here of the movie *2001* but the theme also ran through science fiction literature, for example, in Issac Asimov's short stories. Somewhat later, Jim Moor picked up on this theme and wrote an analytical article, "Are There Decisions That Computers Should Never Make?" (1979).

It could be argued that those very early concerns about computers were not exactly ethical in character. For example, no one explicitly argued that it was immoral to go forward with the development of computers because of the threat to our concept of human beings. And the science fiction literature did not suggest that it was immoral to turn over decision-making power to computers. Rather, the implicit argument seemed to be that there would be terrible consequences—possible catastrophes and degradation of human life—were decision making to be turned over to computers.

These concerns did not come from an effect arising from the use of computers; they arose from the mere idea of computers. The very idea of a technology that could think or do something very close to it was threatening to our understanding of what it means to be human.

Ironically, it could be argued that this idea, the idea that computers do what humans do, has turned out to be rich in its influence on human thinking about thinking, rather than a threat. The model of human thought that computers provide has spawned the thriving new field of cognitive science and changed a number of related disciplines. (See for example, Bynum and Moor, 1999.)

In the late 1970s, the ethical issues began to be more clearly articulated in the works of Joseph Weizenbaum (1979) and Abbe Mowshowitz (1976), and it was in this period that the Privacy Protection Commission did a major study of privacy. The issues that took shape in this period had to do with the threat of big government and large-scale organizations, the related threat to privacy, and concern about the dominance of instrumental rationality. In hindsight, the concern about big government and privacy followed the technology in that in those early days, computers were being used extensively to create and maintain huge databases, databases of a variety of kinds, but especially databases of personal information. Computers were also being used for large numerical calculations. The large-scale calculations were primarily (though not exclusively) for government activities such as weapons development, space travel, and the U.S. census.

The next major technological shift was the development of small computers (*microcomputers* and *personal computers*). Attention turned, for a time at least, to the democratizing aspects of computers. Quietly, at the same time, remote access had come on the scene, first as remote access to large mainframes, later as a web of telecommunications connections between small computers.

Attention turned to software and the ethical issues surrounding it. The development and spread of microcomputers brought computer technology visibly and powerfully into the consumer marketplace. Software was recognized as something with enormous market value, and hence, all the ethical issues having to do with property arose. Should software be owned? If so, how? Would current intellectual property law provide adequate protection? Along with property rights issues came issues of liability and responsibility. In the marketplace, if consumers buy and use computers and software, they want to be able to rely on these tools and when something goes wrong, they want to know who to blame or they want to be compensated for their losses.

During this period, the market in computer games took off and it was also during this period that more attention began to focus on hackers. On the one hand, hackers were responding to the commercialization of computing. They did not like the idea of property rights in software. At the same time, those who were acquiring property rights and/or making a business of computing saw the threat posed by hackers, a threat to property rights and to system security.

In the 1990s, attention turned to the Internet. The coming together of computers, telecommunications, and media was the next major development in the technology. The development and expanded use of the Internet brought a seemingly endless set of ethical issues as the Internet came to be used in so many different ways in so many different domains of life. In effect, we are now in a process of transferring and re-creating much of the world into this new medium. At the same time, the Internet also raised all the concerns of the past. Privacy issues are exacerbated on the Internet; the democracy issue came back into play with new claims about the Internet's democratic character; property rights expanded to Web sites and global property rights became ever more important; and so on.

One other technological development that grew slowly during the 1980s and 1990s was the use of computer technology for a wide variety of visualization activities—not just computer graphics and gaming, but simulation activities including medical imagining and scientific models. This development expanded into the idea of virtual reality, an idea that has captivated many. Very quietly and slowly, ethical concerns have been raised about this thrust of computer technology. Unfortunately, I have been able to give only cursory attention to virtual reality issues.

In summary, during the 1960s and 1970s the dominant uses of the technology were for database creation and large-scale calculations. These uses of the technology brought correlated expressions of concern about centralization of power and big government, and threats to personal privacy. During this time, the very idea of computers seemed to threaten the idea of what it means to be human. During the 1980s, microcomputers were developed and made readily available. Remote access to large mainframe computers also became possible. Quietly, the system of telecommunication lines linking computers, that later became the Internet, was expanding and being made available beyond the "inner circle" of developers. Also, the computer/video game industry began to take off. With these developments came correlative concerns about property rights, liability issues, and the threat posed by hackers. In the 1990s, the coming together of telecommunications and computers reached a pinnacle of development and the Internet and the World Wide Web (Web) became widely available. These technological developments are still being assimilated, but they gave rise to a seemingly endless array of ethical issues as well as exacerbating those that were already there.

This is a story of computer ethical issues following technological developments. The question remains whether this pattern is as it should be. As I suggested before, reversing the order would seem to have some advantages, though scholars in the field of computer ethics do not seem to recognize the possibility of leading rather than following the technology. A central focus on the topic of design of computer technology would go a long way toward reversing this pattern. If the designers of technology were to think about the ethical and social implications of their designs before they became a reality, wouldn't the world be a better place!

CHANGES IN THE THIRD EDITION

Readers who are familiar with earlier editions of *Computer Ethics* will note that in this edition I have added two chapters specifically focused on the Internet, Chapter 4 "Ethics Online" and Chapter 8 "Social Implications and Social

Values." The addition of this new material led to other changes in the organization of the book. First, instead of having a separate chapter on crime, abuse, and hacker ethics, I have situated the discussion of hackers and hacker ethics in the first chapter on the Internet, Chapter 4. This placement recognizes that hacking is a phenomenon made possible by the combination of computers and telecommunications lines that we now call the Internet. In 1994 when the second edition was published, the Internet had already been created, but it was far from clear that it would become what it has. Second, instead of having one chapter on the social implications of computer and information technology and another on the social implications of the Internet, I have combined material on the social implications of computer technology from the second edition with new material on the Internet. While I discuss both, the primary focus of Chapter 8 is on the social implications of the Internet and especially its social implications for democracy. I found this approach useful for focusing discussion of the relationships between technology and social change and between values and technology.

As with previous editions, there are many possible paths a reader might take through the book. The topics from chapter to chapter are interconnected, but each chapter has been written to stand essentially alone. When used as a textbook, the path students take through the book should be determined by the type of students being taught, the length of the course, and other books and materials being used in the course. For example, when teaching a class of computer science majors, it is important that the chapter on professional ethics be read early on. This sets students up to think of the issues as part of their professional responsibility. When teaching nonmajors, this chapter can comfortably be read at the end of a course, and can be presented as a way of thinking about how some of the issues discussed in the book might be addressed—control who becomes a computer professional and give computer professionals more responsibility for the effects of their work.

As in the previous editions, I have started each chapter with a set of short scenarios. The scenarios are intended to entice the reader into the topic, to implicitly make the case for the importance of the topic, and to make the topic concrete for those who are impatient with theory. The cases also provide the content for teaching skills in ethical analysis. As before, I have provided study questions and suggested further reading at the end of each chapter.

OVERVIEW

Chapter 1: Introduction: Why Computer Ethics?

In Chapter 1, I make the case for the importance of computer ethics and I explore why computer and information technology raises ethical questions when many other technologies do not. Building on Moor's idea that the task of computer ethics is to fill policy vacuums, I describe generally how computer and information technology gives rise to ethical issues. I push further addressing how these issues can be resolved and explore the traditionalist account which specifies that we can extend ordinary moral principles to situations created by computer technology. This discussion prepares the way for asking in what ways computer ethical issues are unique and in what ways not. As in the last edition, I argue that it is useful to think of the ethical issues surrounding computer and information technology as new species of generic moral issues. I support this idea by arguing that while ethics is always about human action, technology *instruments* human action and technology makes it possible for individuals and institutions to behave in ways they couldn't behave without technology. Traditional ethics and ethical theories have largely ignored the instrumentation of human action. Computer ethics brings this unexplored area of ethics into focus. I conclude this chapter with a brief discussion of the virtues and dangers of using analogies in analyzing computer ethical issues.

Chapter 2: Philosophical Ethics

This chapter is largely as it was in the second edition though I have added brief descriptions of virtue ethics and John Rawls' theory of justice. As before, the aim of this chapter is to show that ethics is not just a subjective and relativistic enterprise. The aim is to show that ethics and ethical analysis involves giving reasons and making arguments for one's claims and subjecting those reasons and arguments to critical evaluation. By reviewing traditional ethical theories, the chapter provides readers with a useful vocabulary and conceptual tools for thinking through ethical issues. The chapter is not intended to provide *the* theoretical framework from which answers to all ethical questions can be deduced. Rather, the aim of this chapter is to suggest that ethical analysis is a dialectic process.

Chapter 3: Professional Ethics

The organization of this chapter and the ideas explored are fundamentally the same as in the last edition of *Computer Ethics* though I have tried to clarify the ideas further, and I have updated the chapter by addressing the issue of licensing of software engineers. I have also recognized recent changes to the ACM code of ethics. The chapter begins with a discussion of how becoming a member of a profession can lead to somewhat special moral rights and responsibilities. That analysis sets the scene for defining *profession* and *professional,* and for asking whether computing is a *profession.* This is followed by a brief discussion of software engineering licensing. The focus of the chapter then turns to the responsibilities of computer professionals, to employers, to clients, to the public, and to co-professionals, and how they come into conflict. The chapter ends with a brief discussion of professional codes of ethics.

Chapter 4: Ethics and the Internet: Ethics Online

I begin this chapter by identifying what is morally significant and distinct about the Internet. Focusing on the Internet as a medium of communication, what seems morally significant is the many-to-many global scope of the Internet, the availability of a certain kind of anonymity, and the reproducibility of the medium. After drawing out the implications of these features, emphasizing the difficulties of accountability and trust, I move on to discuss hacking and hacker ethics. Here I have included some of the material from the previous edition. I conclude the chapter with a discussion of the problems the Internet seems to pose for controlling socially undesirable behavior and for encouraging civil behavior.

Chapter 5: Privacy

Chapter 5 is a combination of old and new material. As in the previous edition, I begin by asking how computer and information technology has changed the collection and distribution of personal information. I describe the traditional way in which the privacy issue has been framed—as necessarily involving a trade-off between individual interests in controlling information *and* the efficiency and improved decision making of those who can make use of the information. I argue for reframing the issue in a way that recognizes personal privacy not just as an individual good but as a social good, and I try to make clear the importance of privacy for democracy. I conclude the chapter by discussing a variety of possible approaches to improving the protection of personal privacy.

Chapter 6: Property

In the years since I wrote the first edition of *Computer Ethics,* the property rights issues have gotten more and more complicated. While there is dissatisfaction with current law, in fact, the law has not changed fundamentally. I have come to the conclusion that the most useful approach for an introductory text of this kind is to stay with the fundamentals. Thus, this chapter is very similar to the property rights chapter in the second edition. I begin by describing the problem that ownership of software poses. I describe copyright, trade secrecy, and patent law and the inadequacies each has for protecting computer software. Digging deeper into the problem, I explore the philosophical basis for property rights looking first at the natural rights arguments and then at the utilitarian arguments for and against ownership. I conclude with an argument similar to the one I made in the second edition: Making an illegal copy of proprietary software is immoral because it is illegal. While it is immoral because it is illegal, there are other kinds of immorality that would be immoral even if they were legal. I conclude with a brief discussion of how the Internet is likely to exacerbate property rights issues.

Chapter 7: Accountability

Chapter 7 begins with scenarios that pose a wide range of accountability issues: responsibility for rape in a virtual reality game, accountability when software recommends a decision, liability of Internet Service Providers, and responsibility for the Y2K problem. A discussion of the different meaning and uses of terms such as responsibility, accountability, liability, and blame lays the groundwork for the chapter. The focus then turns to the legal environment for the buying and selling of computer and information technology where the distinction between selling a product and providing a service is pivotal. The remainder of the chapter is devoted to issues that are unique to computer and information technology, especially the diffusion of accountability, the Y2K problem, and Internet issues.

Chapter 8: Ethics and the Internet II: Social Implications and Social Values

Chapter 8 is the second chapter devoted to the Internet. Drawing on material from the second edition, I begin this chapter with a general discussion of technology and social change and identify the pitfalls in asking questions such as, Is computer and information technology causing a social revolution? Is it changing things or reinforcing the status quo? Is technology good or bad? Attention is then focused on values embedded in computer and information technology. I emphasize how value-laden technology is. The chapter turns, then, to the Internet and democracy. I examine the arguments that are made to show that the Internet is a democratic technology and I critique these arguments.

Computer and information technology and especially the Internet have been implicated in the widening gap between haves and have-nots within countries and among countries of the world. After examining this issue which has come to be known as "the digital divide," I briefly discuss the gender gap in computing, and then I turn briefly to the value of freedom of expression. I conclude this chapter by pointing to three issues that will be particularly important to watch in the future: jurisdiction, systems of trust, and insularity.

Practical Ethics

Finally it may be helpful to explain what I have and have not tried to do with regard to ethical theory. I have *not* aimed to provide "the" ethical theory from which all ethical beliefs should be derived. Nor have I tried to provide the only possible or adequate ethical analysis of any particular issue. There are both pedagogical and theoretical reasons for taking this stance.

Pedagogically, I believe it is essential for students and other readers to struggle with the cases, the issues, and the relevant moral concepts and theories.

This is crucial to developing skill at ethical analysis and critical thinking, and to developing moral personhood. Hence, it would be somewhat counterproductive to present (what I claim to be) "the" final answers to all the ethical questions raised in this book. Instead I have left a good deal of room for further struggle with the issues. I have tried to present ethics as an ongoing, dialectic enterprise. My analyses are intended to move the discussion forward but not to end it.

Moreover, this book is an undertaking in practical ethics, and practical ethics is the middle ground where abstract ethical theories and concepts meet real-world problems and decisions. It takes an enormous amount of work to understand what theories mean for real-world situations, issues, and decisions, and in some sense, we don't understand theories until we understand what they imply about real-world situations. Practical ethics is best understood as the domain in which there is negotiation between theory and real-world situations. We draw on moral concepts and theories but we must interpret them and draw out their implications for the issues at hand. In practical ethics, we work both ways, from theory to context and from context to theory. Often a theory or several theories provide illumination on a practical matter; other times, struggle with the practical problem leads to new insight into a theory.

TERMINOLOGY

As in earlier editions, I use *ethics* and *morality* interchangeably. Many philosophers draw a distinction between the two, but I find such distinctions too far from conventional usage to be of help.

Since the publication of the previous edition, linguistic conventions around computer technology have changed. Computers have come to be understood as more than simply computational—computing—machines. Moreover, there are a wide variety of computer-related tools for which it may or may not be appropriate to use the term *computer*. It was difficult to decide what terminology to adopt to refer to the technology on which this book focuses—information technology (IT), communication technology, information and communication technology (ICT), and so on. Indeed, it was tempting to change the name of the book to something like *Information Ethics* or *IT Ethics,* but, in the end, I have concluded that it is best to keep the name of the book the same, if for no other reason than that it is a known product. Wherever possible I use the (cumbersome) phrase computer and information technology rather than just computer technology. This more closely reflects current linguistic practice and understanding of the technology. In fact, the focus of the book may more accurately be described as a focus on a family of technologies that deal with a very wide variety of types of information (signals, data, images, words, etc.).

ACKNOWLEDGMENTS

A number of people helped me with this edition by reading chapters and providing comments and suggestions. I particularly want to thank Keith Miller, Fran Grodzinsky, Roberta Berry, Don Gotterbarn, Andy Ward, and Amy Bruckman for their feedback on various chapters. Marc Pang Quek was a wonderful graduate research assistant and wrote several scenarios based on real cases.

I owe much to many others who have helped me in a wide variety of ways. Scholarship is a collective enterprise. I have learned from reading the ideas of others, from listening and talking to students and colleagues. I am always encouraged by those who are willing to tell me what they like and don't like about my writing.

I will always be grateful to my colleagues in the Department of Science and Technology Studies at Rensselaer Polytechnic Institute. My years there shaped my thinking and my career in profound and permanent ways. In 1998, I moved to the School of Public Policy at Georgia Institute of Technology and I have been delighted to find another robust and lively interdisciplinary environment. My new colleagues and students in public policy and in other units of the Ivan Allen College at Georgia Tech have already enriched my thinking.

In writing this edition, I drew on several of my previously published articles. "Ethics Online" published in *Communications of the ACM,* a chapter entitled "Democratic Values" in Duncan Langford's book *Ethics and the Internet,* and "Is the GII a Democratic Technology?" presented at several conferences and then published in *Computers and Society.* I developed Chapter 1 from an unpublished paper that I wrote for the Tangled Web conference.

As I was completing a draft of this edition, Keith Miller, Laurie King, Tracy Camp, and I received a grant from the National Science Foundation's Program on Course, Curriculum and Laboratory Improvement, to develop materials and hold workshops focused on using the Web to teach computer ethics. The first workshop took place in June of 2000. During the workshop I received extremely valuable feedback on a draft of the book. Materials developed as part of the grant are available at: www.uis.edu/~miller/dolce/ and may be useful to teachers who use this book in their courses.

DEBORAH G. JOHNSON

CHAPTER **1**

Introduction: Why Computer Ethics?

SCENARIO 1.1 Should I copy proprietary software?

Since John graduated from college, five years ago, he has been investing small amounts of money in the stock market. A year ago, he discovered an extremely useful software package that helps individual investors choose penny stocks. (Penny stocks are stocks of small companies that sell for a few dollars or less per share.) The software requires users to input information about their attitudes toward risk as well as the names of penny stock companies in which they are interested. The software provides a wide range of information and allows the user to analyze stocks in many different ways. It also recommends strategies given the user's attitudes toward risk, age, size of investment, and so on.

John has several friends who invest in stocks, and one of his friends, Mary, has been getting more and more interested in penny stocks. At a party, they begin talking about investing in penny stocks and John tells Mary about the software package he uses. Mary asks if she can borrow the package to see what it is like.

John gives his disks and documentation to Mary. Mary finds the software extremely useful. She copies the software and documentation onto her computer. Then she gives the package back to John.

John and Mary were both vaguely aware that software is proprietary, but neither read the licensing agreement very carefully. Did John do anything wrong? If so, what? Why is it wrong? Did Mary do anything wrong? If so, what? Why is it wrong?

SCENARIO 1.2 Should my company make use of data mining technology?

Inga has worked hard all her life. Ten years ago, she started her own business selling computer software and hardware. In any given year now, 100,000 to 200,000 customers purchase things in her store. These purchases range from a $5 item to a $10,000 item. As part of doing business, the company gathers

1

information on customers. Sometimes information is gathered intentionally (e.g., when they distribute customer surveys to evaluate the service they are providing and find out their customer preferences). Other times, they gather information embedded in the purchase transaction (e.g., when they record name, address, what is purchased, date purchased).

Recently Inga has been reading about data mining tools. Data mining tools allow the user to input large quantities of information about individuals and then search for correlations and patterns. Inga realizes that she might be able to derive useful information about her customers. The records contain credit card numbers, checking account numbers, driver's license numbers, and so on, but to make use of this information, it would have to be "mined." The zip code alone is extremely valuable in that data mining tools might reveal a correlation between purchasing habits and zip code, and would allow Inga to target advertising more effectively. The correlation between zip codes and purchasing pattern might then be correlated with public records on voting patterns to identify what political sympathies customers in various zip codes have and to see how political affiliation is correlated with size of purchase. This could also be useful in targeting advertising.

Inga is conflicted about using data mining tools. On the one hand, her customers have given information in order to make a purchase and data mining would be using this information in a way that the customers had not anticipated. On the other hand, for the most part, the information would not identify individuals but rather groups of individuals with financial or attitudinal patterns.

Should Inga use data mining tools?

SCENARIO 1.3 Freedom of expression.

In December 1994, Jake Baker, a sophomore at the University of Michigan, posted three sexual fantasies on an Internet newsgroup "alt.sex.stories." The newsgroup was an electronic bulletin board whose contents were publicly available through the Internet. In one of these stories entitled "Pamela's Ordeal," Baker gave his fictional victim the name of a real student in one of his classes. The story describes graphically the torture, rape, and murder of Pamela, and ends with the woman being doused in gasoline and set afire while tied to a chair. In addition to publishing the fantasies on the newsgroup, Baker also exchanged e-mails with another man from Ontario, Arthur Gonda, discussing the sexual acts. In one of these e-mails, Baker said that "[j]ust thinking about it anymore doesn't do the trick . . . I need *to do it*." It should be noted that Gonda's true identity and whereabouts are unknown. The e-mails were private, and not available in any publicly accessible portion of the Internet.

A University of Michigan alumnus in Moscow spotted Baker's stories while browsing the newsgroup and alerted university officials. The campus police and the Federal Bureau of Investigation were then brought in to investigate the case. On February 9, 1995, Baker was arrested and was held in custody for 29 days. A month later, he was charged in a superceding indictment with five counts of transmitting interstate communication of a threat to injure another. The story on which the initial complaint was partially based, however, was not mentioned in the superceding indictment, which referred only to the e-mail exchanges between Gonda and Baker. The charges were dropped in June 1995, on grounds that Baker expressed no true threat of carrying out the acts.

Did Jake Baker do anything wrong? Should the police have arrested him?

This case was written by Marc Quek Pang based on the following sources: *United States v. Baker,* Criminal No. 95-80106, United States District Court for the Eastern District of Michigan, Southern Division, 890 F.Supp. 1375; U.S. Dist. (1995) (LEXIS 8977); 23 Media L. Rep. 2025 (June 21, 1995) decided (June 21, 1995) filed; Philip Elmer-Dewitt, "Snuff Porn on the Net," *Time Magazine,* February 20, 1995, p. 69; Peter H. Lewis, "An Internet Author of Sexually Violent Fiction Faces Charges," *New York Times,* (February 11, 1995), p. 7; other sources include local Michigan newspaper articles.

SCENARIO 1.4 What is my professional responsibility?

Milo Stein supervises new projects for a large software development firm. One of the teams he manages has been working on a new computer game for children in the 8 to 14 age group. It is an educational game that involves working through a maze of challenges and solving inferential reasoning problems. Players of the game get to choose which character they want to be and other characters appear throughout the game. The characters are primarily exaggerated macho guys and sexy women.

While Milo is attending a conference of computer professionals, he decides to attend a session focused on gender and minorities in computing. He listens to several papers focused on various aspects of this matter. One paper discusses the bias in software, especially in the design of children's software. Apparently, when software designers are asked to design games for children, they design games for boys (Huff and Cooper, 1987). The games are not, then, comfortable to female users. Milo also hears another paper about the small number of women and minorities who are majoring in computing in college despite there being a national crisis due to the shortage of technically trained people. The session ends with a panel discussion about what computer professionals can do to make computing more attractive to women and minorities.

When Milo returns to work after the conference, the leader of the team working on the new computer game reports that the game is ready for final testing before being released for marketing. Milo has never thought much about the composition of the team before, but he now realizes that the team consists only of men. Milo wonders if he should ask the team to rethink the game and have it reviewed for gender and/or racial bias. What should he do? Even if the game sells well, should a different message be sent with the game? What is his responsibility in this regard?

These scenarios pose a variety of types of ethical questions. The first raises a question for personal decision making and is inextricably tied to the law. Is it morally permissible for an individual to break the law by making a copy of proprietary software? If so, when is law breaking justified? When it's a bad law? When the law is easy to break? The second scenario also raises a question for individual decision making, but here the decision has to do with establishing a policy for a company. Inga has to decide what her company should do and this means taking into account what is good for the company—its bottom line, its employees, as well as what her responsibilities are to her customers. The third scenario poses an issue that could be addressed either as an individual matter (should I censor myself when I do things on the Internet) or as a public policy matter (should there be free expression online?). Finally, the fourth scenario raises a question of professional ethics. What Milo should do in the situation described is not just a matter of his individual values but has much to do with the profession of computing. That is, computer professionals have a collective responsibility to ensure that computing serves humanity well. Moreover, Milo's behavior will impact the reputation of computer professionals as well as his own and his employer's.

Taken together, the four scenarios illustrate the diverse character of ethical issues surrounding computer and information technology. Among other things, the ethical issues involve property rights, privacy, free speech, and professional ethics. The development and continuing evolution of computer and information technology has led to an endless sequence of ethical questions: Is personal privacy being eroded by the use of computer and information technology? Should computers be used to do anything they can? What aspects of information technology should be owned? Who is morally responsible for errors in software, especially those that have catastrophic effects? Will encryption technology make it impossible to detect criminal behavior? Will virtual reality technology lead to a populace addicted to fantasy worlds? These questions ultimately lead to deeper moral questions about what is good for human beings, what makes an action right and wrong, what is a just distribution of benefits and burdens, and so on.

While the scenarios at the beginning of the chapter illustrate the diversity of ethical issues surrounding computer and information technology, it should be noted that there is still a puzzle about why computer and information technology give rise to ethical questions. What is it about computer and information technology, and not bicycles, toasters, and light bulbs, that creates ethical issues and uncertainty about right and wrong, good and bad? This question and a set of related questions are contentious among computer ethicists. The controversy has focused especially on whether the ethical issues surrounding computer and information technology are unique. Are the issues so different from other ethical issues that they require a "new ethics," or are the ethical issues associated with computer and information technology simply old ethical issues in a new guise?

The uniqueness issue is intertwined with several other important and persistent questions. Why or how does computer and information technology give rise to ethical issues? Is a new field of study and/or separate academic courses needed to address the ethical issues surrounding computer and information technology? What does one "do" when one does computer ethics? That is, is there a special methodology required? The uniqueness issue seems to be at the core of all of these questions. Identification of something unique about computer technology holds the promise of explaining why computer technology, unlike other technologies, gives rise to ethical issues and why a special field of study and/or a special methodology may be needed. Of course, if computer and information technology is *not* unique, these issues will have to be resolved in some other way. I begin with the question why computer and information technology gives rise to ethical issues and proceed from there to a more detailed account of the uniqueness issue.

NEW POSSIBILITIES AND A VACUUM OF POLICIES

Computer and information technology is not the first (nor will it be the last) technology to raise moral concerns. Think of nuclear power and the atom bomb. New technologies seem to pose ethical issues when they create new possibilities for human action, both individual action and collective or institutional action. Should I donate my organs for transplantation? Should employers be allowed to use urine or blood tests to determine if employees are using drugs? Should we build intelligent highways that record automobile license plates and document when cars enter and leave the highway and how fast they go?

As these questions suggest, the new possibilities created by technology are not always good. Often they have a mixed value. New technologies bring benefits as well as new problems, as in the case of nuclear power and nuclear waste, automobiles and air pollution, aerosol cans and global warming.

Because new technological possibilities are not always good or purely good, they need to be evaluated—morally as well as in other ways (e.g., economically, environmentally). Evaluation can and should take place at each stage of a technology's development, and can and should result in shaping the technology so that its potential for good is better realized and negative effects are eliminated or minimized. Technical possibilities are sometimes rejected after evaluation, as in the case of biological weapons, nuclear power (no new nuclear power plant has been built in the United States for several decades), and various chemicals that deplete the amount of ozone in the atmosphere or cause other environmental problems.

So it is with computer and information technology. Enormous possibilities for individual and institutional behavior have been created. We could not have reached the moon without computers, nor could we have the kind of global communication systems we now have. Information technology used in medicine has enormously enhanced our ability to detect, diagnose, and treat illness. Information technology has created thriving new industries and facilitated a growing global economy. Nevertheless, computer and information technology creates potentially detrimental as well as beneficial possibilities. We now have a greater capacity to track and monitor individuals without their knowledge, to develop more heinous weapon systems, and to eliminate the need for human contact in many activities. The possibilities created by computer and information technology, like other technologies, need to be evaluated—morally and in other ways.

Extending the idea that computer and information technology creates new possibilities, James Moor (1985) has suggested that we think of the ethical questions surrounding computer and information technology as policy vacuums. Computer and information technology creates innumerable opportunities. This means that we are confronted with choices about whether and how to pursue these opportunities, and we find a vacuum of policies on how to make these choices. The central task of computer ethics, Moor argues, is to determine what we should do and what our policies should be. This includes consideration of both personal and social policies.

The sense in which there is a vacuum of policies surrounding computer and information technology can be illustrated, first, with examples from the early days of the technology. Consider the lack of rules regarding access to electronically stored data when computers were first developed. Initially there were no formal policies or laws prohibiting access to information stored on a mainframe computer. From our perspective today, it may seem obvious that computer files should be treated as private; however, since most early computing took place in business, government, and educational institutions, the privacy of files was not so obvious. That is, most paper files in these institutions were not considered the personal property of individual employees. Or, consider the lack of policies about the ownership of software when the first software was being written. It wasn't clear whether software should be considered private property at all. It was understood simply to be instructions for a machine.

Since the early days, computer technology has been far from stagnant, and with each new innovation or application, new policy vacuums have been created. Is it ethical for a company with a Web site to place a cookie on the hard drive of those who visit their site?[1] Is data mining morally acceptable? Are Internet domain names being distributed in a fair way? Should surgery be performed remotely with medical imaging technology? Who should be liable for inaccurate or slanderous information that appears on electronic bulletin boards? Should computer graphical recreations of incidents, such as automobile accidents, be allowed to be used in courtrooms? Is it right for an individual

---

[1] A cookie is a mechanism that allows a Web site to record your comings and goings, usually without your knowledge or consent. See www.epic.org/privacy/internet/cookies/ and www.cookiecentral.com.

to electronically reproduce and alter an artistic image that was originally created by someone else? New innovations, and the ethical questions surrounding them, continue to arise at an awe-inspiring pace. Policy vacuums continue to arise and are not always easy to fill.

FILLING THE VACUUM, CLARIFYING CONCEPTUAL MUDDLES

The fact that computer and information technology creates policy vacuums may make the task of computer ethics seem, at first glance, easy. All we have to do is develop and promulgate policies—fill the vacuums. If only it were so simple!

When it comes to figuring out what the policies should be, we find ourselves confronted with complex issues. We find conceptual muddles that make it difficult to figure out which way to go. And, as we begin to sort out the conceptual muddles, often we find a moral landscape that is fluid and sometimes politically controversial. Consider the case of free speech and the Internet. On the one hand, it takes some conceptual work to understand what the Internet is and it takes even more conceptual work to figure out whether it is an appropriate domain for free or controlled expression. Even if information on the Internet is recognized as a form of speech (expression), we are thrust into a complex legal and political environment in which speech is protected by the first amendment but a variety of exceptions are made depending on content, when and where the words are expressed, and so on. So, figuring out what norms or laws apply or should apply is not a simple matter. Can we distinguish different types of expression and protect them in different ways? Can we protect children while not diminishing adult expression and access?

The Traditionalist Account

How policy vacuums are filled is, in part at least, a matter of methodology. How can or should computer-ethical issues be resolved? On one account—call this the *traditionalist account*—all that is necessary is to take traditional moral norms and the principles on which they are based, and apply them to the new situations created by computer and information technology. For example, when it came to filling the policy vacuum with regard to ownership of computer software, lawyers and judges extended existent property law—copyright, patent, and trade secrecy—to the new "thing," computer software (more on this in Chapter 6). To use a more current example, when it comes to online communication, the traditionalist account suggests that we should look at the conventions that are already followed in face-to-face, telephone, and written communication, and "map" these conventions onto computer-mediated communication. Certain words and questions are considered impolite; certain kinds of conversations are considered confidential; and so on. According to the traditionalist account, we should take these conventions from precomputer communication and create similar, parallel conventions regarding computer-mediated communication.

The traditionalist account is important both as a descriptive and as a normative account. That is, it describes both how policy vacuums are often filled and recommends how policy vacuums ought to be filled. Descriptively the account captures what people often do when they are first introduced to computer and information technology. For example, when individuals first begin using e-mail, they probably imagine themselves writing letters or talking on the phone. Hence, they identify themselves when they make contact, without considering the possibilities of being anonymous or pseudononymous. The new communication device is treated as prior communication devices were treated, with norms being carried over from the old to the new. When you hear of someone accessing your computer files, you may think of the parallel with someone breaking into your house or office, and it seems clear that they have violated your property rights. So, the traditionalist account captures the idea that when we develop policies with regard to computer and information technology, we tend to draw on familiar social and moral norms, extending them to fit the new situation.

The traditionalist account is also normative in that it recommends how we should proceed in filling policy vacuums. It recommends that we make use of past experience. For example, we already know a good deal about property and the sorts of situations that are likely to arise when property claims come into conflict. Similarly, when it comes to communication, we already know that words can be harmful and can offend, and we know that individuals have an interest in some conversations being confidential. It makes good sense to draw on these experiences when it comes to a new situation, whether it is one created by computer and information technology or something else. So, the normative thrust of the traditionalist account seems important and valuable. We should take norms and principles from precomputer situations and see how they extend to the circumstances of a computerized environment.

Nevertheless, the traditionalist account has two serious problems. As a descriptive account of how the ethical issues associated with computer and information technology are addressed and resolved, it oversimplifies. And, as a normative account of how we should resolve these ethical issues, it has serious dangers. The traditionalist account over-simplifies the task of computer ethics insofar as it suggests that extending old norms to new situations is a somewhat mechanical or routine process. This hides the fact that the process is fluid and synthetic. When it comes to resolving the ethical issues surrounding computer and information technology, often the technology is not a fixed and determinate entity. That is, the technology is itself still "in the making" so to speak. So in trying to resolve an ethical issue arising from the use of computer and information technology, the first step is to clear up the conceptual muddles and uncertainties that are found. These conceptual muddles have to do with understanding what the technology is or should be and what sort of situations it creates.

I mentioned earlier the uncertainty surrounding how to think about the Internet as a forum for communication. This is a good example of the fluidity and uncertainty of technology. If we don't know what the Internet is exactly, we can't know which rules or principles should be applied.

Another example is computer software. A complex body of law regarding ownership of new inventions existed long before the invention of computers, including patent law, copyright, and trade secrecy. Applying this law to computer software, however, was enormously difficult because nothing with all the characteristics of software programs had existed before; so it was unclear how software programs should be conceptualized or categorized. Is a program the kind of thing that should be treated as property? Is a program the expression of an idea? If so, is it a form of intellectual property for which copyright law is appropriate? Or, is it (should it be seen as) a process for changing the internal structure of a computer? Or perhaps a program should be seen as a series of "mental steps," capable, in principle, of being thought through by a human, and not, thereby, appropriate for ownership. Before existent law or norms could be applied, a concept had to be fixed.

This is not to say that traditional legal or moral norms were irrelevant to the policy vacuum surrounding computer programs. On the contrary, there was a need to clear up the conceptual muddle so that the new entity could be seen in relation to familiar legal and moral norms. It is important to keep in mind that deciding whether computer programs are expressions of ideas or mental steps or design specifications for machines is not an issue with a predetermined right answer. Lawyers, judges, and policy makers had to decide what computer programs should be treated as, and in doing this, they, in a sense, *made* computer software what it is. Deciding that copyright law applied to software defined what software is. Later deciding that patent law applied to certain types of software also defined it. In Chapter 6, we will see that various aspects of new software creations persist in challenging traditional property norms. Filling policy vacuums is not a simple process of applying known laws and principles to entities that can be subsumed under them. A good deal of negotiation is required to get the technology and the law or principle to fit.

Our understanding of the Internet also illustrates the fluid rather than mechanical way that traditional norms and laws are extended to computer and information technology. Writers have had a good deal of fun trying to conceptualize the Internet. Some have conceptualized it as a network of highways, the superhighways of the future. Others have thought of it as a huge shopping mall with an almost infinite number of possible stores, and you navigate your way through the mall, perhaps discovering some places you do not want to go. Yet others have likened the Internet to Disneyland, suggesting that what you find on the Internet should always be treated as a fantasy world. These metaphorical renderings of the Internet are attempts to conceptualize the Internet in a way that will help us fill policy vacuums. Another good illustration of this fluid conceptual activity is the process of trying to understand the act of placing a cookie on the computer of a visitor to a Web site. Is it intrusive surveillance or business as usual? Are cookies comparable to a store asking for your zip code when you buy something, so that it can do marketing analysis and determine in what neighborhoods to advertise? Or is it more like installing a camera in a store to watch and see every customer that enters? Or is going from one Web site to the next more like traveling on a highway in which case cookies seem more like a surveillance technology. Or, since you may be sitting at home when you navigate on the Web, are cookies comparable to cameras in your home watching what you are reading? Needless to say, how we understand the activity makes all the difference in our evaluation of it and in determining what policies seem appropriate. Deciding how to conceptualize the activity and deciding which norms apply go hand in hand.

The traditionalist account is correct insofar as it suggests that in resolving the ethical issues surrounding computer and information technology, we often try to extend norms and principles from familiar situations to new situations. The account goes wrong, however, when it suggests that this process is simple, routine, or mechanical.

A second problem with the traditionalist account arises from its *recommendation* that we resolve the ethical issues involving computer and information technology by extending norms and laws from situations in which there is no technology or old technology. As already suggested, this is a worthy recommendation insofar as it recommends drawing on experience. The norms that are followed in many prevailing practices have survived the test of time. They often embody important social values such as respect for persons, fairness, and so on. Nevertheless, the recommendation has a danger that should be kept in mind. New technologies, as already mentioned, create *new* opportunities. If we simply extend old norms to new situations, we run the risk of missing the new opportunities. In other words, if we treat new situations as if they are comparable to known and familiar situations, we may fail to take advantage of the novel features of the new technology. To fill policy vacuums created by computer and information technology with traditional norms may prevent the creation of new ways of doing things.

Since we do not live in a perfect world, the opportunities created by computer and information technology are opportunities to change the way we do things *for the better.* Computer and information technology creates opportunities for new kinds of practices—new kinds of social arrangements, relationships, and institutions. Extending traditional norms and principles to the new possibilities runs the risk of reproducing undesirable practices or not improving on acceptable practices.

When computer programs were first being developed, many in the computing community saw the potential for software to be readily available to everyone, since programs could be copied without loss to the original developer. They also saw the potential for all kinds of information to be distributed cheaply and easily in the electronic medium. This was recognized to be an invention on the order of the printing press in importance but on an even grander scale. The debate about property rights and how to interpret and apply them to software is, in a sense, a debate about taking advantage of the special features of software to create a system of distribution that has never been possible before. Most recently, this debate is taking place around the distribution of music on the Internet.

To be fair to the traditionalist account, it need not be committed to adopting norms and policies that are identical to those that prevailed before computer and information technology. A traditionalist could take the position that traditional norms and principles must be modified when they are extended to new situations. In modifying their position in this way, the traditionalist moves somewhat away from recommending simply that we extend the old to the new. In this weaker version, there is the suggestion of something new being created in the process of extending old norms and principles.

The traditionalist account is a good starting place for understanding how the ethical issues surrounding computer and information technology are and should be resolved and how policy vacuums are and should be filled, but it has serious limitations. As a descriptive account, it does not capture all that is involved. Filling policy vacuums is not only a matter of mechanically applying traditional norms and principles. Conceptual muddles have to be cleared up, often a synthetic process in which normative decisions are invisibly made. Moreover, as a normative account, the traditionalist position runs the risk of not taking advantage of the new features of, and new opportunities created by, computer and information technology. Hence, we need to move beyond the traditionalist account.

COMPUTERS USED IN A SOCIAL CONTEXT

Clearing up the conceptual muddles and filling policy vacuums involves understanding the social context in which the technology is embedded. Computer and information technology is developed and used in a social context rich with moral, cultural, and political ideas. The technology is used in businesses, homes, criminal justice systems, educational institutions, medicine, science, government, and so on. In each one of these environments, there are human purposes and interests, institutional goals, social relationships, traditions, social conventions, regulations, and so on. All of these have an influence on how a new technology is understood and how policy vacuums are filled.

For example, by some measure of efficiency, it might be best for the United States, as a whole, to create one master database of information on individual citizens, with private and public agencies having access to appropriate segments of the database. There are, however, a variety of reasons why such an arrangement has not yet come about and is not likely to come about in the near future. These reasons include historically shaped social fears of powerful centralized government, beliefs about the inefficiency of centralized control, an already established information industry, a political environment favoring privatization, and so on.

Social context shapes the very character and direction of technological development. This is true at the macro level when we think about the development of computer and information technology over time. It is also true at the micro level when we focus on how specific applications are adopted and used at particular sites such as small businesses, college campuses, or government agencies. Imagine, for example, the process of automating criminal justice records in a local police station. The specifications of the system—who will have access to what, the kind of information that is stored and processed, the type of security, and so on—are likely to be determined by a wide variety of factors, including the unit's understanding of its mission and priorities, the existence of laws specifying the legal rights of citizens who are arrested and accused, the agency's budget, and the relationships the unit has with other criminal justice agencies.

One of the reasons the study of ethical issues surrounding computer and information technology is so fascinating is that in order to understand these issues, one has to understand the environments in which it is being used. In this respect, the study of computer ethics turns out be the study of human beings and society—our goals and values, our norms of behavior, the way we organize ourselves and assign rights and responsibilities. To understand the impact of computer and information technology in education or government, for example, we have to learn a good deal about what goes on and is intended to go on in these sectors. To figure out what the rules governing electronic communication should be in a particular environment, we have to explore the role of communication in whatever sector we are addressing. For example, because universities are educational institutions, they tend to promote free speech much more than would be tolerated in a business environment. And even in a university environment, attitudes toward free speech will vary from country to country.

The study of computer ethics may be seen as a window through which we view a society—its activities and ideals, the social, political, and economic forces at work. Perhaps the most important thing about computer and information technology is its malleability. It can be used to do almost anything that can be thought of in terms of a series of logical steps or operations, with input and output. Because of this malleability, computer and information technology can be used in a wide range of activities touching every aspect of human endeavor.

Computer and information technology can be used as much to keep things the same as to cause change. Indeed, as the traditionalist account suggests, when this technology enters a new environment, we tend, initially at least, to map the way we had been doing things onto the new computer system. The process of computerization often involves looking at the way people have been doing a particular task or set of tasks—bookkeeping, educating, manufacturing, communicating, and then computerizing those activities. Nevertheless, over time, these activities may be profoundly changed by the incorporation of new applications of computer and information technology.

It is important to recognize that while there may be a vacuum of policies with regard to computer and information technology, the technology is never used in a vacuum. Deciding what policies should reign in computerized environments, be they personal policies or policies for organizations, agencies, states, and countries requires understanding the social context in which the technology is used. This includes understanding the nature of the human relationships involved, institutional purposes and values, and prevailing norms of behavior. This social context is inextricably intertwined with the ethical issues that arise in that context. Policy vacuums cannot be filled without taking that social context into account.

MORAL AND LEGAL ISSUES

To say that computer ethical issues arise because there is a vacuum of policies leaves open whether the vacuum should be filled with *laws* or with something else. It is quite possible that some vacuums are better left to personal choices, institutional policies, or social conventions rather than to the imposition of law. It is also important to remember that this need not be an either/or matter. In a wide variety of cases, what seems to be needed is a multiplicity of approaches. For example, when it comes to proprietary software, intellectual property laws define what can and cannot be owned and how property rights are to be respected. Yet, corporations and government agencies supplement these laws with internal policies specifying what their employees can and cannot do in handling intellectual property. The internal policies interpret the law for the company or agency context, and tell employees how to address any vagueness in the law. As well, individuals will develop personal policies on the use of proprietary software (e.g., whether to obey the law or not, how to behave when the law is unclear).

Law is neither the beginning place nor the ending place when it comes to filling policy vacuums and addressing ethical issues. Ethical analysis precedes law when it is the basis for creation of a law. That is, our moral ideas often give rise to and shape the character of our laws. Think, for example, of minimum wage laws, of laws against racial and sexual discrimination, or of the way we have designed our criminal justice system to recognize the rights of the accused as well as the rights of the accuser. These aspects of our system of laws come from a shared sense of what is just and what is good. Criticisms of law and proposals for change in our laws are often based on a shared moral ideal that is not being achieved. In this regard, law is often not the final word. Think of the abortion debate or the debate about whether we should have compulsory or voluntary military service. These are issues that have been decided by legislation, even though individuals persist in having contrary moral opinions.

To say that computer ethics is needed to fill the vacuum of policies surrounding computer and information technology is not simply to say that we need laws. In some cases, we do need laws, while in other cases, we need personal policies or institutional policies or social conventions or several of these. In all cases, we need ethical analysis to help us understand and decide how to fill the policy vacuums.

ARE COMPUTER ETHICAL ISSUES UNIQUE?
FIRST ATTEMPTS

In trying to understand why computer and information technology raises ethical concerns and in what ways it does and does not change the environments in which it is used, the question of uniqueness inevitably arises. Are the ethical issues surrounding computer and information technology new? Are they unique? Or, are they the same old ethical issues that have engaged Western society for centuries?

In support of the idea that there is nothing unique about these issues is the old saying, "There's nothing new under the sun." Computer and information technology may well threaten privacy, but privacy issues have been around for ages, and they have often centered on new technologies. Consider concerns about the publication of photographs in newspapers, wiretapping, hidden cameras, and more recently urine, blood, and genetic testing. There have always been debates about privacy that involve who should have access to, and be able to use information about individuals. The same may be said about accountability and liability in computing. Computer and information technology challenges our traditional conception of responsibility and our system of accountability because it allows us to do many things remotely and anonymously, making it difficult to be identified or diffusing our sense of responsibility for the effects of our actions. However, this is not the first or only technology to disrupt traditional conceptions of responsibility. Nuclear weapons challenged our concept of responsibility insofar as they gave human beings the power to annihilate humanity. According to this argument, therefore, the ethical issues arising around computer and information technology are not unique.

To sort out this uniqueness issue, it is helpful to keep in mind a distinction between the uniqueness of the *technology* and the uniqueness of the *ethical issues*. The argument just described claims that none of the ethical issues surrounding computer and information technology fall outside the realm of ethics as traditionally conceived. It suggests, in other words, that we can categorize and discuss computer-ethical issues in familiar moral terms using traditional moral categories.

On the other hand, most of the arguments in favor of uniqueness seem to be focused on the uniqueness of *computer and information technology*. They suggest that since the technology is unique, the ethical issues must be unique. There are several provocative arguments worth mentioning.

First consider the argument that computer technology has brought about the creation of *new entities*—programs, software, microchips, Web sites, video games, and so on. These things never existed before. The activity of encoding information on silicon chips could not have been conceived of sixty years ago. The ethical issues surrounding computer and information technology are unique, then, insofar as they deal with things that have never been dealt with before.

Another uniqueness argument is that computer and information technology has changed the *scale* of many activities, arrangements, and operations. This includes the scale of data collection, calculations, and statistical analysis, as well as the scale of communication. When it comes to data collection, think of the billions of bits of information about individuals that can now be recorded and analyzed. Much of the information is transaction-generated information (TGI). As you move through your day, most of your activities can be recorded: what you buy with your credit card, where and what you eat, phone calls that you make, where you drive (if you pass through toll booths), what sites you go to on the Web. Information about individuals was gathered and stored before computer and information technology, but not to the extent possible today because of this new technology.

The increased *scale of calculations* has facilitated the creation of more sophisticated machines such as robots, spaceships, and medical imaging equipment. While each of these was possible, in some sense, before computer and information technology, they were not possible on the scale that is possible today. The increased scale means much more sophisticated equipment. Moreover, the increased scale of information processing and statistical analysis has meant *new kinds of knowledge*. Knowledge about the solar system, about weather, and the economy is available only because of the scale (including speed) of data processing in computer and information technology. Transaction-generated information is a new kind of knowledge as is traffic patterns on the Internet.

Another argument that might be made for uniqueness, also connected to increased scale, has to do with the *inherent unreliability* of computer and information technology. Here the argument is that because of the complexity and scale of calculations involved in computer and information systems, the technology cannot be built without some degree of unreliability. That is, since no single individual can understand and check every step in many computer systems, reliability is always an issue, much more so than with other technologies. Techniques for testing computer systems are continuously improving but, the argument goes, testing is very different from having an individual understand what is going on in a computer system. This calls for, some would argue, an entirely new way of thinking about risk, accountability, and liability.

Yet another argument on behalf of the uniqueness of computer-ethical issues might be made by focusing on the *power and pervasiveness* of the technology. Computer and information technology is changing the character of everything that we do. The transformation of our world that is taking place is comparable to that of the industrial revolution. When taken separately, each new application of the technology may not look unique, but when taken as a whole, the impact of computer and information technology has been utterly revolutionary and therefore unique.

These arguments for uniqueness are fascinating, but notice that each one emphasizes something about the technology—the entities and kinds of knowledge it creates, the scale of operations it makes possible, and its powerful effects. None of the arguments touches on ethics or the uniqueness of the ethical issues per se. There seems to be something of a mis-match between those who claim that computer-ethical issues are unique and those who argue that the issues are not unique. On the one side, the fact that all the issues touch some familiar moral notion or ethical principle is emphasized. On the other side, the fact that computer and information technology has features or has created entities and situations that were not possible before, is emphasized. We have to delve more deeply into the matter to sort out this mismatch.

ARE COMPUTER ETHICAL ISSUES UNIQUE?
A DEEPER ANALYSIS

It is helpful, in trying to get a handle on this issue, to clarify what is and is not in dispute. The uniqueness of computer and information technology is *not* in dispute. Computer and information technology is unique. While it has features in common with other technologies and while it may be thought of as an extension of earlier calculating machines, nothing with the power and capabilities of computer and information technology ever existed before. The claim that computer and information technology creates situations that never existed before is, also, *not* in dispute. Before this technology, it was not possible to launch computer viruses, to make images of internal human organs in the detail that is now possible, or to monitor, record, and analyze every second of an employee's activity as we can today. What *is* in dispute is whether this unique technology and the situations it creates pose unique ethical issues. Are the *ethical issues* surrounding computer and information technology special, unusual, or distinct in some way?

New Species of Traditional Moral Issues

The answer to this question seems to lie in putting together the kernel of truth on each side of this debate. I propose that we think of the ethical issues surrounding computer and information technology as *new species of general, or traditional moral issues*. The idea is that the ethical issues surrounding computer and information technology can be understood as variations of traditional ethical problems or issues. They involve familiar moral concepts such as privacy, harm, taking responsibility for the consequences of one's action, putting people at risk, and so on. At the same time, the presence of computer and information technology often means that the issue arises with a new twist—a new feature, a new possibility. The presence of this new feature or new possibility makes it difficult to draw on traditional moral concepts without some interpretation, modification, or qualification.

Once again, the ownership of computer programs in the early days of computing illustrates the point. Issues of ownership and property had been around for centuries, long before the advent of computer technology. However, never before computer technology had property rights issues arisen with regard to the cluster of characteristics distinctive of computer software. Before computers, it was inconceivable that a sequence of steps expressed as a series of ones and zeros could have value, let alone be considered a candidate for ownership. On the one hand, then, software ownership did not create a new type—in the sense of new "category"—of ethical issue. Property disputes were common and familiar. On the other hand, the issue was new in the sense that property in something with the features of software had never been addressed before.

In terms of uniqueness, then, the software ownership issue is not unique in the sense that it is an ownership issue and ownership is an old—familiar, standard—ethical issue. Th software ownership issue is unique, however, in the sense that it involves ownership of something that had never been a candidate for ownership before. Both of these points are captured in the idea of genus and species. The software ownership issue is a new and unusual species of a familiar ethical (and legal) genus of issues.

To put this in yet another way, we know that human beings often want to own and control that which has value. Computer programs have value in our society. This is neither new nor surprising. The only thing new here is that software has features that are distinct from other things that have been defined as property. Software has features that make it difficult (as discussed earlier) to mechanically apply current norms and laws. Whether or not and how various aspects of computer software should be owned poses a new species of a not-so-new ethical issue.

The genus-species account emphasizes the idea that the ethical issues surrounding computer and information technology are first and foremost ethical issues. This is an important point because ethical issues are always about human beings and what they do to one another. Ethics has to do with human interactions, human interests, human harm, and conflicts between human beings. An ethical issue arises when something that human beings value is at stake. It may be something as profound as a right to life or a right to be treated fairly, or it may be something as complicated as assigning liability in a way that will have good consequences. It may be a matter of deciding what the rules should be when it doesn't make a big difference whether it is rule A or B as long as there is a rule (e.g., which side of the road automobiles ride on).

Oddly, the connection between ethics and human interaction is sometimes missed by computer ethicists who are focused on the uniqueness of the technology. Maner (1998) for example, provides a set of examples of ethical issues surrounding computer and information technology that he considers weakly or strongly unique. However, his examples emphasize the uniqueness of the technology or technical arrangement, not the uniqueness of the human situation. One of his examples is the ethical argument for making computer technology available to the handicapped. Maner argues that computer technology is unique because of its general applicability and this generality leads to an obligation to make computer technology available to the handicapped. In other words, Maner argues that because computer technology has the potential to benefit the handicapped in a way that no other technology can, we have a unique obligation to provide computers to the handicapped. He writes:

> My point is that our obligation to provide universal accessibility to computer technology would not have arisen if computers were not universally adaptable. The generality of the obligation is in proportion to the generality of the machine. . . . Even if elevators did provide a comparable case, it would still be true that the availability of a totally malleable machine so transforms our obligations that this transformation itself deserves special study. (p. 145)

The case for making computer technology available to the handicapped may be strong, and I would not want to argue against it. However, Maner's claim is that there is something unique about the obligation to provide *computer technology* to the handicapped. He argues that this case is distinct from others on behalf of providing something to the handicapped. Maner seems to be confusing the uniqueness of the technology with the uniqueness of the moral situation. As an ethical argument, the argument is far from new. It appeals to a familiar moral obligation, an obligation to help those who are in need (i.e., to help those whose lives can be significantly improved with help). At a deeper level and more subtly, the argument appeals to the value of autonomy (i.e., to helping those who could, with our help and the help of computers, become more autonomous).

Maner suggests that the novelty of the argument lies in its inference from the generality (malleability) of computer technology and never before, he claims, has a technology of this kind been available. In other words, he seems to be saying that never before has humanity been in a situation to be able to so powerfully help the handicapped. I am not sure if this is true, but in any case, it illustrates the puzzle around uniqueness.

The puzzle seems to arise because the technology is unique, and since it is unique, an argument for making it accessible has features that other arguments lack. (Compare, for example, this argument with the argument for making public transportation available to the handicapped.) The argument is not unique insofar as it appeals to special features of a technology. There are good arguments for distribution of other technologies, not just to the handicapped but universally. Think of the good that would come from universal access to disease-preventing vaccines, life-saving medical technologies, or food, for that matter. In parallel to Maner's argument, one could argue that because of the enormous power of these things to do good, we have an obligation to make them available to those who will benefit from them.

Maner's argument illustrates the virtue of the genus/species account in allowing us to identify what is and is not unique about the ethical issues surrounding computer and information technology. His argument appealing to the generality of computer technology is a new species of moral arguments of the kind that appeal to an obligation to help people in need and who would benefit from access to something. This genus of argument connects the obligation to help those in need with the power and availability of a technology to help. The genus is not new; it is familiar. At the same time, Maner's argument is a species unlike any that has come before insofar as it appeals to the generality of computer technology, assuming nothing with the generality of computers ever existed before. It is a new version and a unique species of a familiar genus of arguments.

That the ethical issues associated with computer and information technology can all be categorized and analyzed using traditional ethical theories and concepts should not surprise us. We would not be able to recognize these issues as ethical issues unless they were connected in some way or another to our traditional ethical concepts such as harm, responsibility, privacy, and property. Imagine creatures from outer space suddenly appearing. They look somewhat similar to human beings; they walk and talk like us, but every once in a while they behave in strange ways. What would we think about this behavior? We would have no basis for claiming that it was immoral except if the behavior had characteristics that violated or conformed to our moral norms. If, for example, the behavior resulted in the death of a human being or if the behavior could be described as lying, then we would be inclined to call it immoral or bad. This may seem farfetched, but it isn't that off mark when one remembers (as discussed near the beginning of this chapter) that computer and information technology give human beings the capacity to do things they couldn't do before—visiting a Web site, launching a computer virus, anonymously engaging in role playing games with people thousands of miles away. These behaviors might be treated as morally neutral unless they connected in some way to a familiar moral concept such as harm or responsibility or privacy.

Instrumentation of Human Action

Why does computer and information technology create ethical issues? It changes the instrumentation of human action. The physical events that occur when an individual acts in a computerized environment are different from those that occur when an individual makes the same movements in an environment with no computers. When I write a paper by hand, the pencil moves over paper. When I write using a typewriter, levers and gears move. When I write using a computer, electronic impulses change configurations in microchips. In this example, the changes in physical events that take place when I write seem morally *in*significant. In all three cases I create words and a text. However, there are many cases in which the switch from no technology to technology, or from one technology to another changes not just the physical events constituting an action, but the moral character of the action.

As described earlier in this chapter, often what changes are the possibilities for action. A good example here is the act of launching a computer virus. Computer technology and the Internet have made it possible for an individual, sitting alone in a room, to move his or her fingers over a keyboard, pressing various keys, and with these simple movements, launch a virus that wreaks havoc in the lives of thousands of people. The technology has instrumented an action not possible (indeed, not even comprehensible) without it.

A world instrumented with computer and information technology has very different possibilities for human action than a world without it. Consider other illustrations. When a business automates its workplace, it acquires the ability to create and manipulate data in a way that would have been (practically) impossible before. In the new environment, employees who perform routine tasks also create records of their activities. When customers make purchases from an automated business, they no longer simply give cash in exchange for a product; they may simultaneously create an enduring record of their transaction, a record that can be combined with other records to create a profile of the customer. Hence, the act of purchasing something is potentially a very different act in a computerized environment than in a noncomputerized environment. Similarly, when speaking face to face, the default situation is that spoken words disappear after they are spoken (except insofar as they remain in the memory of those who have heard them). On the other hand, in communicating the same words to the same person in an e-mail exchange, the default position is that the words endure. Effort has to be made to remove the words from the system. So, actions or action-types are instrumented differently in computerized and noncomputerized environments, and the difference in instrumentation can have moral significance.

Consider yet other examples of how the change in instrumentation can have moral significance. Driving on an intelligent highway (one that records license plates as cars pass through toll booths) is different than driving on an ordinary highway; the difference is morally significant in that the intelligent highway has the potential to intrude on privacy. Buying a software package is morally different from buying a lawnmower in the sense that you can more easily violate property rights with software by making copies of the software. Communicating on the Internet is morally different from communicating face-to-face because of the potential for anonymity.

In some cases, computerization adds features to the situation while in other cases it seems more accurate to say that certain features of action are enhanced or constrained. In business transactions, for example, even without computer technology, a company could have created and retained records of all their sales, or they could have set up cameras to record every movement of their employees. To do so would have been difficult and costly, but would, nevertheless, have been possible. Computerization facilitates the capacity for recording and maintaining records of transactions and employee activities; it makes the recording cheap, instantaneous, and practically effortless. In this case it may be more accurate to say that a possibility has been facilitated or enhanced rather than created. Similarly, prior to the development of computer and information technology we had the ability to communicate with colleagues in other countries via mail or expensive telephone calls. The development of the Internet did not create a new possibility; rather, it enhanced and facilitated the possibility of international communication by making it more convenient and quicker.

Computer technology creates a new instrumentation for human action, both for individual action and for institutional arrangements. The new instrumentation changes the character of some actions and enhances and facilitates others. It creates the possibility of actions and arrangements that weren't possible before.

Ethical analysis has not traditionally or explicitly focused on the instrumentation of action. Rather, ethicists have emphasized ethical theory, leaving the details for practice and not recognizing that the instrumentation of action can have moral significance. Yet, ethical analysis always presupposes an instrumentation of action; it presupposes a physical world of a particular kind and human bodies with particular features. The ethical issues surrounding computer and information technology draw attention to this largely ignored aspect of ethics.

The character of the physical world in which humans act has continuously changed over time, often because of technology. Think of dams, plumbing, electricity, automobiles, and so on. One could argue that computer and information technology is just another step in a series of ongoing changes that have altered the instrumentation of human action. Airplanes, guns, bombs, and computers have all changed what human beings can do with movements of their bodies. These technologies have all changed the configuration of the physical world in which human beings act and live. They have all made it possible for human beings to perform actions not possible before (without) a given technology—firing guns, flying, giving and receiving organs, dropping bombs, and cloning. They have all facilitated and burdened various aspects of human action.

New possibilities and newly favored and disfavored features give rise to ethical issues because traditional moral concepts and norms presupposed a world instrumented in a different way. The new instrumentation gives rise to new species of general types of moral issues.

This account of the ethical issues surrounding computer and information technology, as new species of familiar moral issues, is meta-ethical. It is about how ethical issues are identified, classified, and then addressed. To say that the ethical issues surrounding computer and information technology are new species of familiar moral issues is not to say, however, that the new species always fit neatly into familiar categories. It is not uncommon for a new species to challenge traditional categories or straddle several categories. Sometimes, computer and information technology instrument human action in ways that seem to challenge our ordinary moral concepts or categories.

The ethical issues surrounding computer and information technology are not new in the sense that we have to create a new ethical theory or system. They call upon us to come to grips with new species. This means understanding the new issue in familiar moral terms, using traditional moral concepts. For the most part this is consistent with the traditionalist account because once connected to standard moral categories and concepts, the new issue can be addressed by extending familiar moral concepts to the new situation and drawing on our experience with other cases. However, the new species may not fit easily into standard categories and concepts; allowances for the special or new features of the new situation have to be taken into account. New species have special features and, as pointed out earlier, if we simply treat them as the same as other, familiar cases, we may fail to recognize how the new features change the situation in morally significant ways.

THE ROLE OF ANALOGY IN COMPUTER ETHICS

Analogical Reasoning Is Useful

Earlier I explained how policy vacuums surrounding computer and information technology can and should be filled by working through conceptual muddles and understanding the environment in which the technology is being used. One very useful way to do this is *reasoning by analogy*. Reasoning by analogy involves looking for familiar situations comparable to the one involving computer and information technology, and then either accepting the equivalence of certain actions, or identifying the significant differences between the cases.

Consider computer hacking. This activity will be discussed more extensively in Chapter 4, but for now let us consider a simple case. A hacker breaks into someone's computer and looks around at the various files. How are we to conceptualize this behavior? One way is to make an analogy with breaking into someone's office and then into their file cabinet. Is there a moral difference between the one act and the other? Certainly it is true that the physical movements required to get access to electronic files are quite different from those required to break into an office and into a file cabinet. Nevertheless, both actions involve obtaining access to information an individual has stored with the intention that others would not have access. In this respect the analogy seems to work. If we can't find any morally significant difference between the two cases, then we cannot (with consistency) claim that one type of behavior is morally permissible and the other is not.

Consider a slightly more complicated example of reasoning by analogy. Isn't going online and "playing around" by seeing just what systems or files you can get access to, comparable to walking down a street and testing the doors of every house on the street to see if they are locked? Suppose when you find a door unlocked (a file accessible), you go in and look around. You may not change or take anything from the house (file). You simply look at what the owner has put in her or his drawers (what she or he has stored in various files). Now, what, if anything, is different about these two cases? Is testing to see if you can get access to computer systems comparable to testing doors on houses, or is it different? From the point of view of the person who is being intruded upon, both types of actions may be felt to be intrusions of privacy and a violation of property rights. Whatever one says about the comparability or non-comparability of these cases, the analogy helps to focus attention on the character of the action at issue. Analogies help us to understand the human relationships and action types that are at issue. They help us to classify and connect behavior in computerized environments to familiar ethical notions and principles.

The hacker analogy can be carried a bit further. Am I partially responsible if someone enters my house after I forgot to lock my door? Alternatively, suppose the analogy is made to yards and gates. I left my gate unlocked and I have a swimming pool in my yard. The law generally recognizes that individuals have a responsibility to take measures to protect others from the dangers of their swimming pool. Many local statutes require that one build a fence around the pool. There are computer comparables here. Perhaps, we should expect individuals to take measures to protect their files, especially if they contain sensitive data. We could pass legislation to this effect, or through court cases set precedents that make the responsibilities of computer users clear, and diminish the responsibility of trespassers where owners have not made efforts to protect their files. The point here is that analogical thinking can often be helpful in sorting out an ethical issue arising around computer and information technology.

Analogical Reasoning Is Dangerous

While analogical reasoning can be useful in sorting out an ethical issue arising in a computerized environment, caution is, nevertheless, in order. Reasoning by analogy has some dangers which can only be avoided by fully developing the analogy. Analogies are useful because they allow us to draw upon situations or technologies with which we are familiar. They help us to see rules or principles that might be relevant in the computer situation. The danger is that we may be so taken with the similarities of the cases that we fail to recognize important differences. For example, in arguing about online break-ins and the dissemination of computer viruses, hackers sometimes put forth the argument that they are providing a service by identifying and revealing the flaws and vulnerabilities in computer systems, so that they can be fixed. Countering this argument, Eugene Spafford (1992) uses a powerful analogy. He suggests that the hacker's argument is comparable to arguing that it is morally permissible to set a fire in a shopping mall to show the flaws in the fire protection system. Launching a computer virus on the Internet has some parallels to starting a fire in a shopping mall but this analogy is so powerful that we might immediately jump to the conclusion that since one is wrong, the other must also be wrong. We should first ask whether there are any important differences. Some might argue that lighting a fire in a shopping mall puts individual lives at risk, while most computer viruses do not. Both actions cause property damage, but the damage done by most computer virus can be repaired more easily.

It is important to remember that while analogical reasoning can be extremely useful in understanding the ethical issues surrounding computer and information technology, it also has dangers. When reasoning by analogy it is important to identify the differences as well as the similarities between the computer and noncomputer cases.

CONCLUSION

A variety of ethical issues surrounding computer and information technology have now been introduced. We began with what might be thought of as meta-ethical questions. Why does computer and information technology create ethical issues? How can and should we understand and resolve ethical issues around computer and information technology. Ethical issues arising around computer and information technology arise in a social context and often they involve conceptual muddles. In analyzing computer ethical issues, we can and should draw on traditional moral concepts and theories, but in doing so, we should be careful not to miss new opportunities created by the technology. We should be aware that we are making the technology, not just discovering it. Computer and information technology creates new possibilities; it instruments human action in new ways. The ethical issues that are thereby created are not out of the realm of human understanding, but they have unique features with which we must come to grips. The issues are best understood as new species of generic moral issues.

STUDY QUESTIONS

1. Explain what it means to say that computer and information technology creates new possibilities for human behavior. Give examples.
2. How does computer and information technology create policy vacuums? Give examples.
3. What is the central task of computer ethics according to J. Moor?
4. Why are the policy vacuums arising from computer and information technology sometimes difficult to fill?

5. What is the traditionalist account? Explain it as a descriptive account of how computer ethics is done and as a normative account of how computer ethics should be done.

6. What are the limitations of the traditionalist account as a descriptive account? As a normative account?

7. Why is the social context in which computer and information technology is used so important to computer ethics?

8. Why isn't law sufficient to fill all the policy vacuums?

9. What aspects of computing and computers support the claim that computer ethical issues are unique?

10. Why isn't Maner's example of a unique ethical issue successful at illustrating uniqueness?

11. Explain the author's claim that computer ethical issues are new species of generic moral issues.

12. When human action is instrumented with computer and information technology how is human action changed?

13. What is analogical reasoning? What are the benefits and the dangers of using analogical reasoning in computer ethics.

SUGGESTED FURTHER READING

BAASE, SARA, *The Gift of Fire Social, Legal, and Ethical Issues in Computing* (Upper Saddle River, NJ: Prentice-Hall, 1997).

JOHNSON, DEBORAH G., and HELEN NISSENBAUM, eds., *Computer, Ethics, and Social Values* (Englewood Cliffs, NJ: Prentice-Hall, 1995).

SPINELLO, RICHARD, *Ethical Aspects of Information Technology* (Englewood Cliffs, NJ: Prentice-Hall, 1995).

TAVANI, HERMAN, "A Computer Ethics Bibliography," *Computers & Society SIGCASE Reader* (New York: AMC, 1996). Available: www.rivier.edu/faculty/htavani/biblio.htm

WEB SITES

www.2ncsu.edu:8010/eos/info/computer_ethics/
www.ethics.ubc.ca/resources/computer/pubs.html
www.ccsr.cse.dmu.ac.uk/contents/
www.wolfson.ox.ac.uk/~floridi/ie.htm

CHAPTER 2

Philosophical Ethics

Before embarking on analysis of the ethical issues surrounding computer and information technology, it will be helpful to discuss the nature of ethical analysis, and to become familiar with some traditional ethical concepts and theories. This chapter shows how ethical analysis can proceed so as to produce insight and better understanding. The chapter also explains concepts and theories that philosophers have found particularly useful in discussing ethical issues.

We often overhear or participate in discussions of ethical issues. Think, for example, of the heated discussions you have heard about government restrictions on individual freedom (e.g., censorship of the Internet, the right to assisted suicide). Or think of discussions about abortion, affirmative action, and the distribution of wealth in our society. Often when individuals are asked to explain why they think a behavior or policy is wrong, they have difficulty articulating their reasons. Sometimes it seems that individuals who are expressing moral opinions are simply reacting as they think most people in their society react or they espouse ideas they heard friends or relatives espouse. Many who have fairly strong moral beliefs have only a very vague sense of why the behavior or policy is unfair or irresponsible or harmful. These unexamined beliefs can be the starting place for ethical analysis, though it is important to understand that they are only starting places.

Discussions at this level may quickly end unresolved because the individuals involved are not able to provide good reasons for believing as they do. It is difficult or impossible to discuss the issues rationally, let alone resolve them. If discussion stays merely at the level of statements of belief, discussants will walk away thinking that everyone is entitled to his or her own opinion and there is no point talking about ethics, except perhaps to see where others stand. Discussants won't have learned anything or come to understand the ethical issues any better.

This book is an undertaking in philosophical analysis, and philosophical analysis proceeds on the premise that we must examine the reasons we have for our moral or ethical beliefs. In philosophical, ethical analysis the reasons for moral beliefs are articulated, and then critically evaluated. The reasons you give for holding an ethical belief or taking a position on an ethical issue can be thought of as an argument for a claim. The argument has to be "put on the table," and once there, it can be evaluated in terms of its plausibility, coherence, and consistency. Once stated, we can ascertain whether the argument does, indeed, support the claim being made or the position being taken.

This critical evaluation is often done in the context of trying to convince someone to reject a position, or to adopt another position, but it may also be done simply to explore a claim. When you critically evaluate the argument supporting a claim, you come to understand the claim more fully. A critical examination of the underpinnings of moral beliefs sometimes leads to a change in belief, but it may also simply lead to stronger and better understood beliefs.

In philosophical analysis, not only must you give reasons for your claims, you are also expected to be consistent from one argument or topic to the next. For example, instead of having separate, isolated views on abortion and capital punishment, philosophical analysis would lead you to recognize that both your views on abortion and your views on capital punishment rest on a claim about the value of human life and what abrogates it. Philosophical analysis would lead you to inquire whether the claim you made about the value of human life in the context of a discussion of capital punishment is consistent with the claim you made about the value of human life in the context of a discussion of abortion. If the claims appeared to be inconsistent from the one context to the next, then you would be expected to change one of your claims or provide an account of how the two positions can be understood as consistent. In other words, you would show that seemingly inconsistent views are in fact consistent.

Philosophical analysis is an ongoing process. It involves a variety of activities. It involves expressing a claim and putting forward an argument or reasons for the claim, and it involves critical examination of the argument. If the argument does not hold up to critical examination, then it might be reformulated into a revised argument, perhaps rejecting aspects of the original argument but holding on to a core idea. The revised argument, then, has to be critically examined, and so on, with ongoing reformulation and critique. Philosophers often refer to this process as a *dialectic* (which is related to the word *dialogue*). We pursue an argument to see where it goes and to find out what you would have to know or assert to defend the argument and establish it on a firm footing.

In addition to moving from claims to reasons and arguments, and from one formulation of an argument to another, better formulation, the dialectic also moves back and forth from cases to principles or theory. To illustrate, take the issue of euthanasia. Suppose you start out by making the claim that euthanasia is wrong. You articulate a principle as the reason for this claim. Say, the principle is that human life has the highest value and, therefore, human life should never be intentionally ended. You might then test this principle by seeing how it applies in a variety of euthanasia cases. For example, is it wrong to use euthanasia when the person is conscious but in extreme pain? When the person is unconscious and severally brain damaged? When the person is terminally ill? When the person is young or elderly? Since your principle concerns the value of human life, it has implications beyond the issue of euthanasia. Hence, you might also test it by applying it to completely different types of cases. Is the intentional taking of human life wrong when it is done in a war situation? Is intentional killing wrong when it comes to capital punishment? Given your position on these cases, you may want to qualify the principle or you may hold to the principle and change your mind about the cases. For example, after seeing how the principle applies in various cases, you may want to qualify it so that you now assert that one should never intentionally take a human life *except* in self-defense or *except* when taking a life will save another life. Or you might reformulate the principle so that it specifies that the value of human life has to do with its quality. When the quality of life is significantly and permanently diminished, while it is still not permissible to intentionally kill, it is morally permissible to let a person die.

The dialogue continues as the dialectic leads to a more and more precise specification of the principle and the argument. The process clarifies what is at issue and what the possible positions are. It moves from somewhat inchoate ideas to better and better arguments, and more defensible and better-articulated positions.

The dialectic (from an initial belief to an argument, from argument to better argument, and from theory to case, and back) does not always lead to definitive conclusions or unanimous agreement. Therefore, it is important to emphasize that understanding can be improved, progress can be made, even when one has not reached definitive conclusions. Through the dialectic we learn which arguments are weaker and stronger and why. We come to understand the ideas that underpin our moral beliefs. We develop deeper and more consistent beliefs and we come to understand how moral ideas are interrelated and interdependent.

As you will see in a moment, a familiarity with traditional ethical theories will help in articulating the reasons for many of your moral beliefs. Ethical theories provide frameworks in which arguments can be cast. Moreover, ethical theories provide some common ground for discussion. They establish a common vocabulary and frameworks within which, or against which, ideas can be articulated.

DISTINGUISHING DESCRIPTIVE AND NORMATIVE CLAIMS

In any discussion of ethics, it is important to recognize the distinction between descriptive and normative claims. In a sense and partly, this is the distinction between facts and values, but the matter of what counts as a fact is very contentious in philosophy. So, it will be better to stay with the terms descriptive and normative. *Descriptive* statements are statements that describe a state of affairs in the world. For example, "The car is in the driveway." And "Georgia is south of Tennessee." In addressing ethical issues and especially the ethical issues surrounding computer and information technology, it is quite common to hear seemingly factual statements about human beings. The following are descriptive statements: "Such and such percentage of the people surveyed admitted to having made at least one illegal copy of computer software." "The majority of individuals who access pornographic Web sites are males between the ages of 14 and 35." "Such and such percentage of U.S. citizens use the Internet to obtain information on political candidates." "In all human societies, there are some areas of life that are considered private." These statements describe what human beings think and do. They are *empirical* claims in the sense that they are statements that can be verified or proven false by examining the state of affairs described. To be sure, it may not be easy to verify or disconfirm claims like these, but in principle it is possible. Observations can be made, surveys can be administered, people can be asked, and so on.

Social scientists gather empirical data and report their findings, both on moral and nonmoral matters. When it comes to morality, psychologists and sociologists might do such things as identify the processes by which children develop moral concepts and sensibilities. Or they may measure how individuals value and prioritize various goods such as friendship, privacy, and autonomy. When anthropologists go to other cultures, they may describe complex moral rules in that culture. They are describing lived and observed moral systems. Similarly, historians may trace the development of a particular moral notion in an historical period.

All of these social scientific studies are descriptive studies of morality; they examine morality as an empirical phenomenon. They don't, however, tell us what is right and wrong. They don't tell us what people *should* think or do, only what people, in fact, think and do.

In contrast, philosophical ethics is *normative*. The task of philosophical ethics is to explore what human beings ought to do, or more accurately, to evaluate the arguments, reasons, and theories that are proffered to justify accounts of morality. Ethical theories are prescriptive. They try to provide an account of why certain types of behavior are good or bad, right or wrong. Descriptive statements may come into play in the dialectic about philosophical ethics, but normative issues cannot be resolved just by pointing to the facts about what people do or say or believe. For example, the fact (if it were true) that many individuals viewed copying proprietary software as morally acceptable would not make it so. The fact that individuals hold such a belief is not an argument for the claim that it is morally permissible to copy proprietary software. You might wish to explore why individuals believe this to see if they have good reasons for the belief. Or you might wish to find out what experiences have led individuals to draw this conclusion. Still, in the end, empirical facts are not alone sufficient to justify normative claims. Figuring out what is right and wrong, what is good and what is bad, involves more than a descriptive account of states of affairs in the world.

The aim of this book is *not* to describe how people behave when they use computers. For this, the reader should consult social scientists—sociologists, anthropologists, political scientists, and psychologists. Rather the aim of this book is to help you understand how people ought to behave when they use computers and what rules or policies ought to be adopted with regard to computer and information technology.

ETHICAL RELATIVISM

We can begin our examination of ethical concepts and theories by examining a prevalent, often unexamined moral belief. Many believe that "ethics is relative." This seems like a good starting place. This claim can be examined carefully and critically. We can begin by formulating the idea as a theory consisting of a set of claims backed by reasons.

The idea of ethical relativism seems to be something like this: "What is right for you may not be right for me," or "I can decide what is right for me, but you have to decide for yourself." When we take this idea and formulate it into a more systematic account, it seems to encompass a negative claim (something that it denies), and a positive claim, (something it asserts). The negative claim appears to be: "There are no universal moral norms." According to this claim, there isn't a single standard for all human beings. One person may decide that it is right for him to tell a lie in certain circumstances, another person may decide that it is wrong for her to tell a lie in exactly the same circumstances, and both people could be right. So, the claim that "right and wrong are relative" means in part that there are no universal rights and wrongs.

The positive claim of ethical relativism is more difficult to formulate. Sometimes ethical relativists seem to be asserting that right and wrong are relative to the individual, and sometimes they seem to assert that right and wrong are relative to the society in which one lives. I am going to focus on the latter version, and on this version the relativist claims that what is morally right for me, an American living in the twenty-first century, could be different than what is right for a person living, say, in Asia in the fifth century. The positive claim of relativism is that right and wrong are relative to your society.

Ethical relativists often cite a number of descriptive facts to support these claims:

1. They point to the fact that cultures vary a good deal in what they consider to be right and wrong. For example, in some societies, infanticide is acceptable while in other societies it is considered wrong. In some societies, it is considered wrong for women to go out in public without their faces being covered. Polygamy is permissible in some cultures; in others it is not. Examples of this kind abound.

2. Relativists also point to the fact that the moral norms of a given society change over time so that what was considered wrong at one time, in a given society, may be considered right at another time. Slavery in America is a good example of this since slavery was considered morally permissible by many in the United States at one time, but is now illegal and almost universally considered impermissible.

3. Relativists also point to what we know about how people develop their moral ideas. We are taught the difference between right and wrong as children, and what we come to believe is right or wrong is the result of our upbringing. It depends on when, where, how, and by whom we were raised. If I had been born in certain Middle Eastern countries, I might believe that it is wrong for a woman to appear in public without her face covered. Yet because I was raised in the

United States in the twentieth century, by parents who had Western ideas about gender roles and public behavior, I do not believe this. Of course, parents are not the only determinant of morality. A person develops moral ideas from the experiences he or she has in school, at work, with peers, and so on.

It is useful to note that we have already made progress simply by clearly and systematically formulating the idea of ethical relativism, an idea you may have entertained or heard expressed, but never had a chance to examine carefully. Moreover, we have been able to identify and articulate some reasons thought to support ethical relativism. With the idea and supporting evidence now "on the table," we can carefully and critically examine them.

The facts which ethical relativists point to cannot be denied. For example, I would not want to take issue with the claims that:

1. There is and always has been a good deal of diversity of belief about right and wrong.
2. Moral beliefs change over time within a given society.
3. Social environment plays an important role in shaping the moral ideas you have.

However, there does seem to be a problem with the connection between these facts and the claims of ethical relativism. Do these facts show that there are no universal moral rights or wrongs? Do they show that right and wrong are relative to your society?

On more careful examination, it appears that the facts cited by ethical relativists do not support their claims. To put this another way, we can, without contradiction, accept the facts and still deny ethical relativism. The facts do not necessitate that there are no universal moral standards or that ethics is relative. Lest there be no confusion, you should recognize that "ethics is relative" could be interpreted either as an empirical or a normative claim. As an empirical claim, it asserts that ethical beliefs vary; as a normative claim it asserts that right and wrong (not just beliefs about, but what is actually right and wrong) vary.

If we understand the claim "ethics is relative" to be a description of human behavior, then it *does* follow from the facts sited. Indeed, it is redundant of the facts cited, for as a description of human behavior, it merely repeats what the facts have said. Ethical beliefs vary. Individuals believe different things are right and wrong depending on how and by whom they have been raised and where and when they live.

On the other hand, if we understand "ethics is relative" to be a normative claim, a claim asserting the negative and/or positive parts of ethical relativism, then it is not redundant, and the facts do not support the claims. Here the leap from facts to conclusion is problematic for a number of reasons. For one, the argument goes from a set of "is" claims to an "ought" claim and the ought-claim just doesn't follow (in a straightforward way) from the is-claims.

The argument goes like this: "People do a; people do b; people do c; and therefore people ought to do x."

Moreover, the facts are compatible with the opposite conclusion. That is, it is possible that a universal moral code applies to everyone even though some or all fail to recognize it. Centuries ago when some people believed the earth was flat and others claimed that it was round, the earth's shape was not relative. The fact that there is diversity of opinion on right and wrong does not tell us anything about whether right and wrong are relative. The facts are compatible both with the claim that there is no universal right and wrong and with the claim that there is a universal right and wrong.

Taking this one step further, let's consider the fact that our moral beliefs are shaped by our social environment. While it is true that our moral beliefs are shaped by our social environment, this says nothing about the rightness or wrongness of what we believe. Racism and sexism are good examples of moral attitudes we may acquire from our environment but which turn out on reflection to be unjustifiable (bad) ideas.

We must also be careful about what is inferred from the fact that there is diversity in moral beliefs. This diversity may be misleading; that is, it may be superficial rather than deep. Relativists seem to be focusing on specific practices and there is still the possibility that universal norms underlie these. Moral principles such as "never intentionally harm another person" or "always respect human beings as ends in themselves" are of such generality that they could be operative in many or all cultures but expressed in different ways. What is meant by "harm," "respect," and "human being" may vary although there is some principle to which all people adhere. So, it is possible that there are some universal principles at work, but they are hidden from sight due to the diversity of expression or interpretation of the principle.

Social scientists have certainly tried to find patterns within the apparent diversity. Some have asserted, for example, that all cultures have prohibitions on incest or, more recently, that while there is a great deal of diversity about what is considered private, all cultures consider some aspect of the lives of individuals private.

Even so, while such patterns have important implications for the study of ethics, we have to remember that establishing patterns across cultures is descriptive, and it is another matter to determine what these claims imply about how people ought to behave. In a moment, when we examine utilitarianism, we will see an example of a very general normative principle that is compatible with a diversity of practices. Utilitarianism is a form of consequentialism, and such theories assert that individuals should always do what will maximize good consequences. Individuals in quite different situations may be doing very different things but all in accordance with this same principle.

In any case, the facts pointed to by relativists do not support their claim that there are no universal moral rights and wrongs. Nor do the facts cited support the ethical relativist's claim that right and wrong are relative to one's society. Pointing to what people believe to be right and wrong tells us nothing about what is right or wrong. The fact that people behave in accordance with the norms of their society is not evidence for the claim that they ought to.

It is important to keep in mind that the criticism I have just made of the ethical relativist's argument does not establish that there are universal rights and wrongs. The criticisms show only that the arguments ethical relativists might put forward to support their position do not work. You may be able to come up with a different argument on behalf of ethical relativism, and then your argument would have to be carefully and critically examined.

Before you try to defend ethical relativism, however, there are some serious problems with the theory and you ought to be aware of these. Ethical relativism, as I have formulated it, appears to be self-contradictory. The negative and positive claims appear to contradict each other. In saying that right and wrong are relative to one's society, ethical relativists seem to be asserting that one is bound by the rules of their society. The relativist seems to be saying that what is right for me is defined by my society, and what is right for a member of an African tribe is what is set by the standards of her or his tribe. It would seem, then, that I ought to do what is considered right in my society, and everyone else ought to do what is considered right in their society. Notice, however, that if this is what ethical relativists mean, they are affirming a universal moral principle. On the one hand, they deny that there are universal rights and wrongs, and, on the other hand, they assert one. If I have accurately depicted ethical relativism, then it appears to be an utterly incoherent (self-contradictory) theory.

If this were a book about ethical relativism alone, I would try to resurrect the theory by reformulating its claims and bringing in other arguments to support it. All I will do instead is to point to what I think is an important moral motive buried in relativism. Often what ethical relativists are trying to do is make the point that no one should denigrate, ridicule, and disrespect people who have beliefs that are different from their own. In other words, you shouldn't judge people from other times or places by the standards of your own morality. It is arrogant, relativists might say, to believe that you as an individual or a member of a particular society have the correct moral views and that anyone who doesn't agree with you is wrong. Such relativists would argue that we ought to respect people with moral beliefs different from our own.

This seems an important and worthy point that some relativists want to make. Still, it should be noted that to take this position is, again, to take a universal position. You are claiming that "everyone ought" to adopt a position which might be characterized as tolerance or respect for others.

So, it would seem that we cannot assert both that everyone ought to respect the views of others and at the same time hold that ethics is relative. If toleration is the motive behind relativism, this motive has an implicit universal character and that conflicts with relativism's claim that there is no universal right and wrong. To see the contradiction, consider the case of someone who lives in a society that does not believe in toleration. According to relativism, this person need not be tolerant of others. Relativism says right and wrong is relative to your society and in this person's society there is nothing wrong with being intolerant. Thus, it would seem that if underlying one's belief in relativism is the belief that everyone should be tolerant of the beliefs of others, relativism is not going to be an acceptable theory, at least not if it is formulated as I have formulated it.

Case Illustration

To see these and other problems with ethical relativism, consider a hypothetical case. Suppose, by a distortion of history, that computers were developed to their present sophistication in the late 1930s and early 1940s. World War II is in progress. You are a German citizen working for a large computer company. You are in charge of the sales division and you personally handle all large orders. You are contacted by representatives of the German government. The German government has not yet fully automated its operations (computers are still relatively new) and it wants now to purchase several large computers and several hundred smaller computers to be networked.

You read the newspapers and know how the war is proceeding so you have a pretty good idea of how the German government will use the computers. It is quite likely they will use the computers to help keep track of their troops and equipment, to identify Jews and monitor their activities, to build more efficient gas chambers, and so on. The question is, if you were an ethical relativist would it be permissible for you to sell the computers to Hitler and his government?

The question reveals some practical problems with relativism. Relativism specifies that what is right for you is what is considered right in your society. But, how do you figure out what the standards of your society are? Are the standards of your society what the political leaders say and do or what the majority in the society believe? If these are different, what should you do? To put this in another way, is Hitler necessarily abiding by the standards of his society or is he going against these? If he is going against these standards, then perhaps he is doing wrong and you would be doing wrong to support him. It may not be easy to tell whether Hitler is adhering to or rejecting the standards of his society. Hence, it may not be so easy to use relativism to guide your actions.

This leads to another problem with relativism. Suppose Hitler and most German citizens agree that Hitler's agenda is right. Nevertheless, you disagree. Relativism seems to rule out the possibility of resistance or rebellion in such a situation. If someone rebels against the standards of her society, it would seem she is doing wrong for she is acting against relativism's claim that what is right for you is what is considered right in your society. Many of our greatest heros, Socrates, Martin Luther King, Ghandi, even Jesus, would, on this account, be considered wrong or bad. They acted against the standards of their societies.

So, if Hitler and most Germans agreed that the German agenda was right, it would seem that you, as a relativist, would have to conclude that it is right for you to sell the computers to the German government (even if you personally objected to Hitler's agenda).

Now suppose that one of your friends from the United States or somewhere else finds out about the sale and asks you why you did this. What do you say? You answer: It was the right thing to do because it was consistent with the standards and beliefs in my society. From your friends perspective, this may seem a very feeble answer. The fact that some type of behavior is the standard in your society seems an inadequate moral reason for adopting the standard as your own. It doesn't seem a very good reason for acting in a certain way, especially when the act has significant negative consequences.

Summarizing what has been said so far about the problems with relativism, it suffers from three types of problems. First, the evidence that is used to support it, does not support it. Second, proponents cannot assert both the negative and the positive claims of relativism without inconsistency. By claiming that everyone is bound by the rules of his or her society, the ethical relativist makes a universal claim and yet the relativist claims there are no universal rights and wrongs. And, third, the theory, as the Hitler case illustrates, does not seem to help in making moral decisions. Relativism, at least as I have formulated it, does not help us figure out what to do in tough situations. It recommends that we adhere to the standards in our society and yet it doesn't help us figure out what these standards are. Moreover, doing something because it is the standard in your society does not seem a good reason for doing something.

Where do we stand now? It is important to note that we have made progress even though we have not formulated a moral theory that is defensible. Partly our progress is negative. That is, we have identified some arguments that don't work. At the same time, we have learned about some of the difficulties in taking a relativist position and are therefore in a better position to reformulate the theory. Perhaps, most important of all, we have seen the challenge of developing and defending ethical claims.

Our exploration of ethical relativism has hardly scratched the surface. You may want to reformulate ethical relativism so as to avoid some of the arguments given against it. You may want, for the time being, to take what might be called "an agnostic position." As an agnostic, you claim that you don't yet know whether there are universal rights and wrongs but you would also claim that you do not have sufficient reasons for ruling out the possibility either. You will wait and see, keeping an open mind, and being on the alert for implausible and inconsistent claims.

UTILITARIANISM

Utilitarianism is an ethical theory claiming that what makes behavior right or wrong depends wholly on the consequences. In putting the emphasis on consequences, utilitarianism affirms that what is important about human behavior is the outcome or results of the behavior and not the intention a person has when he or she acts. On one version of utilitarianism, what is all important is happiness-producing consequences (Becker and Becker, 1992). Crudely put, actions are good when they produce happiness and bad when they produce the opposite, unhappiness. The term *utilitarianism* derives from the word *utility*. According to utilitarianism actions, rules, or policies are good because of their usefulness (their utility) in bringing about happiness.

Lest there be no confusion, philosophers are not always consistent in the way they use the terms utilitarianism and consequentialism. Sometimes, consequentialism is seen as the broadest term referring to ethical theories that claim that what makes an action right or wrong is the consequences and not the internal character of action. Utilitarianism is, then, a particular version of this type of theory with the emphasis specifically on happiness-producing consequences. That is the way I shall use these terms, though I warn readers that the distinction sometimes is made in just the opposite way, that is, with utilitarianism seen as the broadest theory and consequentialism as a particular form of utilitarianism.

In any case, in the version on which I will focus, the claim is that in order to determine what they should do, individuals should follow a basic principle. The basic principle is this: *Everyone ought to act so as to bring about the greatest amount of happiness for the greatest number of people.*

But, what, you may ask, is the "proof" of this theory? Why should each of us act to bring about the greatest amount of happiness? Why shouldn't we each seek our own interest?

Intrinsic and Instrumental Value

Utilitarians begin by focusing on values and asking what is so important, so valuable to human beings, that we could use it to ground an ethical theory. They note that among all the things in the world that are valued, we can distinguish things that are valued because they lead to something else from things that are valued for their own sake. The former are called *instrumental* goods and the latter *intrinsic* goods. Money is a classic example of something that is instrumentally good. It is not valuable for its own sake, but rather has value as a means for acquiring other things. On the other hand, intrinsic goods are not valued because they are a means to something else. They have qualities or characteristics that are valuable in themselves. Knowledge is sometimes said to be intrinsically valuable. So, is art because of its beauty. You might also think about environmental debates in which the value of nature or animal or plant species or ecosystems are said to be valuable independent of their value to human beings. The claim is that these things have value independent of their utility to human beings.

Having drawn this distinction between instrumental and intrinsic goods, utilitarians ask what is so valuable that it could ground a theory of right and wrong? It has to be something intrinsically valuable, for something which is instrumentally valuable is dependent for its goodness on whether it leads to another good. If you want x because it is a means to y, then y is what is truly valuable and x has only secondary or derivative value. Utilitarianism, as I am using the term, claims that happiness is the ultimate intrinsic good, because it is valuable for its own sake. Happiness cannot be understood as simply a means to something else. Indeed, some utilitarians claim that everything else is desired as a means to happiness and that, as a result, everything else has only secondary or derivative (instrumental) value.

To see this, take any activity that people engage in and ask why they do it. Each time you will find that the sequence of questions ends with happiness. Take, for example, your career choice. Suppose that you have chosen to study computer science so as to become a computer professional. Why do you want to be a computer professional? Perhaps you believe that you have a talent for computing, and you believe you will be able to get a well-paying job in computer science—one in which you can be creative and somewhat autonomous. Then we must ask, why are these things important to you? That is, why is it important to you to have a career doing something for which you have a talent? Why do you care about being well paid? Why do you desire a job in which you can be creative and autonomous? Suppose that you reply by saying that being well paid is important to you because you want security or because you like to buy things or because there are people who are financially dependent on you. In turn, we can ask about each of these. Why is it important to be secure? Why do you want security or material possessions? Why do you want to support your dependents? The questions will continue until you point to something that is valuable in itself and not for the sake of something else. It seems that the questions can only stop when you say you want whatever it is because you believe it will make you happy. The questioning stops here because it doesn't seem to make sense to ask why someone wants to be happy.

A discussion of this kind could go off in the direction of questioning whether your belief is right. Will a career as a computer professional make you happy? Will it really bring security? Will security or material possessions, in fact, make you happy? Such discussions center on whether or not you have chosen the correct means to your happiness. However, the point that utilitarians want to make is that any discussion of what you should seek in life, and what is valuable, will not stop until we get to happiness.

It makes no sense, utilitarians argue, to ask why people value happiness. Happiness is the ultimate good. All our actions are directly or indirectly aimed at happiness. It is happiness for which we all strive. Utilitarians seem to believe that this is simply part of our human nature. Human beings are creatures who seek happiness. And, since happiness is the ultimate good, utilitarians believe that morality must be based on creating as much of this good as possible. Thus, all actions should be evaluated in terms of their "utility" for bringing about happiness.

According to utilitarianism, when an individual is faced with a decision about what to do, the individual should consider his or her alternatives, predict the consequences of each alternative, and choose that action which brings about the most good consequences, that is, the most happiness. So, the utilitarian principle provides a decision procedure. When you have to decide what to do, consider the happiness-unhappiness consequences that will result from your various alternatives. The alternative that produces the most overall net happiness (good minus bad) is the right action. To be sure, the right action may be one that brings about some unhappiness, but that is justified if the action also brings about so much happiness that the unhappiness is outweighed, or as long as the action has the least net unhappiness of all the alternatives.

Be careful not to confuse utilitarianism with *egoism*. Egoism is a theory that specifies that one should act so as to bring about the greatest number of good consequences for yourself. What is good is what makes "me" happy or gets me what I want. Utilitarianism does not say that you should maximize your own good. Rather, total happiness is what is at issue. Thus, when you evaluate your alternatives, you have to ask about their effects on the happiness of everyone. This includes effects on you, but your happiness counts the same as the happiness of others. It may turn out to be right for you to do something that will diminish your own happiness because it will bring about a marked increase in overall happiness.

The decision-making process proposed in utilitarianism seems to be at the heart of a good deal of social decision making. That is, legislators and public policy makers seem to seek policies that will produce good consequences, and they often opt for policies that may have some negative consequences but on balance, bring about more good than harm. Cost-benefit or risk-benefit analysis aims at quantifying net good consequences. This involves weighing the potential benefits of a project, such as construction of a new waste disposal plant, against the risks of harm in undertaking the project. It involves calculating and weighing the negative and positive effects of a project in deciding whether to go forward with it. In the case of a waste disposal plant, for example, we look at alternative ways to handle the waste, the various costs and benefits of each alternative, the good and bad effects of locating the plant here or there, and so on. We balance the benefits of the plant against the risk of harm and other negative consequences to all those who will be affected.

Acts versus Rules

As mentioned earlier, there are several formulations of utilitarianism and proponents of various versions disagree on important details. One important and controversial issue of interpretation has to do with whether the focus should be on *rules* of behavior or individual *acts*. Utilitarians have recognized that it would be counter to overall happiness if each one of us had to calculate at every moment what all the consequences of every one of our actions would be. Not only is this impractical, because it is time consuming and because sometimes we must act quickly, but often the consequences are impossible to foresee. Thus, there is a need for general rules to guide our actions in ordinary situations.

Rule-utilitarians argue that we ought to adopt rules that, if followed by everyone, would, in the long run, maximize happiness. Take, for example, telling the truth. If individuals regularly told lies, it would be very disruptive. You would never know when to believe what you were told. In the long run, a rule obligating people to tell the truth has enormous beneficial consequences. Thus, "tell the truth" becomes a utilitarian moral rule. "Keep your promises," and "Don't reward behavior that causes pain to others," are also rules that can be justified on utilitarian grounds. According to rule-utilitarianism, if the rule can be justified in terms of the consequences that are brought about from people following it, then individuals ought to follow the rule.

Act-utilitarians put the emphasis on individual actions rather than rules. They believe that even though it may be difficult for us to anticipate the consequences of our actions, that is what we should be trying to do. Take, for example, a case where lying may bring about more happiness than telling the truth. Say you are told by a doctor that tentative test results indicate that your spouse *may* be terminally ill. You know your spouse well enough to know that this knowledge, at this time, will cause your spouse enormous stress. He or she is already under a good deal of stress because of pressures at work and because someone else in the family is very ill. To tell your spouse the truth about the test results will cause more stress and anxiety, and this stress and anxiety may turn out to be unnecessary if further tests prove that the spouse is not terminally ill. Your spouse asks you what you and the doctor talked about. Should you lie or tell the truth? An act-utilitarian might say that the right thing to do in such a situation is to lie, for little good would come from telling the truth and a good deal of suffering (perhaps unnecessary suffering) will be avoided from lying. A rule-utilitarian would agree that good might result from lying in this one case, but in the long run, if we cannot count on people telling the truth (especially our spouses), more bad than good will come. Think of the anxiety that might arise if spouses routinely lied to one another. Thus, according to rule-utilitarians, we must uphold the rule against lying; it would be wrong to lie.

Act-utilitarianism treats rules simply as "rules of thumb," general guidelines to be abandoned in situations where it is clear that more happiness will result from breaking them. Rule-utilitarians, on the other hand, take rules to be strict. They justify moral rules in terms of the happiness consequences that result from people following them. If a rule is justified, then an act that violates the rule is wrong.

In either case, it should be clear that the utilitarian principle can be used to formulate a decision procedure for figuring out what you should do in a situation. In fact, many utilitarians propose that the utilitarian principle be used to determine the laws of a society. Laws against stealing, killing, breaking contracts, fraud, and so on can be justified on utilitarian grounds. Utilitarianism is also often used as a principle for evaluating the laws that we have. If a law is not producing good consequences or is producing a mixture of good and bad effects, and we know of another approach that will produce better net effects, then that information provides the grounds for changing the law. Punishment is a good example of a social practice that can be evaluated in terms of its utility. According to utilitarianism, since punishment involves the imposition of pain, if it does not produce some good consequences, then it is not justified. Typically utilitarians focus on the deterrent effect of punishment as the good consequence counterbalancing the pain involved.

Earlier I mentioned that utilitarianism might be said to capture part of the idea in relativism. According to utilitarianism, the morally right thing to do in a given situation will depend entirely on the situation. In one situation, it may be right to lie, in another situation in which the circumstances are different, it may be wrong to lie. Even rule-utilitarians must admit that the rule that will produce the most happiness will vary from situation to situation. A simple example would be to suppose a natural environment in which water is scarce. In such a situation, a rule prohibiting individuals from putting water in swimming pools and watering lawns would be justified. The rule would be justified because the alternative would lead to bad consequences. On the other hand, in a natural environment in which water is abundant, such a rule would not be justified.

So, even though utilitarians assert a universal principle, the universal principle has varying implications depending on the situation. This means that utilitarianism is consistent with varying laws and practices at different times or in different places depending on the specific circumstances.

Now that the fundamentals of utilitarianism have been explained, it is worth remembering, once again, that we are engaged in a dialectic. We have developed the idea of utilitarianism; we have made the case for the theory. The theory has been "put on the table," so to speak. Even though it has been developed only in its most rudimentary form, the theory now needs to be critically scrutinized.

Critique of Utilitarianism

One of the important criticisms of utilitarianism is that when it is applied to certain cases, it seems to go against some of our most strongly held moral intuitions. In particular, it seems to justify imposing enormous burdens on some individuals for the sake of others. According to utilitarianism, every person is to be counted equally. No one person's unhappiness or happiness is more important than another's. However, since utilitarians are concerned with the total amount of happiness, we can imagine situations where great overall happiness might result from sacrificing the happiness of a few. Suppose, for example, that having a small number of slaves would create great happiness for a large number of individuals. The individuals who were made slaves would be unhappy, but this would be counterbalanced by significant increases in the happiness of many others. This seems justifiable (if not obligatory) according to utilitarianism. Another more contemporary example would have us imagine a situation in which by killing one person and using all their organs for transplantation, we would be able to save ten lives. Killing one to save ten would seem to maximize good consequences. Critics of utilitarianism argue that since utilitarianism justifies such practices as slavery and killing of the innocent, it has to be wrong. It is, therefore, unacceptable as an account of morality.

In defending the theory from this criticism, some utilitarians argue that utilitarianism does not justify such unsavory practices. Critics, they argue, are forgetting the difference between short-term and long-term consequences. Utilitarianism is concerned with all the consequences and when long-term consequences are taken into account, it becomes clear that such practices as slavery and killing innocent people to use their organs could never be justified. In the long run, such practices have the effect of creating so much fear in people that net happiness is diminished rather than increased. Imagine the fear and anxiety that would prevail in a society in which anyone might at any time be taken as a slave. Or imagine the reluctance of anyone to go to a hospital if there was even a remote possibility that they might be killed if by chance they were there when multiple organs were needed to save lives. The good effects of such practices could never counterbalance these bad effects.

Other utilitarians boldly concede that there are going to be some circumstances in which what seem to be repugnant practices should be accepted because they bring about consequences having a greater net good than would be brought about by other practices, that is, because they are consistent with the principle of utility. So, for example, according to these utilitarians, if there are ever circumstances in which slavery would produce more good than ill, then slavery would be morally acceptable. These utilitarians acknowledge that there may be circumstances in which some people should be sacrificed for the sake of total happiness.

In our dialogue about ethics, it is important to pick up on our strongly held moral intuitions for they are often connected to a moral principle or theory. In the case of utilitarianism, the intuition that slavery is always wrong (or that it is wrong to kill the innocent for the sake of some greater good) points to an alternative moral theory. A concrete case will help us further understand utilitarianism and introduce a different theory, one that captures the moral intuition about the wrongness of slavery and killing the innocent.

Case Illustration

Not long ago, when medical researchers had just succeeded in developing the kidney dialysis machine, a few hospitals acquired a limited number of these expensive machines. Hospitals soon found that the number of patients needing treatment on the machines far exceeded the number of machines they had available or could afford. Decisions had to be made as to who would get access to the machines, and these were often life-death decisions. In response, some hospitals set up internal review boards composed of medical staff and community representatives. These boards were charged with the task of deciding which patients should get access to the dialysis machines. The medical condition of each patient was taken into account, but the decisions were additionally made on the basis of the personal and social characteristics of each patient: age, job, number of dependents, social usefulness of job, whether the person had a criminal record, and so on. The review committees appeared to be using utilitarian criteria. The resource—kidney dialysis machines—was scarce and they wanted to maximize the benefit (the good consequences) of the use of the machines. Thus, those who were most likely to benefit and to contribute to society in the future would get access. Individuals were given a high ranking for access to the machines if they were doctors (with the potential to save other lives), if they had dependents, if they were young, and so on. Those who were given lower priority or no priority for access to the machines were those who were so ill that they were likely to die even with treatment, those who were older, those who were criminals, those without dependents, and so on.

As the activities of the hospital review boards became known to the public, they were criticized. Critics argued that your value as a person cannot be measured by your value to the community. The review boards were valuing individuals on the basis of their social value and this seemed dangerous. Everyone, it was argued, has value in and of themselves.

The critique of this method for deciding who should live and who should die suggested a principle that is antithetical to utilitarianism. It suggested that each and every person, no matter what their social role or lot in life, has value and should be respected. To treat individuals as if they are a means to some social end seems the utmost in disrespect. And, that is exactly what a policy of allocating scarce resources according to social value does. It says, in effect, that people have value only as means to the betterment of society, and by that criteria some individuals are much more valuable than others.

The critics of distribution of kidney dialysis on the basis of social utility proposed as an alternative that scarce medical resources should be distributed by a lottery. In a lottery, everyone has an equal chance. Everyone counts the same. This, they argued, was the only fair method of distribution.

The kidney dialysis issue is just a microcosm of all medical resources. Doctors, medical equipment, and medical research are expensive and we have a finite amount of money to spend. Hence, lines have to be drawn—on what level of care goes to who, at what stage in their life, and so on. Distributive decisions have to be made.

The important point for our purposes is that the formulation of utilitarianism we have been considering leads to methods of distribution that seem to be unfair or unjust. So while the core idea in utilitarianism seems plausible (i.e., that everyone's happiness or well-being should be counted), utilitarianism does not seem to adequately handle the distribution of benefits and burdens. The criticism of the hospital review boards for distributing access to kidney machines according to social value goes to the heart of this criticism. Critics argue that people are valuable in themselves, not for their contribution to society. They argue that utilitarian programs are often unfair because in maximizing overall good, they impose an unfair burden on some individuals, and as such treat those individuals merely as means to social good.

I will now turn to an ethical theory that articulates the reasoning underlying the critique of utilitarianism. Before doing so, however, it is important to note that the dialectic could go off in a different direction. The debate about utilitarianism is rich and there are many moves that could be made in reformulating the theory and defending it against its critics. It is also important to note that whatever its weaknesses, utilitarianism goes a long way in providing a systematic account of many of our moral notions.

DEONTOLOGICAL THEORIES

In utilitarianism, what makes an action or a rule right or wrong is outside the action; it is the consequences of the action or rule that make it right or wrong. By contrast, deontological theories put the emphasis on the internal character of the act itself.[1] What makes an action right or wrong for deontologists is the principle inherent in the action. If an action is done from a sense of duty, if

---

[1] The term *deontology* is derived from the Greek words *deon* (duty) and *logos* (science). Etymologically, then, deontology means the science of duty. According to the *Encyclopedia of Philosophy*, its current usage is more specific, referring to an ethical theory which holds that "at least some acts are morally obligatory regardless of their consequences for human weal or woe." (Edwards, 1967)

the principle of the action can be universalized, then the action is right. For example, if I tell the truth (not just because it is convenient for me to do so, but) because I recognize that I must respect the other person, then I act from duty and my action is right. If I tell the truth because I fear getting caught or because I believe I will be rewarded for doing so, then my act is not morally worthy.

I am going to focus here on the theory of Immanuel Kant. If we go back for a moment to the allocation of dialysis machines, Kant's moral theory is applicable because it proposes what is called a categorical imperative specifying that we should never treat human beings merely as means to an end. We should always treat human beings as ends in themselves. Although Kant is not the only deontologist, I will continue to refer to him as I discuss deontology.

The difference between deontological theories and consequentialist theories was illustrated in the discussion of allocation of dialysis machines. Deontologists say that individuals are valuable in themselves, not because of their social value. Utilitarianism is criticized because it appears to tolerate sacrificing some people for the sake of others. In utilitarianism, right and wrong are dependent on the consequences and therefore vary with the circumstances. By contrast, deontological theories assert that there are some actions that are always wrong, no matter what the consequences. A good example of this is killing. Even though we can imagine situations in which intentionally killing one person may save the lives of many others, deontologists insist that intentional killing is always wrong. Killing is wrong even in extreme situations because it means using the person merely as a means and does not treat the human being as valuable in and of himself. Deontologists do often recognize self-defense and other special circumstances as excusing killing, but these are cases when, it is argued, the killing is not exactly intentional. (The person attacks me. I would not, otherwise, aim at harm to the person, but I have no other choice but to defend myself.)

At the heart of deontological theory is an idea about what it means to be a person, and this is connected to the idea of moral agency. Charles Fried (1978) put the point as follows:

> [T]he substantive contents of the norms of right and wrong express the value of persons, of respect for personality. What we may not do to each other, the things which are wrong, are precisely those forms of personal interaction which deny to our victim the status of a freely choosing, rationally valuing, specially efficacious person, the special status of moral personality. (pp. 28–29)

According to deontologists, the utilitarians go wrong when they fix on happiness as the highest good. Deontologists point out that happiness cannot be the highest good for humans. The fact that we are rational beings, capable of reasoning about what we want to do and then deciding and acting, suggests that our end (our highest good) is something other than happiness. Humans differ from all other things in the world insofar as we have the capacity for rationality. The behavior of other things is determined simply by laws of nature. Plants turn toward the sun because of photosynthesis. They don't think and decide which way they will turn. Physical objects fall by the law of gravity. Water boils when it reaches a certain temperature. In contrast, human beings are not entirely determined by laws of nature. We have the capacity to legislate for ourselves. We decide how we will behave. As Kant describes this, it is the difference between acting in accordance with law (plants and stones do) and acting in accordance with *the conception* of law.

The capacity for rational decision making is the most important feature of human beings. Each of us has this capacity; each of us can make choices, choices about what we will do, and what kind of persons we will become. No one else can or should make these choices for us. Moreover, we should recognize this capacity in others.

Notice that it makes good sense that our rationality is connected with morality, for we could not be moral beings at all unless we had this rational capacity. We do not think of plants or fish or dogs and cats as moral beings precisely because they do not have the capacity to reason about their actions. We are moral beings because we are rational beings, that is, because we have the capacity to give ourselves rules (laws) and follow them.

Where utilitarians note that all humans seek happiness, deontologists emphasize that humans are creatures with goals who engage in activities directed toward achieving these goals (ends), and that they use their rationality to formulate their goals and figure out what kind of life to live. In a sense, deontologists pull back from fixing on any particular value as structuring morality and instead ground morality in the capacity of each individual to organize his or her own life, make choices, and engage in activities to realize their self-chosen life plans. What morality requires is that we respect each of these beings as valuable in themselves and refrain from valuing them only insofar as they fit into our own life plans.

As mentioned before, Kant put forward what he called the *categorical imperative*. While there are several versions of it, I will focus on the second version which goes as follows: *Never treat another human being merely as a means but always as an end.* This general rule is derived from the idea that persons are moral beings because they are rational, efficacious beings. Because we each have the capacity to think and decide and act for ourselves, we should each be treated with respect, that is with recognition of this capacity.

Note the "merely" in the categorical imperative. Deontologists do not insist that we never use another person as a means to an end, only that we never "merely" use them in this way. For example, if I own a company and hire employees to work in my company, I might be thought of as using those employees as a means to my end (i.e., the success of my business). This, however, is not wrong if I promise to pay a fair wage in exchange for work and the employees agree to work for me. I thereby respect their ability to choose for themselves.

What would be wrong would be to take them as slaves and make them work for me. It would also be wrong to pay them so little that they must borrow from me and remain always in my debt. This would be exploitation. This would show disregard for the value of each person as a "freely choosing, rationally valuing, specially efficacious person." Similarly, it would be wrong for me to lie to employees about the conditions of their work. Suppose, for example, that while working in my plant, employees will be exposed to dangerous, cancer-causing chemicals. I know this but don't tell the employees because I am afraid they will quit. In not being forthcoming with this information, I am, in effect, manipulating the employees to serve my ends. I am not recognizing them as beings of value with their own life-plans and the capacity to choose how they will live their lives.

Case Illustration

Though utilitarianism and Kantian theory were contrasted in the case illustration about allocation of scarce medical resources, another case will clarify even more. Consider a case involving computers. Suppose a professor of sociology undertakes research on attitudes toward sex and sexual behavior among high school students. Among other things, she interviews hundreds of high school students concerning their attitudes and behavior. She knows that the students will never give her information unless she guarantees them confidentiality, so before doing the interviews, she promises each student that she alone will have access to the raw interview data, and that all publishable results will be reported in statistical form. Thus, it would be impossible to identify information from individual students.

Suppose, however, that it is now time to analyze the interview data and she realizes that it will be much easier to put the data into a computer and use the computer to do the analysis. To assure the confidentiality she promised, the professor will have to code the data so that names do not appear in the database and will have to make an effort to secure the data. She has hired graduate students to assist her and she wonders whether she should let the graduate students handle the raw data. Should she allow the graduate assistants to code and process the data?

At first glance it would seem that from a consequentialist point of view, the professor should weigh the good that will come from the research, and from doing it quickly on a computer, against the possible harm to herself and her subjects if information is leaked. The research may provide important information to people working with high school students and may help her career to prosper. Still, the advantage of doing it quickly may be slight. She must worry about the effect of a leak of information on the students. Also, since she has explicitly promised confidentiality to the student-subjects, she has to worry about the effects on her credibility as a social researcher and on social science research in general if she breaks her promise. That is, her subjects and many others may be reluctant in the future to trust her and other social scientists if she breaks the promise and they find out.

Thus, there seem good reasons to say that from a consequentialist point of view the professor should not violate her promise of confidentiality. Fortunately, there are ways to code data before putting it into the computer or turning it over to her graduate students. She must do the coding herself and keep the key to individual names confidential.

This is how a consequentialist might analyze the situation. Interestingly, a deontologist might well come to the same conclusion though the reasoning would be quite different. The sociologist is doing a study that will advance human knowledge and, no doubt, further her career. There is nothing wrong with this as long as it does not violate the categorical imperative. The question here is whether she is treating her subjects merely as means to knowledge and her own advancement, or whether she is truly recognizing those subjects as ends in themselves. Were the sociologist to ignore her promise of confidentiality to the students, she would not be treating each subject as an end. Each student made a choice based on her pledge of confidentiality. She would be treating them merely as means if she were to break her promise when it suited her. Thus, out of respect for the subjects, the sociologist must code the data herself so as to maintain the promised confidentiality.

The two theories do not, then, come to very different conclusions in this case. However, the analysis is very different in that the reasons given for coming to the conclusion are very different. In other cases, these theories lead to dramatically different conclusions.

Our dialogue on utilitarianism and Kantian theory could continue. I have presented only the bare bones of each theory. However, in the interest of getting to the issues surrounding computers, we must move on and put a few more important concepts and theories "on the table."

RIGHTS

So far, very little has been said about rights though we often use the language of rights when discussing moral issues. "You have no right to tell me what to do." "I have a right to do that." Ethicists often associate rights with deontological theories. The categorical imperative requires that each person be treated as an end in himself or herself, and it is possible to express this idea by saying that individuals have "a right to" the kind of treatment that is implied in being treated as an end. The idea that each individual must be respected as valuable in himself or herself implies that we each have rights not to be interfered with in certain ways, for example, not to be killed or enslaved, to be given freedom to make decisions about our own lives, and so on.

An important distinction that philosophers often make here is between negative rights and positive rights. Negative rights are rights that require restraint by others. For example, my right not to be killed requires that others refrain from killing me. It does not, however, require that others take positive action to keep me alive. Positive rights, on the other hand, imply that others have a duty to do something to or for the right holder. So, if we say that I have a positive right to life, this implies not just that others must refrain from killing me, but that they must do such things as feed me if I am starving, give me medical treatment if I am sick, swim out and save me if I am drowning, and so on. As you can see, the difference between negative and positive rights is quite significant.

Positive rights are more controversial than negative rights because they have implications that are counter-intuitive. If every person has a positive right to life, this seems to imply that each and every one of us has a duty to do whatever is necessary to keep all people alive. This would seem to suggest that, among other things, it is our duty to give away any excess wealth that we have to feed and care for those who are starving or suffering from malnutrition. It also seems to imply that we have a duty to supply extraordinary life-saving treatment for all those who are dying. In response to these implications, some philosophers have argued that individuals have only negative rights.

While, as I said earlier, rights are often associated with deontological theories, it is important to note that rights can be derived from other theories as well. For example, we can argue for the recognition of a right to property on utilitarian grounds. Suppose we ask why individuals should be allowed to have private property in general and, in particular, why they should be allowed to own computer software. Utilitarians would argue for private ownership of software on grounds that much more and better software will be created if individuals are allowed to own (and then license or sell) it. Thus, they argue that individuals should have a legal right to ownership in software because of the beneficial consequences of acknowledging such a right.

Another important thing to remember about rights is the distinction between legal and moral (or natural or human) rights. Legal rights are rights that are created by law. Moral, natural, or human rights are claims independent of law. Such claims are usually embedded in a moral theory or a theory of human nature.

The utilitarian argument is an argument for creating or recognizing a legal right; it is not an argument to the effect that human beings have a natural right, for example, to own what they create. In Chapter 6 we will focus on property rights in computer software and there we will explore both natural and utilitarian property rights.

Rights and Social Contract Theories

Rights are deeply rooted in the tradition of social contract theories. In this tradition the idea of a social contract (between individuals, or between individuals and government) is hypothesized to explain and justify the obligations that human beings have to one another. Many of these theories imagine human beings in a state of nature and then show that reason would lead individuals in such a state to agree to live according to certain rules, or to give power to a government to enforce certain rules. The depiction of a state of nature in which human beings are in a state of insecurity and uncertainty is used to suggest what human nature is like and to show that human nature necessitates government. That is, in such a state any rational human beings would agree (make a contract) to join forces with others even though this involves giving up some of their natural freedom. The agreement (the social contract) creates obligations and these are the basis of moral obligation.

An argument of this kind is made by several social contract theorists and each specifies the nature and limits of our obligations differently. One important difference, for example, is in whether morality exists prior to the social contract. Hobbes argues that there is no justice or injustice in a state of nature; humans are at war with one another and each individual must do what they must to preserve themselves. Locke, on the other hand, specifies a natural form of justice in the state of nature. Human beings have rights in the state of nature and others can treat individuals unjustly. Government is necessary to insure that natural justice is implemented properly because without government, there is no certainty that punishments will be distributed justly.

Rawlsian Justice

In 1971, John Rawls, a professor at Harvard University, introduced a new version of social contract theory (though some argue it is not a social contract theory in the traditional sense). Rawls introduced the theory in a book entitled simply *A Theory of Justice*. The theory may well be one of the most influential moral theories of the twentieth century, for not only did it generate an enormous amount of attention in the philosophical community, it influenced discussion among economists, social scientists, and public policy makers.

Rawls was primarily interested in questions of distributive justice. In the tradition of a social contract theorist, he tries to understand what sort of contract between individuals would be just. Rawls recognizes that we can't arrive at an account of justice and the fairness of social arrangements by reasoning about what rules particular individuals would agree to. He understands that individuals are self-interested and therefore will be influenced by their own experiences and their own situation when they think about fair arrangements. Thus, if some group of us were to get together in something like a state of nature (suppose a group is stranded on an island or a nuclear war occurs and only a few survive), the rules we would agree to would not necessarily be a just system. It would not necessarily exemplify justice.

The problem is that we would each want rules that would favor us. Smart people would want rules that favored intelligence. Strong people would want a system that rewarded strength. Women would not want rules that were biased against women, and so on. The point is that there is no reason to believe that the outcome of a negotiation in which people expressed their preferences would result in rules of justice and just institutions. In this sense, Rawls believes that justice has to be blind in a certain way.

Rawls specifies, therefore, that in order to get at justice, we have to imagine that the individuals who get together to decide on the rules for society are behind a veil of ignorance. The veil of ignorance is such that individuals do not know what characteristics they will have. They do not know whether they will be male or female, black or white, highly intelligent or moderately intelligent or retarded, physically strong or in ill-health, musically talented, successful at business, indigent and so on.

At the same time, these individuals would be rational and self-interested and would know something about human nature and human psychology. In a sense, what Rawls is suggesting here is that we have to imagine *generic* human beings. They have abstract features that human beings generally have (i.e., they are rational and self-interested). And, they have background knowledge (i.e., general knowledge of how humans behave and interact and how they are affected in various ways).

According to Rawls, justice is what individuals would choose in such a situation. Notice that what he has done, in a certain sense, is eliminate bias in the original position. Once a society gets started, once particular individuals have characteristics, their views on what is fair are tainted. They cannot be objective.

So, justice, according to Rawls is what people would choose in the original position where they are rational and self-interested, informed about human nature and psychology but behind a veil of ignorance with regard to their own characteristics. Rawls argues that individuals in the original position would agree to two rules. These are the rules of justice and they are "rules of rules" in the sense that they are general principles constraining the formulation of specific rules. The rules of justice are:

1. Each person should have an equal right to the most extensive basic liberty compatible with a similar liberty for others.
2. Social and economic inequalities should be arranged so that they are both (a) reasonably expected to be to everyone's advantage and (b) attached to positions and offices open to all.

These general principles assure that no matter where an individual ends up in the lottery of life (in which characteristics of intelligence, talents, physical abilities, and so on, are distributed), he or she would have liberty and opportunity. He or she would have a fair shot at a decent life.

While Rawls' account of justice has met with criticism, it goes a long way in providing a framework for envisioning and critiquing just institutions. This discussion of Rawls is extremely abbreviated as were the accounts of Kant and utilitarianism. Perhaps the most important thing to keep in mind as we proceed to the issues surrounding computer and information technology is that rights-claims and claims about justice and fairness generally presume a much more complicated set of claims. Such claims should never be accepted as primitive truths. The underlying argument and embedded assumptions should be uncovered and critically examined.

VIRTUE ETHICS

Before moving on to the ethical issues surrounding computer and information technology, one other tradition in ethical theory should be mentioned. In recent years, interest has arisen in resurrecting the tradition of virtue ethics, a tradition going all the way back to Plato and Aristotle. These ancient Greek philosophers pursued the question: What is a good person? What are the virtues associated with being a good person? For the Greeks *virtue* meant excellence, and ethics was concerned with excellences of human character. A person possessing such qualities exhibited the excellences of human good. To have these qualities is to function well as a human being.

The list of possible virtues is long and there is no general agreement on which are most important, but the possibilities include courage, benevolence, generosity, honesty, tolerance, and self-control. Virtue theorists try to identify the list of virtues and to give an account of each—What is courage? What is honesty? They also give an account of why the virtues are important.

Virtue theory seems to fill a gap left by other theories we considered, because it addresses the question of moral character, while the other theories focused primarily on action and decision making. What sort of character should we be trying to develop in ourselves and in our children. We look to moral heroes, for example, as exemplars of moral virtue. Why do we admire such people? What is it about their character and their motivation that are worthy of our admiration?

Virtue theory might be brought into the discussion of computer technology and ethics at any number of points. The most obvious is, perhaps, the discussion of professional ethics, where we want to think about the characteristics of a good computer professional. Good computer professionals will, perhaps, exhibit honesty in dealing with clients and the public. They should exhibit courage when faced with situations in which they are being pressured to do something illegal or act counter to public safety. A virtue approach would focus on these characteristics and more, emphasizing the virtues of a good computer professional.

INDIVIDUAL AND SOCIAL POLICY ETHICS

One final distinction will be helpful. In examining problems or issues, it is important to distinguish levels of analysis, in particular that between macro and micro level issues or approaches. One can approach a problem from the point of view of social practices and public policy, or from the point of view of individual choice. Macro level problems are problems that arise for groups of people, a community, a state, a country. At this level of analysis, what is sought is a solution in the form of a law or policy that specifies how people in that group or society ought to behave, what the rules of that group ought to be. When we ask the following questions, we are asking macro level questions: Should the United States grant software creators a legal right to own software? Should software engineers be held liable for errors in the software they design? Should companies be allowed to electronically monitor their employees?

On the other hand, micro level questions focus on individuals (in the presence or absence of law or policy). Should I make a copy of this piece of software? Should I lie to my friend? Should I work on a project making military weapons? Sometimes these types of questions can be answered simply by referring to a rule established at the macro level. For example, legally I can make a back-up copy of software that I buy, but I shouldn't make a copy and give it to my friend. Other times, there may be no macro level rule or the macro level rule may be vague or an individual may think the macro level rule is unfair. In these cases, individuals must make decisions for themselves about what they ought to do.

The theories just discussed inform both approaches, but in somewhat different ways, so it is important to be clear on which type of question you are asking or answering.

CONCLUSION

While the focus of our attention will now shift to the ethical issues surrounding computer and information technology, the deep questions and general concerns of ethical theories will continue to haunt us. The dialogue is ongoing. Remember that science is never done. In both science and ethics, we look for reasons supporting the claims that we make, and we tell stories (develop arguments and theories) to answer our questions. We tell stories about why the physical world is the way it is, why human beings behave the way they do, why lying and killing are wrong, and so on. The stories we tell often get better and better over time. They get broader (more encompassing) and richer, sometimes more elegant, sometimes allowing us to see new things we never noticed before. The stories generally lead to new questions. So it is with ethics as well as science.

Computer ethics should be undertaken with this in mind, for the task of computer ethics involves working with traditional moral concepts and theories, and extending them to situations with somewhat new features. The activity brings insight into the situations arising from use of computer and information technology, and it may also bring new insights into ethical concepts and theories.

STUDY QUESTIONS

1. What are the activities involved in doing philosophical ethics?
2. How do descriptive (empirical) claims and prescriptive (normative) claims differ? Give examples of each kind of claim.
3. What is ethical relativism? What is its positive claim? What is its negative claim?
4. What are the three types of evidence often used to support ethical relativism?
5. Does this evidence support ethical relativism?
6. What are the three problems with ethical relativism?
7. What is utilitarianism?
8. What is the difference between an instrumental good and an intrinsic good?
9. Why do utilitarians believe that happiness is the ultimate basis for morality?
10. What is the difference between act-utilitarianism and rule-utilitarianism?
11. What is the traditional criticism of utilitarianism?
12. Why can't happiness be the highest good for humans according to deontologists?
13. What is the categorical imperative?
14. How can rights be based on deontological theory? How can rights be based on utility theory?
15. What are the two principles of justice according to John Rawls?
16. How does virtue ethics differ in focus from other theories discussed in this chapter?
17. What is the difference between macro and micro level issues?

SUGGESTED FURTHER READING

BECKER, LAWRENCE and CHARLOTTE BECKER, *The Encyclopedia of Ethics* (New York: Garland Publishing, 1992).
RACHELS, JAMES, *Elements of Moral Philosophy*. 3rd ed. (Boston: McGraw-Hill, 1999).
SINGER, PETER, *Practical Ethics*. 2nd ed. (Cambridge, MA: Cambridge University Press, 1993).

CHAPTER 3

Professional Ethics

SCENARIO 3.1 **Concerns about safety.**

Carl Babbage is an experienced systems designer. He has been working for the Acme Software Company for three years. Acme develops and sells computer hardware and software. It does this both by designing and marketing general purpose systems and by contracting with companies and government agencies to design custom systems for their exclusive use.

During the first two years that Carl worked for Acme he worked on software that Acme was developing for general marketing. A year ago, however, he was reassigned to work on a project under contract from the U.S. Department of Defense. The project involves designing a system that will monitor radar signals and launch nuclear missiles in response to these signals.

Carl initially had some reluctance about working on a military project, but he put this out of his mind because the project was technically challenging and he knew that if he did not work on it, someone else would. Now, however, the project is approaching completion and Carl has some grave reservations about the adequacy of the system. He is doubtful about the system's capacity for making fine distinctions (for example, distinguishing between a small aircraft and a missile) and the security of the mechanism that can launch missiles; for example, it may be possible for unauthorized individuals to get access to the controls under certain circumstances. Carl expressed his concern to the project director but she dismissed these concerns quickly, mentioning that Acme is already behind schedule on the project and has already exceeded the budget that they had agreed to with the Defense Department.

Carl feels that he has a moral responsibility to do something, but he doesn't know what to do. Should he ask for reassignment to another project? Should he go to executives in Acme and tell them of his concerns? It is difficult to imagine how they will respond. Should he talk to someone higher up in the hierarchy of the Defense Department? Should he go to newspaper or television news reporters and "blow the whistle"? If he does any of these things, he is likely to jeopardize his job. Should he do nothing?

SCENARIO 3.2 How much security?

After getting an undergraduate degree in computer science, Leikessa Jones was hired by a large computer company. She initially worked as a programmer, but over the years was promoted to technical positions with increasing responsibility. Three years ago she quit her job and started her own consulting business. She has been so successful that she now has several people working for her.

At the moment, Leikessa is designing a database management system for the personnel office of a medium-sized company that manufactures toys. Leikessa has involved the client in the design process informing the CEO, the Director of Information Technology, and the Director of Personnel about the progress of the system and giving them many opportunities to make decisions about features of the system. It is now time to make decisions about the kind and degree of security to build into the system.

Leikessa has described several options to the client. The client has decided to opt for the least secure system because the system is going to cost more than was planned. She believes that the information that will be stored in the system is extremely sensitive. It will include performance evaluations, medical records for filing insurance claims, and salaries. With weak security, it may be possible for enterprising employees to figure out how to get access to this data, not to mention the possibilities for online access from hackers. Leikessa feels strongly that the system should be more secure.

She has tried to explain the risks to her client, but the CEO, Director of Information Technology, and Director of Personnel are all willing to accept little security. Should she refuse to build the system as they request?

SCENARIO 3.3 Conflict of interest.

Juan Roriguez makes a living as a private consultant. Small businesses hire him to advise them about their computer needs. Typically a company asks him to come in, examine the company's operations, evaluate their automation needs, and make recommendations about the kind of hardware and software that they should purchase.

Recently, Juan was hired by a small, private hospital. The hospital was interested in upgrading the hardware and software it uses for patient records and accounting. The hospital had already solicited proposals for upgrading their system. They hired Juan to evaluate the proposals they had received. Juan examined the proposals very carefully. He considered which system would best meet the hospital's needs, which company offered the best services in terms of training of staff and future updates, which offered the best price, and so on. He concluded that Tri-Star Systems was the best alternative for the hospital, and he recommended this in his report, explaining his reasons for drawing this conclusion.

What Juan failed to mention (at any time in his dealings with the hospital) was that he is a silent partner (a co-owner) in Tri-Star Systems. Was Juan's behavior unethical? Should Juan have disclosed the fact that he had ties to one of the companies that made a proposal? Should he have declined the job once he learned that Tri-Star had made a bid?

WHY PROFESSIONAL ETHICS?

Carl, Leikessa, and Juan find themselves in difficult situations. The ethical theory discussed in the last chapter should help each of them to figure out what to do, but we have to be careful here. While it is tempting to jump in and see what course of action utilitarian or deontological theory would require, such analyses will not be useful unless they take into account the context in which each person is acting. Carl, Leikessa, and Juan have each taken on a professional role and these roles carry responsibilities with them. Moreover, when we take on professional roles, others have expectations about how we will behave. Thus, the situations in which Carl, Leikessa, and Juan must act are morally complex. Carl is a computer professional but he is also an employee in a company and his company has a client that is a public agency pursuing a public good. Leikessa is also a computer professional but she is the owner of a company and her company has a contract with a client. These roles and relationships constrain and facilitate her actions in a variety of ways. Juan's situation seems, at first sight, the simplest. He has been hired by a company to do a job. He owes the company whatever services he has promised and the company owes him whatever support and payment it promised upon completion of the work. However, this seemingly simple relationship is made more complex because of another relationship Juan has.

Whether the situation is simple or complex, we cannot accurately understand the ethical aspects of these scenarios if we view them simply as situations in which individuals act in ways that affect other individuals. We must consider what it means to act in a professional or occupational role. What responsibilities or obligations do employees have to their employers? What can employers rightfully expect of their employees? What can clients expect from professionals? What can the public rightfully expect of computer professionals? What moral responsibilities do employed professionals have for the effects of their work?

Having completed the previous chapter on ethical theory you might have turned to this chapter and had the following sort of response: Why do we need to talk about professional ethics at all? If I find myself with an ethical problem I should think it through using ethical theory, try to understand what rules or principles are at stake, and then act accordingly. That I act as a computer professional, or any other kind of professional, seems irrelevant.

There is some truth to this, for when you act as a professional, you do not cease to be a moral agent. Nevertheless, acting in a professional role is special in several respects. For one thing, professional roles often carry with them special rights and special responsibilities. Indeed, sometimes professional rights and responsibilities are so special that they are exceptions or additions to ordinary morality. Doctors, for example, are allowed to prescribe drugs, perform surgery, and keep patient information confidential, and they are expected to help individuals who are hurt in accidents or emergencies. Lay persons are neither allowed to do what doctors may nor expected to help others in the way doctors are. Similarly, the signature of a licensed engineer is required before certain structures can be built; no one but a licensed engineer has the power to determine what gets built.

There are several professional roles that, like doctor and licensed engineer, might be called *strongly differentiated* (Goldman, 1980), that is, the role gives the role-holder powers and/or responsibilities that are *exceptions to ordinary morality*. Doctors and licensed engineers, as described above, are two examples, but think also of lawyers and the right that they have to keep information confidential. Lawyers cannot be compelled to reveal confidential information given to them by a client, even when the information would affect the outcome of a trial. Or, think of the physical harm that police officers may inflict in the course of their work. The use of this kind of force is prohibited for everyone else. And police officers have a duty to intervene when a crime is taking place, while ordinary citizens would not be expected to intervene. So, when you become a member of these strongly differentiated professions, you acquire special rights and responsibilities that are exceptions to ordinary morality.

On the other hand, most occupational roles are not strongly differentiated; they do not allow or require that the role-holder act outside ordinary morality. For example, sales personnel, construction workers, secretaries, and auto mechanics have no special powers or privileges because they are members of an occupational group. They are expected to adhere to the demands of ordinary morality (e.g., refraining from using force, testifying at trials when they are subpoenaed, and never performing surgery or distributing drugs). Indeed, the terms *profession* and *professional* are often used to refer only to strongly differentiated professions.

The role of computer professional is not strongly differentiated. That is, when you become a computer professional, you do not acquire any special, socially recognized power or privilege *by virtue of being a computer professional.*

Nevertheless, when you are hired by a company, you may acquire the power to make certain decisions within that company (e.g., to give orders to others or to sign-off on budget items [spending the company's money]). And, employees certainly acquire responsibilities—to perform tasks, to meet deadlines, attend meetings, and so on. The point here is that you acquire these powers and responsibilities by virtue of being an employee of a company or organization, not by virtue of being a computer professional.

When it comes to strongly differentiated professions, special ethical analysis is required—to take into account the distinct ethical rights and responsibilities that a member of such a profession has. In the case of nondifferentiated professions, special ethical analysis is also required but for different reasons.

Here what is special is the employment context. Employees enter into special relationships and take on special responsibilities when they become employed.

Employment roles are generally part of a complex institutional context and this context creates powers and responsibilities for individuals acting in various roles. As mentioned before, one acquires powers and responsibilities by being employed in an organization (even if not by being a member of a professional group). Think, for example, of Carl in Scenario 3.1. Though he may not be obligated to do any and everything his supervisor requests, he does have some obligation to the company that has hired him. Similarly, even though Leikessa in Scenario 3.2 owns her own company, she is not morally free to do whatever she pleases. She has obligations to her clients and her employees. To fully understand the moral situation of computer professionals such as Carl, Leikessa, and Juan, we must take the complexity of their professional/occupational roles into account.

Though there is a good deal of variation, typically computer professionals are employed by private corporations seeking profit in a highly competitive environment and constrained by law in a variety of ways. This context—in no small way—affects the powers and responsibilities of computer professionals. More on this later.

Another way in which occupational roles have to be taken into account in ethical analysis has to do with the *efficacy* of individuals acting in employment roles. By efficacy I mean the power to affect the world. The work of employed individuals in nondifferentiated professional roles has effects; it may produce new and improved products, provide services that benefit others, create risks to society, and so on. While they are *not* morally allowed to do things that are exceptions to ordinary morality, employed professionals are able to do things that others do not have the capacity to do.

Employed professionals often have some skill or knowledge and they use this skill and knowledge to produce a product or provide a service. Sometimes they do this on their own; for example, when an architect designs a house or an auto mechanic fixes a car. More often than not, however, professionals use their knowledge and abilities in ways that contribute to a larger enterprise, wherein their contribution, together with that of others, leads to a product or service. For example, an engineer may use her skill to design one component of a whole airplane, or a research scientist may work with a team of other scientists each making contributions to the development of a cure for some disease.

Knowledge and skill are important parts of the efficacy of professionals, but they are not all of it, for mere possession of skill and knowledge is not enough to produce an effect. You must exercise the skill and use the knowledge, and in most professions this cannot be done in isolation. You need a business, clients, consumers, equipment, legal protection, and so on. Thus, professionals, especially computer professionals, create their own businesses or obtain employment in companies or government agencies. Creating or filling a position in one of these larger enterprises is usually what gives professionals the opportunity to use their knowledge and skill.

So, individuals acting in professional/occupational roles affect the world (they are efficacious) when they exercise their skills and knowledge in a context in which their actions have an effect. A computer professional, for example, may use his or her knowledge and skill to create software used for medical imaging or networking or record keeping. The computer professional has efficacy because he or she works in an institution organized in a certain way and supported by a broader set of social institutions (economic, legal, and political systems). This complex arrangement is what makes it possible for the skill and knowledge of the computer professional to be transformed into an effect on the world. The actions of computer professionals may directly or indirectly have powerful effects, on individuals and on the social and physical world in which we live. These effects may be good or bad and may be foreseen or unforeseen.

Because professionals have this efficacy, they bear special responsibility. That is, precisely because professionals have the ability and opportunity to affect the world in ways that others cannot, they have greater responsibility to ensure that their actions do not harm individuals or public safety and welfare. (More on this later.)

To summarize, when it comes to analyzing the ethical dilemmas of computer professionals, it is not sufficient to think of them merely as individuals acting in complex situations. To fully account for the ethical dilemmas of computer professionals, the domain of professional ethics must be recognized. This means recognizing that the moral dilemmas of computer professionals (as well as other professionals) are different from those of lay persons. It means recognizing the moral complexity of the environments in which computer professionals work as well as the special efficacy that computer professionals have in those environments. While some professionals (members of strongly differentiated professions) have special rights and responsibilities (powers and privileges) by virtue of being members of a profession, computer professionals do not. Computer professionals have special powers and privileges by virtue of their skill and knowledge and the positions they hold in organizations.

CHARACTERISTICS OF PROFESSIONS

As suggested earlier, the term *profession* is sometimes restricted to occupations that are strongly differentiated. More often than not, however, profession is used rather loosely to refer to occupational groups that for one reason or another have acquired higher social status and higher salaries. In theory we could use the term simply to refer to occupational groups such as house painters, x-ray technicians, and receptionists, as well as doctors and lawyers. But this term is more often used to refer to a subset of occupations that, even if not strongly differentiated, have a somewhat distinct set of characteristics.

While there is no hard and fast definition, professions are often associated with the following set of characteristics:

1. Mastery of an Esoteric Body of Knowledge. Professions seem to require mastery of an esoteric body of knowledge, usually acquired through higher education. A member of the profession needs this body of knowledge in order to practice; those who do not master the knowledge cannot do the work. Because a distinct body of knowledge is so important to a profession, a related characteristic of professions is that they often embrace a division between researchers and practitioners, with the researchers devoting themselves to continuous improvement in the body of knowledge—medical researchers and clinicians, academic engineers and practicing engineers.

2. Autonomy. Members of professions typically have a good deal of autonomy in their work (as compared to other occupations in which members take orders). This autonomy is justified in part on grounds that the work of the professionals depends on esoteric knowledge; those with the esoteric knowledge should be making decisions rather than taking orders from those who don't have the knowledge, and therefore, cannot fully understand the situation.

Professions typically have autonomy both at the collective level as well as in individual practice. At the collective level, professions are often organized in a way that allows the membership to make decisions about the profession's organization and practice. Rather than being regulated by outsiders, the profession sets its own admission standards and standards of practice. Members of professions generally have more autonomy in their daily work—doctors making decisions about treatment for their patients, lawyers deciding the best strategy for defending a client, or architects deciding on the design of a building. These professionals have much more autonomy when compared to, say, sales personnel, assembly-line workers, and office clerks. In the latter occupations, members may have some say in the details of their work, but, for the most part, they are told what to do and how to do it.

3. Formal Organization. Professions generally have a single unifying, formal organization recognized by state and/or federal government, and this organization may control admission to the profession, as well as set standards for practice. The organization may also be involved in accreditation of educational institutions. In some cases, the professional organization is involved in licensing of its members. The formal organization will also generally have the power to expel individual members from the profession. In the United States, the American Medical Association and the American Bar Association are prominent examples of this type of organization.

4. Code of Ethics. Professions generally have a code of ethics (or a code of professional conduct). The code of ethics is both a way of setting standards in the field and a mechanism for maintaining autonomy. Members of professions with a code of conduct must adhere to the code no matter what their employment context; an employer—be it in a small or large business or government or a nonprofit—cannot require a professional to do anything that goes against the professional code. In many cases, professions require their members to take an oath to a code when they become members. A code of

ethics also serves as a statement from the profession to the public as to what to expect from its members. In this way, codes of ethics promote public trust.

5. Social Function. Professions are generally understood to fulfill an important social function. Medicine, for example, is committed to promoting health, and while lawyers are not alone responsible for justice, they play a vital role in the system of legal institutions aimed at achieving justice. Engineering is more difficult to describe because engineering is not committed to a single social good; rather engineering is devoted to developing technologies that facilitate a variety of social endeavors (transportation, communication, commerce, etc.). Nevertheless, as stated in several codes of conduct, engineers are committed to protecting safety and welfare in any projects they pursue.

These five characteristics are associated with a subset of occupational groups that have typically been labeled professions—doctors, lawyers, engineers, architects, accountants, and clergy. However, as already suggested, the concept of profession or professional is not hard and fixed. Moreover, it would be a mistake to think of this as a simple dichotomy; that is, it would be a mistake to think that any occupational group can be classified either as a profession or not a profession. These five characteristics are better seen as describing a model or paradigm against which various occupational groups can be measured. Occupational groups (such as computer professionals) can be examined in terms of these characteristics, some of which they exhibit and some they do not. Think of a continuum of professions/nonprofessions: Several occupations can be placed at one end of the continuum because they possess all of the characteristics mentioned and possess them to a high degree. At the other end of the continuum are occupations that exhibit none of these characteristics. There are many other occupational groups falling in between and closer or farther from each end of the continuum.

THE SYSTEM OF PROFESSIONS

Another way of thinking about professions that may be particularly helpful in understanding the field of computing is to think of the five characteristics listed as implicitly describing a process of professionalization. Many occupational groups want the power of self-regulation and the status and high salaries that go with it. To achieve this status and power, they must acquire and maintain a monopoly of control over a particular domain of activity. The characteristics listed implicitly describe how this is typically achieved.

An occupational group must organize itself into a formal unit. It must demonstrate that in a certain domain of activity (e.g., distributing therapeutic drugs, building bridges, auditing financial records, producing software), it is dangerous for just anyone to be doing the job. The activity will be safer, more effective, and, therefore, better for all who are affected, if that domain of activity is restricted to persons who have mastered a particular body of knowledge and have undergone special training. Moreover, the occupational group must convince the public that lay people cannot judge who is appropriately trained and qualified. Only those who have mastered the relevant body of knowledge can truly judge whether someone is qualified. In this way, the group convinces the public and government that for the good of society, a monopoly of control should be given to that group. The group is then given a monopoly of control in a certain domain of activity. The monopoly means that only members of that profession can engage in certain activities and the group can control who is qualified to be a member (i.e., who can practice the profession).

This type of monopoly is not granted simply on the basis of special expertise; nor is it granted unconditionally. The occupational group must regulate itself so as to protect and further the interests of the public (including clients, patients, and all those affected by the work of the profession). In other words, the occupational group must continuously demonstrate that it is worthy of the monopoly and this means controlling who becomes a member and how they practice, as well as expelling those who don't live up to the standards.

The system of professions makes clear the role of each of the characteristics mentioned above. To obtain a monopoly of control and self-regulation, an occupational group must organize itself and convince the public that there is *special knowledge* in its domain of activity and only those who have that knowledge should engage in the activity. It must also convince the public that only members of the profession are qualified to evaluate/determine who should be allowed to practice. The group must make clear that an important *social function* is at stake and can best be achieved by granting the knowledgeable group control of the particular domain of activity. In order to convince the public to trust the group, the group adopts a *code of ethics* committing itself to certain standards of conduct. If the group succeeds, the public (through state or federal government) recognizes the *formal organization* of the occupational group, gives it a monopoly of control in its domain, and prohibits nonmembers from engaging in the activity. The monopoly of control gives the group *collective autonomy* and recognition of the profession as such may justify *individual autonomy* in the practice of the profession.

It is useful to think of this process as establishing a social contract between a profession and society. "Society" here refers to the public though the contract is negotiated, so to speak, through state and/or federal government. Each side takes on responsibilities in exchange for something it perceives to be valuable. Members of a profession organize themselves and promise to pursue or protect a social good in exchange for recognition by the state. The state grants the profession a monopoly of control of certain activities in exchange for the commitment by the profession that it will self-regulate in ways that serve the public interest. So, the profession gets the power of self-regulation in exchange for the commitment to protect and pursue a social good. Society gets better quality of services in a particular domain of activity in exchange for the commitment to support and enforce the profession's monopoly.

The social contract idea makes clear that there is always the possibility that the contract may be broken. If the occupational group violates its part of the contract, by failing to do a good job of setting standards and controlling admission, then the state could take away its monopoly and begin to regulate the domain of activity from the outside. On the other hand, a professional group can go to the state and complain that it is not being given the support it has been promised. For example, doctors would justifiably complain if courts began to demand that doctors reveal confidential information about their patients.

IS COMPUTING A PROFESSION? ARE COMPUTER PROFESSIONALS "PROFESSIONALS"?

Where does computing fit in this scheme of things? What does the field of computing look like when described in terms of the five characteristics mentioned above? Where is computing in the process of professionalization?

To fully answer these questions would take us too far afield, not because they are difficult questions, but because the field of computing is so diverse and complex. The field of computing as an occupation (or set of occupations) is still young and evolving. The range of those who are called computer professionals is extremely broad, including those who design, sell, and maintain software and hardware; those who write documentation; those who advise on the security of information systems; those who design, monitor, and maintain Web sites; those who work for Internet service providers; those who work as academic computer scientists; and on and on. It is difficult to figure out what these jobs have in common except that, in one way or another, they involve the use of computer and information technology. This is in sharp contrast with older professions that are organized around a domain of life (law enforcement, medicine, religion, accounting) rather than a technology.

I will not try to sort out all the subfields and emerging divisions within computing. Instead, I will mention two trends in the organization of computing that seem worth watching, and then I will examine, in very broad terms, where the field of computing seems to fit on the continuum of professions/ nonprofessions. I will also briefly discuss the emergence of software engineering as a distinct field within computing.

One trend to watch in the evolving organization of computing is the specification of occupations in ways that push computing out of sight or into the background. Remember that a distinct feature of computer technology is its malleability. Because of this malleability, computer technology is used in a wide variety of domains and fields. As computing becomes more and more a routine part of particular domains, it may well be that individuals will come to identify with the domain rather than computing. Computing may become an assumed part of many jobs, just as reading and writing are essential skills for doing many jobs. Where this happens, a worker will not be considered a computer professional per se, but simply a manager, a librarian, a graphic artist, an engineer, a security expert, a teacher, and these occupations require having and using knowledge of computers and information technology. Being able to use word processors, e-mail, and Web browsers is now standard for many occupations. As computer technology becomes more and more user friendly, this trend is likely to continue.

A trend that might be watched for clues as to how the organization of computing is evolving is the new curriculums being developed on college campuses and other educational institutions. There are computer engineering degrees as well as computer science degrees, but there are also new degree programs in business, for example, information management or MIS (management of information systems), and in communication, information studies, and so on. The curriculums that evolve are likely to be connected to categories of future professions and subfields.

With this as a backdrop, we can now discuss the field of computing in terms of the five characteristics of professions. At first glance, it would seem that computing possesses all of these characteristics, though it possesses them in complex and, perhaps, diffused ways.

Most computer professionals must master an esoteric body of knowledge to do what they do. Many people who work in the field have acquired their knowledge of computing through higher education.[1] Moreover, it appears that computing has a division between researchers and practitioners with knowledge of computing being continuously improved upon by those who do research and innovate.

Nevertheless, there are many points of controversy with regard to the esoteric body of knowledge on which computing is based. First, because the field is new and because of the huge demand for computing expertise, there are many people working in the field who do not have college degrees and many people who have college degrees but not in the field of computing.

Whether or not computing is actually based on mastery of an esoteric body of knowledge is a matter of contention. Some argue that computer science does not yet have its own body of knowledge; it relies on other fields (e.g., mathematics, engineering, physics). Others argue that computing does not really rely on a *systematic* or *abstract* body of knowledge and in this sense the body of knowledge on which it draws is not *esoteric;* rather computing relies on knowing how to do things. It is more application than science.

This is an important issue because, as mentioned earlier, identifying a special body of knowledge is part of the process of becoming recognized as a distinct occupational group. Indeed, the importance of identifying a distinct body of knowledge can be seen in recent events surrounding the licensing of software engineers (to be further discussed in the next section of this chapter). The Association for Computer Machinery (ACM), one of the largest organizations

---

[1] This is more true now than in the early days of computing when there were no educational programs in computing.

of computer professionals in the United States, recently took a position opposing the licensing of software engineers *at this time*. ACM took this position on the grounds that there is not yet an identifiable body of knowledge in software engineering. The ACM committee appointed to explore the issue of licensing of software engineers found that: "There is no widely accepted body of knowledge defining competency in software engineering."

When it comes to autonomy, the situation is again complex. As mentioned earlier, computing is not a strongly differentiated profession. That is, computer professionals are not allowed to do or required to do anything that an ordinary person (non-computer professional) cannot do. Strong differentiation aside, computer professionals have varying degrees of autonomy depending on where they work and what their positions are in an organizational hierarchy. Yes, those who work in private practice, by owning their own companies or consulting firms, and those who have worked their way up the ladder in corporate or government agencies, have greater decision making authority. They have greater autonomy than those who are newly employed in companies and lower in the organizational hierarchy.

At the collective level, it would seem that computer professionals do not have a great deal of autonomy, though they do have some. There is no single professional organization comparable to the AMA or the ABA; no single organization to which all members of the profession must belong. There is no formal process of admission that you must go through to become a computer professional. Nevertheless, computing has several large formal organizations. ACM and IEEE-CS (Institute for Electronics and Electrical Engineering Computer Society) are probably the largest and most visible. In recent years, these organizations have worked together to come up with curriculum requirements for accreditation of degree programs in computing and computer engineering. While these organizations have little in the way of enforcement power, attention is paid to their recommendations, and this effectively gives them some degree of self-regulation.

While there is no single code of ethics binding all computer professionals, ACM and IEEE, as well as other more specialized computer professional organizations have codes, and they are relatively similar in what they specify as the responsibilities of computer professionals.

Finally, as for fulfilling a social function, it seems clear that computing is now a crucial part of our society and will continue to be important. I hesitate to say that computing fulfills an important social function for computing is not a good in itself, in the way that health and justice are. Computing is closer to engineering in this respect. Engineering and computing are activities that help us to achieve other social goods such as health, safety, efficiency, communication, and transportation. Computing supports a variety of social functions but is not itself a social function.

So, computing has several of the features associated with professions though it exhibits these characteristics in complex ways. It seems fair to say that computing is not at the far end of either side of the continuum of professions/nonprofessions, though it also seems fair to say that it is much closer to the profession side of the continuum than many other occupations.

SOFTWARE ENGINEERING

Software engineering appears to be one area of computing that is emerging as a distinct profession within the field of computing. This trend seems to have been created by the initiative of individuals in the field who are concerned about the quality and safety of the software currently being produced and sold. Developing software engineering as a distinct field involves several of the activities that have already been discussed. For example, it means identifying a unique body of knowledge that a person must possess to be a competent software engineer. It means developing educational requirements (curriculum components) such that the person who meets the requirements is much more likely to produce high quality, safe software than someone without the training. It means developing mechanisms for licensing of members. This will include identifying or creating the proper organization for issuing licenses and identifying requirements for obtaining a license, such as passing an exam or acquiring a certain number of years of experience.

The state of Texas has boldly taken the first steps in this process and has established software engineering licensing in its state. Texas has developed a set of requirements and an exam that candidates must pass in order to receive a license.

Another requirement for professionalization is a code of ethics. While the Texas licensing initiative is not explicitly associated with a code of ethics, in its early stages of development Texas asked for assistance from the ACM and IEEE and these two organizations established a joint task force to design a code of ethics and professional conduct specifically for software engineering. Even though the ACM subsequently decided not to support efforts at licensing of software engineers, the code of ethics was developed jointly by ACM and IEEE-CS.

The Texas licensing process, at this point, does not make software engineering a strongly differentiated profession; that is, it does not give those with licenses the power to do anything that nonlicensed engineers cannot do. Rather, Texas licensing seems aimed at helping those who contract for creation of software in identifying competent qualified professionals, that is, those who have obtained licenses. Though it is difficult to predict what will follow, the Texas initiative could be the first step in a sequence that will lead to granting licensed software engineers the power to determine whether software is released for sale (or not).

The Texas initiative is important for many reasons. Among them is that Texas defined software engineering as *engineering*. In doing this, Texas was able to make use of the apparatus (agencies, procedures, and practices) already in place for the licensing of other kinds of engineers. This will not be possible for all areas of computing, but it helps to give shape to the field of software development. Classifying software engineers as engineers provides a context and framework for thinking about the work of software designers. It helps the public to understand how to think about the products and services being provided by software engineers.

The Texas initiative is a serious attempt at setting standards in a field in which, in many contexts, there are none. Moreover, it looks like the first steps in a process of negotiating the social contract between computer professionals and those who are affected by their work. While the process is far from over, other groups of computer professionals can learn a great from observing how the process proceeds.

PROFESSIONAL RELATIONSHIPS

The work-life of computer professionals is, as already suggested, far from simple morally. When computer professionals take on jobs, depending on the details, they may enter into relationships with any one or several of the following: (1) an employer, (2) a client, (3) coprofessionals, and (4) the public. Each of these relationships have ethical parameters.

Employer-Employee

When a person accepts a job in an organization, he or she enters into a relationship with an employer. While many conditions of this relationship will be made explicit when the employee is hired—responsibilities, salary, hours of work—many conditions will not be mentioned. Some conditions are not mentioned because they are specified by law (for example, an employee may not be required to do anything illegal); they are assumed by both parties. Some aspects of the relationship may be negotiated through a union (for example, employees with more seniority cannot be laid off before employees with less seniority). Yet many other conditions of the relationship will not be mentioned because neither party has an interest in them at the moment, because no one can anticipate all the situations which may arise, and probably because it is better not to press the uncertainties of some aspects of employer-employee relations. For example, when you accept a job, do you, thereby, agree to work overtime whenever your supervisor requests it? If you work for a local government and it gets into financial trouble, will you accept your salary in script? Do you agree never to speak out publicly on political issues that may affect your employer? Do you agree to a dress code?

The moral foundation of the employer-employee relationship is contractual. Each party agrees to do certain things in exchange for certain things. Generally, the employee agrees to perform certain tasks and the employer agrees to pay compensation and provide the work environment. Since the relationship is contractual in character, we may think of it as fulfilling the requirements of the categorical imperative. Each party exercises his or her autonomy in consenting to the terms of the contract since each party is free to refuse to enter into the contract.

According to the categorical imperative, each individual should be treated with respect and never used merely as a means. Thus, it is wrong for either the employer or the employee to take advantage of the other. This means, among other things, that each party must be honest. An employee must be honest with her employer about her qualifications for the job and must do the work promised. Otherwise, she is simply using the employer to get what she wants without respecting the employer's interests. Likewise, the employer must pay a decent wage and must be honest with the employee about what she will be expected to do at work.

Workplace hazards illustrate the potential for exploitation here. If your employer says nothing about the dangers involved in a job and simply offers you a big salary and good benefits, making the job so attractive that it is hard to turn down, then the employer has not treated you with respect. He or she has not recognized you as an end in yourself, with interests of your own and the capacity to decide what risks you will or will not take. Your employer has kept important information from you in order to insure that you will do what he or she wants. You are used merely as a means to what your employer wants. On the other hand, if your employer explains that you will be exposed to toxic substances at work and explains that this will increase the likelihood of your developing cancer, then if you agree to take the job, your employer has not exploited you.

For professional ethics, one of the most difficult areas of the employer-employee relationship has to do with what you rightfully owe an employer in the name of loyalty (or what an employer can rightfully expect/demand of an employee). While loyalty is generally thought to be a good thing, closer examination reveals that it has both good and bad aspects. The bad effects of loyalty include the following (Baron, 1984): (1) it invites unfairness, (2) it eschews reliance on good reasons, and (3) it invites irresponsibility. For example, if I am responsible for hiring a new employee, and I, out of loyalty, choose my friend without considering the qualifications and experience of all other applicants, I have not treated the other applicants fairly. I have not used good reasons in making the decision and I have acted irresponsibly in not taking fully into account the interests of my employer.

On the other hand, loyalty is a good thing insofar as it allows us to have special relationships that are extremely valuable. Parenting and friendship are two powerful examples. Being a parent means treating certain people in special ways. If I were obligated to use my time and resources to help all children equally (that is, if "my" children had no special claims to my care and attention), then the idea that I was someone's parent would be without meaning. It is the same with friendship. If I treated my friends exactly as I treated all other persons, it would be hard to understand what it means to have a friend.

Both the good and bad implications of loyalty come into play in employer-employee relationships. Organizations could probably not function unless individuals recognized that they owe something special to their employers. Having individuals that will take orders and make efforts to coordinate their activities with others allows organizations to accomplish tasks that could not be accomplished otherwise. Hence, a certain degree of loyalty to employer seems necessary and even worthy.

Nevertheless, we should not jump to the conclusion that employees owe their employers whatever they demand in the name of loyalty. There are limits. The hard part, of course, is to figure out where to draw the line. Clearly, employers cannot demand every form of behavior that will serve the interests of the company. For example, companies have been known to pressure their employees, in the name of loyalty, to vote in public elections for candidates who the company believes will further the company's interests. Such pressure threatens an employee's right as a citizen to vote as he or she sees fit. Indeed, it threatens democracy. Companies have also been known to expect their employees, again in the name of loyalty, not to buy any products made by a competitor. This, especially when coupled with sanctions against those who do not comply, seems to overstep the bounds of legitimate employer expectations.

Trade secrecy is one area where the line is particularly difficult to draw. While employers have a legal right to expect their employees to keep trade secrets, it is unclear how far employers should be allowed to go to protect their trade secrets. (Trade secrecy law will be discussed more in Chapter 6.) For example, an employer may try to prevent an employee from taking a job at another company for fear that the employee will, intentionally or unintentionally, reveal their secrets to the new employer. Typically employers have employees sign agreements promising not to reveal secrets and they sometimes require employees to agree not to work in the same industry for a certain period of time after they leave the company.

Needless to say, employees often want to move on to another job and their best opportunities are likely to be, if not in the same industry, at least, doing the same kind of work. Employees learn a great deal of what might be called "generic" knowledge while working at a company. It is not considered wrong for employees to take this knowledge with them to their next job. It is this knowledge and experience that makes an employee attractive to another company. So, the employer's legitimate concern about a trade secret has to be balanced against the right of an employee to work where he or she wants.

The employer-employee relationship is more complicated and less well-defined than you might expect. Employees do incur special responsibilities to their employers, but there are limits to this. The Carl Babbage scenario, at the beginning of this chapter, illustrates the point clearly enough. We cannot say that Babbage has no responsibilities to Acme. If he were to blow the whistle, a great deal of damage could be done to the company. And, the damage would be done even if his concerns turned out to be wrong. On the other hand, it is hard to say that out of loyalty to the company he should do nothing. What he owes the company and when he should "break ranks" is not easy to figure out.

Client-Professional

The Carl Babbage scenario can also be understood to involve a conflict between an employee's responsibilities to an employer and to a client. The client in this case is the Defense Department, and technically it is Acme's client, only indirectly Babbage's. The Defense Department has entrusted its project to Acme, and it would seem that to be true to this trust, Acme should inform its client of the unanticipated problems. The problem here, of course, is that Acme does not appear to be behaving well. This creates the problem for Babbage. He is expected by Acme to use the channels of authority in the organization. One can think of Acme's organizational structure as a mechanism for managing its responsibilities. Babbage has tried to work through this structure but it has not been effective.

In both the Leikessa Jones scenario and the Juan Roriguez scenario, the layers of bureaucracy are removed so that there is a more direct client-professional relationship. These are, perhaps, the better cases to use when first thinking through the character of client-professional relationships.

As with the employer-employee relationship, the client-professional relationship can be thought of as essentially a contractual relationship. Each party provides something the other wants, and both parties agree to the terms of the relationship. They agree about what will be done, how long it will take, how much the client will pay, where the work will be done, and so on. The important thing to keep in mind about client-professional relationships is the disparity in knowledge or expertise of the parties.

The client seeks the professional's special knowledge and expertise, but because the client does not possess that knowledge, the client must depend on the professional. "Trust" is the operative term here. The client needs the professional to make or help make decisions that may be crucial to the client's business, and must *trust* that the professional will use his or her knowledge competently, effectively, and efficiently. This is true of doctor-patient, lawyer-client, architect-client, and teacher-student relationships, as well as in relationships between computer professionals and clients.

Different models have been proposed for understanding how this disparity in knowledge in professional-client relationships should be handled. Perhaps the most important models are: (1) agency, (2) paternalism, and (3) fiduciary (Bayles, 1981).

Briefly, on the agency model, the professional is to act as the agent of the professional and simply implement what the client requests. Here the implication is that the client retains all decision-making authority. The professional may make decisions but they are minor, that is, they are simply implications of the client's choice. I call a stock broker, tell her what stocks I want to buy, how many, what price, and she executes the transaction. She is my agent.

Some client-professional relationships are like this, but the problem with this model is that it does not come to grips with the special knowledge or expertise of the professional. Often the professional has knowledge that reflects back on what the client ought to be deciding. Professional advice is needed not just to implement decisions but to help make the decisions.

At the opposite extreme is the paternalistic model. Here the client transfers all decision-making authority to the professional. The professional acts in the interests of the client making decisions that he or she believes will benefit the client. This model clearly recognizes the special expertise of the professional, so much so that the client has little "say." We used to think that the doctor-patient relationship followed this model. I go to a doctor, report my symptoms, and the rest is up to the doctor. He or she decides what I need and prescribes the treatment. I am simply expected to accept what the doctor prescribes. How can I question the doctor's authority when I don't have the expert knowledge?

The problem with the paternalistic model of client-professional relationships is that it expects the client to turn over all autonomy to the professional and cease to be a decision maker. The client must place him or herself at the complete mercy of the professional.

The third model attempts to understand client-professional relationships as relationships in which both parties have a role and are working together. Clients retain decision-making authority but make decisions on the basis of information provided by the professional. This is called the "fiduciary" model. "Fiduciary" implies trust. On this model, both parties must trust one another. The client must trust the professional to use his or her expert knowledge and to think in terms of the interest of the client, but the professional must also trust that the client will give the professional relevant information, will listen to what the professional says, and so on. On this model, decision making is shared.

Using the fiduciary model, computer professionals serving clients have the responsibility to be honest with clients about what they can and can't do, to inform them about what is possible, give them realistic estimates of time and costs for their services, and much more. They also have the responsibility to give clients the opportunity to make decisions about various features of the software or hardware being developed. Leikessa Jones seems to be working on the assumption of this sort of relationship in that she has informed her client of the possibilities and has made a recommendation. The problem now is that she doesn't think her client is making the right decision. The fiduciary model would seem to call upon her to go back to her client and try to explain. It is hard to say what she should do if she is unsuccessful at convincing them. What is clear is that she owes her clients the benefits of her judgment.

In the Juan Rodriguez scenario, we see a computer professional doing something that threatens to undermine the trust that is so important to client-professional relationships. Juan has allowed himself to enter into a conflict of interest situation. His client—the hospital—expects him to exercise professional judgment on behalf of (in the interest of) the hospital. While Juan may think he will be able to evaluate the offers made by each software company objectively, he has an interest in one of those companies that could affect his judgment. If representatives of the hospital find out about this, they might well conclude that Juan has not acted in the hospital's best interest. Even if Juan recommends that the hospital buy software from another company (not Tri-Star), there is the possibility that Juan's judgment has been distorted by his "bending over backwards" to treat the other companies fairly. In that case, the hospital would not have gotten the best system either.

Society-Professional

When professionals exercise their skill and act in their professional roles, their activities may affect others who are neither employers nor clients. For example, you may design a computer system that will be used in a dangerous manufacturing process. Use of the system may put workers at risk or it may put residents in the neighborhood of the plant at risk. Or, you might simply design a database management system for a company, where the security of the system has implications for those who are in the database. Because the work of computer professionals has these potential effects, computer professionals have a relationship with those who may be affected.

This relationship is, to a certain extent, shaped by law. That is, regulatory laws setting safety standards for products and construction are made in order to protect the public interest. But the law does not and cannot possibly anticipate all the effects that the work of professionals may have. At the same time, professionals, including computer professionals, are often in the best position to see what effects their work will have or to evaluate the risks involved. Carl Babbage, for example, because of his expertise and familiarity with the system being designed, is in a better position than anyone outside of Acme to know whether or not the missile detecting system needs further evaluation.

The relationship between professionals and the individuals indirectly affected by their work can also be understood in terms of a social contract (as suggested earlier). In this framework, society grants the members of a profession (or the profession as a whole) the right to practice their profession in exchange for their promise to practice the profession in ways that serve society, or, at least in ways that do no harm to society. This means maintaining professional standards and looking out for the public good. On this model, both parties give something and receive something in the exchange. Society gives professionals the right to practice and other forms of support, and receives the benefits of having such professionals. Professionals receive the right to practice and other forms of societal support (protection of law, access to educational systems, and so on), and in exchange take on the burden of responsibility for managing themselves so as to serve the public interest. If a profession were not committed to public good, it would be foolish for society to allow members to practice.

Another way to understand the relationship between professionals and the public is by returning to the idea of professions possessing special knowledge and skill, and the power of positions. What distinguishes computer professionals from others is their knowledge of how computers work, what computers can and cannot do, and how to get computers to do things. This knowledge, one might insist, carries with it, some responsibility. When a person has knowledge—special knowledge—he has a responsibility to use it for the benefit of humanity, or, at least, not to the detriment of humanity. Special knowledge coupled with the power of position gives computer professionals efficacy; they can do things in the world which others cannot. Thus, they have greater responsibility than others.

The only problem with this account is that it seems to simply assert a correlation between knowledge and responsibility without showing the connection. The connection is left as a primitive without explanation. Thus, we cannot help but ask: Why does responsibility come with knowledge? Why does it have to be so?

One way to establish the correlation between knowledge and responsibility is to base it on a principle of ordinary morality. Alpern (1983) argues that the edict "do no harm" is a fundamental principle of ordinary morality that no one should or will question. He has to qualify the principle somewhat so that it reads, "other things being equal, one should exercise due care to avoid contributing to significantly harming others." He then adds a corollary, the corollary of proportionate care: "whenever one is in a position to contribute to greater harm or when one is in a position to play a more critical part in producing harm than is another person, one must exercise greater care to avoid so doing."

Focusing on engineers, Alpern argues that while engineers are no different from anybody else in having the responsibility to avoid contributing to significant harm, they are different in that they are in positions (because of their work) in which they can do more harm than others. Thus, they have a responsibility to do more, to take greater care.

All of this would seem to apply to computer professionals—at least, to many of them. Computer professionals often hold positions in which they can use their expertise to contribute to projects which have the potential to harm others, as in the case of Carl Babbage. Since they act in ways that have the potential to do more harm, they have greater responsibility.

Alpern's account does seem to apply to computer professionals, though it is worth noting that according to this account it is not just computer professionals that bear responsibility but all those who contribute to projects with the potential to harm. Employed computer professionals can argue that they do not have nearly as much power as corporate managers, CEOs, or anyone above them in an organizational hierarchy. Alpern's proportionality thesis implies that the greater a person's power, the greater his or her responsibility. Of course, this need not be an either/or matter. Everyone, by Alpern's account, bears some responsibility, and so computer professionals bear their share of the responsibility along with managers and executives (Johnson, 1992).

Professional-Professional

Many professionals believe that they have obligations to other members of their profession. For example, professionals are often reluctant to criticize each other publicly and they often help each other in getting jobs or in testifying at hearings when one of them is being sued. However, whether or not such behavior can be justified as a moral obligation is controversial.

It seems that the special treatment one professional gives to another may at times be good and other times not. The earlier discussion of loyalty is relevant here. If one of your coprofessionals is an alcoholic and, as a result, not doing a competent job, it is good that you try to help the person. On the other hand, if you keep your coprofessionals' problem a secret, not wanting to jeopardize his or her career, this may result in injury to the person's employer or client. Similarly, when professionals get together to fix prices, this may be good for the professionals in that they can demand higher and higher prices, but it is not good for consumers who might benefit from a more competitive market.

We can take the cynical view that professionals only unite with one another to serve their shared self-interest but even this line of thinking, when extended to the long-term interests, justifies professionals treating clients and the public well. Every professional has an interest in the reputation of the profession because it affects how individual members are perceived and treated. Hence, each member of a profession may further his or her self-interest by forming alliances with other coprofessionals and agreeing to refrain from certain types of behavior. For example, even though some might benefit from lying about their qualifications, or taking bribes, or fudging test results, in the long run such practices hurt the reputation of the profession and, therefore, individual practitioners. The trust that clients and society must place in professionals is undermined and eroded when members of a profession behave badly. All members of the profession are hurt. Clients become more reluctant to use computer systems and to rely on computer experts.

One way to think about what professionals owe to one another is to think of what they owe each other in the way of adherence to certain standards of conduct. This is different from thinking only of what they might do to help and protect one another in the short term. Rules about being honest, avoiding conflicts of interest, giving credit where credit is due, and so on can be understood to be obligations of one member of a profession to other members (Davis, 1992).

CONFLICTING RESPONSIBILITIES

The complexity of managing responsibilities in the relationships just discussed should not be underestimated. Indeed, your work environment is not always structured so as to make it easy to keep your responsibilities in harmony. Issues of professional ethics often arise from conflicts between responsibilities to different parties.

Possibly the most common—at least, the most publicized—conflict is that between responsibilities to an employer and responsibility to society. The Carl Babbage case illustrates the typical situation. The employed professional is working on a project and has serious reservations about the safety or reliability of the product. For the good of those who will be affected by the project, the professional believes the project should not go forward yet. On the other hand, the employer (or supervisor) believes that it is in the interest of the company for the project to go forward. The professional has to decide whether to keep quiet or do something that will "rock the boat."

To see why this conflict arises, we can return to our discussion of the characteristics of the work life of professionals and compare the situation of a typical employed computer professional with that of a stereotypical doctor. Perhaps the most striking difference is that the typical computer professional employed in a large private corporation has much less autonomy than a doctor working in private practice. Computer professionals often work as employees of very large corporations or government agencies and have little autonomy.

Another characteristic of the work of computer professionals in contrast with that of doctors, is its relatively fragmented nature. Computer professionals often work on small parts of much larger, highly complex projects. Whatever authority they have is limited to the small segment, with someone else having the designated responsibility for the whole project. As well, computer professionals are often quite distant from the ultimate effects of their activities. They may work on a project at certain stages of its development and then never see the product until it appears in the market place, having no involvement in how it is used, distributed, or advertised. Doctors, on the other hand, see in their patients the direct results of their decisions, and lawyers know whether they have won or lost cases, furthered or impeded the interests of their clients, and so on.

Often computer professionals find themselves in a tension between their need for autonomy and the demands for organizational loyalty made by their employers (Layton, 1971/1986). On the one hand, they need autonomy because they have special knowledge. If they are to use that knowledge in a responsible manner and for the good of society, they must have the power to do so. However, insofar as they work for corporations with complex, highly bureaucratized organizational structures, and insofar as such large organizations need coordination of their various parts, there must be a division of labor, and they must often simply do what they are told. Carl Babbage's dilemma arises from this tension.

Acts of whistle-blowing arise out of precisely this sort of situation. Whistle-blowers opt against loyalty to their employer in favor of protecting society. Whistle-blowing is, perhaps, the most dramatic form of the problem. Other issues that come up for computer professionals are more subtle aspects of this same tension—between loyalty to employer and social responsibility or professional responsibility. Should I work on military projects or other projects I believe are likely to have bad effects? What am I to do when I know that a certain kind of system can never be built safely or securely enough, but I need the money or my company needs the contract? What do I do when a client is willing to settle for much less safety or security than is possible?

In the case of computer professionals, because the profession is relatively new and not well organized, the commitment to public safety and welfare is neither well entrenched in everyday practice nor well articulated in professional codes or literature. Nevertheless, the tension exists between protecting public good or adhering to professional standards *and* staying loyal to a higher organizational authority. It comes into clear focus now and then when cases involving public safety come to public attention. One of the first cases of whistle-blowing to be written about extensively involved three computer specialists working on the Bay Area Rapid Transit (BART) system (Anderson et al., 1980). The computer professionals in this case were concerned about the safety of the system controlling train speeds. They feared that under certain circumstances trains might be speeded up when they should be slowed. When their concerns were dismissed by their supervisors and then by the board monitoring the project, they went to newspaper reporters. In another case drawing public attention, David Parnas, a well-recognized computer scientist, spoke out against funding for the Strategic Defense Initiatives (Parnas, 1987).

CODES OF ETHICS AND PROFESSIONAL CONDUCT

The role of a code of ethics and professional conduct was discussed earlier in this chapter in relation to the process of professionalization. However, codes of ethics serve a variety of functions, so they are worthy of further discussion. It is important to keep in mind that a code of ethics may, at one and the same time, be directed to members of the profession, the public, and employers and clients of members of the profession.

Perhaps the most important function of a code of ethics is as a statement embodying the collective wisdom of members of the profession. You can read a code of ethics as a statement of what members of the profession, with many years of experience, have found to be the most important things to think about and do when working as a computer professional. The code expresses both the experience of many members and the consensus of many members.

Currently, there are several codes of ethics in computing. Perhaps the most visible codes are those produced by the ACM and the IEEE. These codes as well as the newly developed Software Engineering Code of Ethics and Professional Practice are available on the Web. The addresses are provided at the end of this chapter. I mentioned earlier that the latter code was developed by a joint ACM-IEEE taskforce with an eye to the licensing of software engineers.

While these codes are somewhat different in their emphasis, they are re-markably similar in what they identify as important for computer professionals. As you review these codes, you should keep in mind that codes of ethics serve multiple functions. Earlier in this chapter, I discussed the role of codes of ethics in establishing public trust. Even if a profession does not win a monopoly of control, the code helps to fend off external regulation. In effect, the code says to the public that this profession will serve the interests of the public and will adhere to certain standards of behavior as well as aspire to certain ideals. In making this statement, the profession wants to show that it is worthy of trust as well as special status. In this way, the code also sets expectations; it informs employers and clients as well as the public of what to expect in their dealings with members of the profession.

Insofar as codes of ethics are aimed at the public, they may appear to be a public relations tool; they make the profession look good. So it is important to remember that regardless of the motive for its creation, if the code contains rules that protect the public, and promote worthy practices, then their self-serving character is not problematic.

Codes of ethics are not just statements to the public; they are also state-ments to and for members of the profession. They can serve several functions here. First, a code may be understood to be a statement of the shared commit-ments of the members. As such we might think of a code as the embodiment of agreed upon values and concerns. Second, a code may be a statement of agreed upon rules or standards. In creating a code, members of a profession may be understood to be saying to each other, "these are the standards we all agree to follow." A third function of a code in relation to its members is to sen-sitize members to issues that they might not be aware of. As new members read the code for the first time (or experienced members re-read the code), they may become aware of issues surrounding computing that they had not fully recognized before.

Related to the standard setting function, a code of professional conduct might be designed to provide guidance to professionals who find themselves in tough ethical situations. In other words, a professional who finds herself in a tight spot might look to the code to help figure out what to do. This is a par-ticularly difficult goal to achieve with a code since the situations that com-puter professionals find themselves in are so diverse and the details can make all the difference. Codes of ethics must be general enough to apply to most, if not all, computer professionals, and in order to do this, they must stay very gen-eral. In the 1992 ACM Code of Ethics, the taskforce developing the Code rec-ognized the tension between generalities and specifics and between ideals and guidelines by dividing the Code into two parts. The first part of the Code con-sists of a set of short statements of what every ACM member will do. A second section of the code consists of guidelines that provide much more detail about the meaning of each short statement. This section gives some guidance but the discussion is still in broad terms.

Finally, a code of conduct could be used as a mechanism for educating or socializing. Here the idea is that those entering the field, when introduced to the code will quickly learn what the standards in the profession are. Without a code, there is little quality control on what members of an occupational group learn about the standards in the field. In fields like computing, the educational requirements tend to emphasize technical subject matter to the neglect of professionalism. Members of such professions often learn about their profession in their first job. If your first job happens to be in a place where the standards are sloppy and unprofessional, you may come to believe that this is the way all computer professionals behave. On the other hand, you may luck out and land a first job in an environment in which the tone is highly professional. The problem is that what you learn will, largely, be a matter of luck. If, however, there is a code of ethics and all individuals entering the field get some exposure to it, then there is some assurance that all new members will, at least, know about the standards that have been explicated in the code.

It is probably impossible for a code to serve all of these functions. The process of developing and adopting a code is extremely complex and political. Some functions must give way to others depending on where a profession is in its development. Nevertheless, the variety of functions that a code can serve is important to recognize in evaluating codes and thinking about how they might be changed.

COLLECTIVE RESPONSIBILITY

It is important in thinking about issues of professional ethics not to fall into the trap of thinking only about individuals—individual responsibility and individual decision making. A profession (be it an occupational group or a profession in the stronger sense of the term) can do a great deal as a collective unit. The group can act effectively and powerfully to improve the development and use of computer and information technology as well as to improve the work life of computer professionals.

Often collective action can be more powerful than individual action. It can prevent problems and make it easier for individual professionals to act in ethical ways. For example, organizations of computer professionals such as the ACM and the IEEE can work to create better public policies affecting computing. Remember that computer professionals know more about computing and are in a better position than the average citizen to understand the risks and benefits of computing. Think also of what the profession as a whole might do on such issues as protection for whistle-blowers and assistance for those who find themselves in moral tight spots. Policies that protect and support computer professionals who express legitimate professional concerns about safety and security can do more in the long run than one or two individuals acting alone even though they are acting in morally heroic ways.

In fact, there are many important issues that can effectively be addressed by the collective action of computer professionals. Remember Scenario 1.4 in Chapter 1 in which a computer professional wonders about gender bias in the field of computing and in particular in software development. While computer professionals can address this problem individually, they can also address it collectively. Collective action can make individual professionals aware of the problem and aware that it is an important concern. Collectively computer professionals can be pro-active in discovering why the problem arises and recommend strategies for addressing the problem.

Another example of an issue that can be addressed both collectively and effectively is security. This is a matter that every computer professional should be concerned about but this is also a matter that can greatly benefit from a pooling of ideas, cooperation, and collaboration regardless of where individuals are employed. Computer professional organizations can raise awareness of the issue, undertake research that individuals alone cannot do, and make recommendations that are backed by the power and authority of the entire profession.

CONCLUSION

In this chapter I have discussed a variety of issues surrounding the role of the computer professional. When an individual acquires special knowledge and skill with regard to computer and information technology, the individual acquires efficacy. With efficacy comes responsibility. When one becomes a computer professional, one may acquire responsibilities to an employer, clients, and other members of the profession. All computer professionals have a responsibility to protect public safety and well-being. Hence, ethics is central to the role of the computer professional.

While I have pointed to a variety of strategies for ensuring that computer professionals act ethically, the bottom line is that all of us (computer professionals, the public, employers, and clients) benefit when computer professionals take responsibility for computing. Ideally, all computer professionals, individually and collectively, work to shape computer systems for the good of humanity.

STUDY QUESTIONS

1. What is special about acting in a professional role?
2. What is special about *strongly differentiated* professional roles? Is the role of computer professional a *strongly differentiated* role?
3. What is meant by the "efficacy" of professionals?
4. What characteristics are usually associated with professions?
5. How can professions and the process of professionalization be understood as systems?

6. Is computing a profession? What are the arguments for? What are the arguments against?

7. Should software engineers be licensed? What are the advantages? The drawbacks?

8. Name the primary relationships that individuals have when they work as computer professionals. Can each type of relationship be thought of as contractual in character? Explain.

9. How does the categorical imperative apply to the employer-employee relationship? How does it constrain employers in treating employees?

10. What is valuable about loyalty? What is problematic about loyalty?

11. How do the agency, paternalistic, and fiduciary models of client-professional relationships deal with the disparity in knowledge of the client and professional? What is wrong, if anything, with each of these models?

12. On the fiduciary model of client-professional relationships, what might a computer professional owe to a client, and what might a client owe to a computer professional?

13. How would a social contract theory account for the responsibility of professionals to those who may be affected by their work?

14. What is the corollary of proportionate care? How might it apply to computer professionals?

15. How does the issue of whistle-blowing arise for computer professionals?

16. What functions can a code of professional conduct aim to serve?

17. What are the responsibilities of computer professionals according to the ACM and IEEE codes of conduct?

SUGGESTED FURTHER READING

ABBOTT, ANDREW, *The System of Professions An Essay on the Division of Expert Labor* (Chicago: University of Chicago Press, 1988).

ANDERSON, RONALD E., DEBORAH G. JOHNSON, DONALD GOTTERBARN, and JUDITH PEŘOLLE, "Using the New ACM Code of Ethics in Decision Making," *Communications of the ACM*, vol. 36, no. 2 (1993), 98–105.

COLLINS, W. R., and KEITH MILLER, "Programming and Public Trust," National Forum 29 (1991), pp. 28–29.

GOLDMAN, ALAN, *The Moral Foundations of Professional Ethics* (Totowa, NJ: Rowman and Littlefield, 1980).

GOTTERBARN, DON, "How the New Software Engineering Code of Ethics Affects You," *IEEE Software* (November/December 1999), pp. 58–64.

GOTTERBARN, DON, "Software Engineering: A New Professionalism," in *The Responsible Software Engineer,* ed. Colin Myers (London: Springer Verlag, 1997).

JOHNSON, DEBORAH G., *Ethical Issues in Engineering* (Englewood Cliffs, NJ: Prentice-Hall, 1991).

WEB SITES

For codes of ethics from many professions, see www.csep.iit.edu/codes/computer.html
For a broad range of materials, see www.onlineethics.org/
For the AMC Code of Ethics, see www.acm.org/constitution/code.html
For the IEEE Code of Ethics, see www.services5.ieee.org/about/whatis/code.html
For CS/ACM Code of Ethics, see www.computer.org/tab/code11.html

CHAPTER 4

Ethics and the Internet I: Ethics Online

SCENARIO 4.1 **The Robert Morris case.**

Around 6 P.M. EST on Wednesday, November 2, 1988, a computer "worm" was discovered in a system in Pennsylvania. Soon the worm was spreading itself across the Internet. By 10 P.M. the worm had managed to infect the Bay Area Research Network (BARnet), which was at the time one of the most sophisticated and fastest in the nation. At this time, the worm exploded quickly throughout the Internet, and teams of computer wizards combined forces to stop the threat.

The worm attacked the system in three different ways. First, it would simply crack various passwords by force. Next, the worm would attack the core of UNIX, a program widely used in the network, by attacking a main function known as "sendmail" and adjust its commands. Finally, the worm would overstack data into a status report function known as "finger demon" or "fingerd." The worm would do this so as not to attract notice by making itself look like legitimate commands. After completing infection of a site, the worm would replicate itself and go to another system. When a site was successfully infected, the worm would send a signal to "Ernie," a popular computer system at Berkeley. To avoid quick detection, the worm program would, in effect, role a 15-sided die to see if it could infect a new system. A positive role, a 1-in-15 chance, would instruct the worm to go ahead. Unfortunately, the program was faulty and was infecting on a 14-in-15 chance instead. This caused systems to slow down and operators to take notice.

The infector was eventually identified as Robert T. Morris, Jr., a Cornell computer science graduate student. Within 48 hours, the worm had been isolated, decompiled, and notices had gone out explaining how to destroy the pest. While the worm did no permanent damage, it slowed systems to a standstill and acquired passwords into these systems.

Morris was suspended from Cornell by a university board of inquiry for irresponsible acts, and went to trial in January 1990. A federal court in Syracuse charged him with violating the Federal Computer Fraud and Abuse Act of

1986. The Morris case was unprecedented in U.S. courts; it was the first to test the 1986 Act. During the trial, Morris revealed that he had realized he had made a mistake and tried to stop the worm. He contacted various friends at Harvard to help him. Andrew Sudduth testified at the trial that he had sent messages out with the solution to kill the program, but the networks were already clogged with the worm.

Morris was found guilty, was placed on three years' probation, fined $10,000, and ordered to perform 400 hours of community service. He could have been jailed for up to five years and fined $250,000.

During the trial, the seriousness of Morris' behavior was debated in newspapers and magazines. On one side, some said that his crime was not serious, and that release of the worm had managed to alert many systems managers to the vulnerability of their computers. Those who thought this, also thought that no jail time was appropriate, but community service was. On the other side, some argued that Morris should go to jail. The argument put forth was that a jail sentence would send a clear message to those attempting similar actions on computer systems.

This case summary was written by Dave Colantonio based on the following: "The Worm's Aftermath" *Science* (November 11, 1988); "Hacker's Case May Shape Computer Security Law," *The Washington Post* (January 9, 1990); "Student Testifies His Error Jammed Computer Network," *New York Times* (January 19, 1990); "From Hacker to Symbol," *New York Times* (January 24, 1990); "Revenge on the Nerds," *The Washington Post* (February 11, 1990); "U.S. Accepts Hacker's Sentence," *New York Times* (June 2, 1990); "No Jail Time Imposed in Hacker Case," *The Washington Post* (May 5, 1990); "Computer Intruder Is Put on Probation and Fined $10,000," *New York Times* (May 5, 1990).

SCENARIO 4.2 The Melissa virus.

In March 1999, David Smith created the Melissa virus. The virus was constructed to evade anti-virus software and to infect computers using Windows operating systems, and the Microsoft Word 97 and Word 2000 word processing programs. On March 26, 1999, Smith, who lived in New Jersey, accessed the AOL account of a civil engineer in Lynwood, Washington. He proceeded to post on the newsgroup "Alt.Sex" a message with an attachment infected with the Melissa virus, indicating that the attachment contained a list of pass codes to pornographic Web sites.

Opening and downloading the message caused Melissa to infect victim computers. Once launched, Melissa alters programs such that any document created is infected with the virus. The virus then proliferates by starting Microsoft Outlook and sending copies of the infected document as an attachment to the first 50 addresses in the address book. The e-mail carrying the attachment is thus disguised as an important message from a colleague or friend, and reads as "Here is that document that you asked for . . . don't show anyone else" to entice the reader to open the attachment. In this manner, the Melissa virus was said to have infected over a million computers in the United States alone. Its rapid distribution disrupted computer networks by overloading e-mail servers, causing indirectly a denial of service on mail servers and substantial costs to repair the computer systems. Damages were estimated to be more than $80 million.

Smith was arrested by New Jersey authorities on April 1, 1999, and pleaded guilty on December 9, 1999 in the U.S. District Court in Newark, New Jersey, to a one-count accusation charging the second-degree offense of computer-related theft. He is currently awaiting sentencing.

This scenario was researched and written by Marc Pang Quek based on the following: U.S. Department of Justice Press Release, *Creator of Melissa Computer Virus Pleads Guilty to State and Federal Charges* (December 9, 1999). Available: www.usdoj.gov/criminal/cybercrime/melipres.htm (accessed on February 14, 2000, 1400 EST); other DOJ Press releases; CERT Advisory CA-99-04-Melissa-Macro-Virus. Available: www.cert.org/advisories/CA-99-04-Melissa-Macro-Virus.html (accessed on February 14, 2000 1400 EST); Erich Luening, "Smith Pleads Guilty to Melissa Virus Charges," CNET News.com (December 9, 1999, 1:40 P.M. PT); Stephanie Miles, "Melissa Virus Still Circulating," CNET News.com (October 15, 1999, 6:35 P.M. PT); Stephen Shankland, "Melissa suspect arrested in New Jersey," CNET News.com (April 2, 1999, 2:55 P.M. PT).

SCENARIO 4.3 Credit card extortion.

Maxis (alias), a self-described 19-year-old Russian, had been involved in the illegal use of credit cards since 1997. In 1998, he discovered a flaw in the credit card verification program called ICVerify, which was used to protect financial information on Internet Web sites. Maxis proceeded to steal the 300,000 credit card numbers stored on an online music store CDUniverse.

On December 1999, Maxis sent a fax to CDUniverse extorting US$100,000 in exchange for the destruction of his cache of stolen information. ("pay me $100,000 and I'll fix your bugs and forget about your SHOP FOREVER . . . or I'll sell your cards and tell about this incident in news"). When the company did not respond to his demands, Maxis created a Web site called Maxus Credit Card Pipeline, and posted the credit card files on the Web site on December 25, 1999. The Web site was shut down on January 9, 2000, but while it was up several thousand visitors had downloaded more than 25,000 credit card numbers from the Maxus Web site.

American Express and Discover, credit card companies based in the United States, reacting to the incident, replaced about 300,000 credit cards belonging to those customers who had made purchases from CDUniverse.

This scenario was researched and written by Marc Pang Quek based on the following: John Markoff, "Thief Reveals Credit Card Data When Web Extortion Plot Fails," *New York Times* (January 10, 2000), section A, p. 1; Louise Kehoe, "Hacker Forces Card Recall," *The Financial Times (London)* (January 20, 2000), p. 8; Mark Ward, "Internet Hacker in Credit Card Plot," *The Electronic Telegraph* (January 12, 2000). Available: www.telegraph.co.uk/et?ac=002444936927410&rtmo=02xGssGq&atmo=t . . . /whak12.htm (accessed on February 19, 2000 at 1100 EST).

SCENARIO 4.4 Cyberstalking.

Gary Dellapenta was a former security guard living in North Hollywood. In 1996, Dellapenta met a 28 year-old woman at church. He took an interest in her, but when she did not reciprocate, Dellapenta started following her. In 1998 when the woman spurned his romantic advances, Dellapenta decided to solicit her rape. He impersonated her in various Internet chat rooms and on-line bulletin boards; disclosed her telephone number and address; and posted messages stating that she has fantasies of being raped. On at least six occasions, sometimes in the middle of the night, the woman received propositions by strangers to rape her. Dellapenta was eventually arrested and prosecuted under California's cyberstalking law. He pleaded guilty on April 28, 1999, to one count of stalking and three counts of solicitation of sexual assault.

This scenario was researched and written by Marc Pang Quek based on the following: Rebecca F. Raney, "Internet Stalking Case Ends in Plea," *New York Times* (April 29, 1999). Available: www.search.nytimes.com/search/daily/b . . . ?getdoc+site+74+_0+wAAA+computer (accessed on April 29, 1999, 11.43 EST); Department of Justice, "1999 Report on Cyberstalking: A New Challenge for Law Enforcement and Industry." Available: www.usdoj.goc/criminal/cybercrime /cyberstalking.htm (accessed on February 14, 2000, 11.10 EST).

SCENARIO 4.5 Flaming.

The term "flame" was coined by computer hackers to refer to lengthy, often insulting, debate in an electronic community. In the case described here, all of the participants were subscribers to Communet. Communet was an unmoderated mailing listserv (all messages were sent directly to all subscribers) devoted to community computing. At six o'clock on Tuesday, March 29, 1993, in response to a request for information regarding community computing, Grundner posted a message that read ". . . we can send a 15-minute videotape on community computing—suitable for showing to potential funders, recalcitrant computer center managers, wives . . . , and other informationally challenged individuals." The message immediately elicited numerous responses from members of the online community.

One member, Mabel, sent a private e-mail to Grundner, reprimanding him for his use of sexist language that alienates women. Grundner thought Mabel had responded publicly to the entire listserv, so he apparently felt embarrassed. He responded to Mabel by sending a message to the entire listserv stating his opinion that online communication has the potential to transcend all barriers so long as "professional victim-mongers" do not "screw it up." Nolan, like many other subscribers, regarded Grundner's reply to Mabel as a personal attack, and questioned Grundner's personal tone.

Other subscribers began voicing their opinions on Grundner's comments and on issues of gender online. The e-mails chided Grundner for his behavior on his two messages. The flame spread and grabbed the attention of the entire community.

Grundner posted a conciliatory message proposing a new discussion forum on encouraging women (and other minorities) to use this technology and solicited volunteers to keep official records of the suggestions presented. His suggestions were met with immediate support from the community, and positive responses were received from even Nolan and Mabel. The subscribers were generally forgiving of Grundner's earlier action.

This scenario was researched and written by Marc Pang Quek based on the following: V. Franco, R. Piirto, H. Y. Hu, and B. V. Lewenstein, "Anatomy of a Flame: Conflict and Community Building on the Internet," *IEEE Technology and Society*(Summer 1995), pp. 12–21.

SCENARIO 4.6 Spamming.

In 1994, two immigration attorneys, Laurence Canter and Marsha Siegel, posted identical copies of an e-mail to thousands of newsgroups, offering their services to people with "green card" problems. This spam outraged most of the newsgroup subscribers. In response, they sent a number of e-mail flames back to Canter and Siegel, overloading the lawyers' service system and causing a shutdown. In addition, a "cancelbot" program was set up to block off any future messages from Canter and Siegel. Although the program was not mobilized, its creation generated discussion among fellow newsgroup subscribers urging that the program be deployed. The lawyers' Internet service provider (ISP), reacting to public pressure, decided to close their account.

On their part, Canter and Siegel were unapologetic. As a result of the spam, they received "25,000 customer inquiries for one night's work—and $100,000 worth of business for a $20 investment." They also threatened to file suit against their ISP for denying them their First Amendment access rights.

On February 9, 2000, undeterred by the negative publicity generated by their first attempt, Canter and Siegel dispatched a similar spam to over 10,000 newsgroups. The newsgroup subscribers each received the identical message that read: "GUARANTEED CREDIT REPAIR BY LAW FIRM." Canter and Siegel also managed to send their electronic advertisement to the newsgroups' emergency channel which was reserved for urgent messages addressed to everyone. The message also carried the false statement that the lawyers' activity had the permission of the newsgroup managers.

This scenario was researched and written by Marc Pang Quek based on the following: Anne Wells Branscomb, Symposium: Emerging Media Technology and the First Amendment: Anonymity, Autonomy, and Accountability: Challenges to the First Amendment in Cyberspaces, 104 Yale L.J. 1639 (May 1995); Roy V. Leeper, and Philip Heeler, "Commercial Speech in Cyberspace: The Junk E-mail Issue," in Real Law @ Virtual Space, eds. Susan J. Drucker, and Gary Gumpert (Creskill, NJ: Hampton Press, 1999), p. 351; Anne E. Hawley Comments: Taking Spam Out of Your Cyberspace Diet: Common Law Applied to Bulk Unsolicited Advertising Via Electronic Mail, 66 UMKCL. Rev. 381 (winter 1997).

Current estimates are that as of January, 2000, approximately 248 million people were connected to the Internet worldwide (*NUA Internet Surveys*, February 2000).

In a speech delivered on January 28, 2000, William E. Kennard (Chairman of U.S. Federal Communications Commission) reported that while there were 27 million Internet users in the United States in 1996, there were now 80 million users. This means an increase of almost 200 percent in four years. It seems almost an understatement to say that in an amazingly short period of time, the Internet has become an integral part of the daily lives of millions and millions of individuals who use it for work, education, shopping, keeping in touch with family and friends, access to news, political campaigning, and so on.

Like many new technologies, the Internet makes life easier in some ways while at the same time creating some problems; it enhances and improves certain aspects of our lives while diminishing other aspects; it brings social costs along with social benefits. The Internet brings individuals from across the globe closer together, in principle increasing the potential for tolerance and peace. Yet at the same time, it intensifies economic competition among nation-states which in turn increases the potential for conflict. The Internet extends the power and reach of individuals, governments, and businesses, but it also extends the power and reach of criminals and terrorists. It increases the potential for individuals to be informed as well as the potential for individuals to be misinformed and manipulated. It provides a new arena for entertainment and sociability while at the same time providing a new arena for those whom would exploit, harass, stalk, and torment others.

The scenarios at the beginning of this chapter are all descriptions of real incidents. They suggest the range of problematic behavior that arises on the Internet. Roughly, the scenarios fall into three categories. The first two scenarios describe incidents in which individuals engaged in behavior that disrupted the smooth functioning of the Internet. While the motive was different in each case, the behavior was destructive in both cases. I will refer to this category of behavior as *hacking* (and those who engage in the behavior as *hackers*) and will include in this category such actions as gaining unauthorized access to computer systems, releasing viruses, taking control of Web sites, and making denial of service attacks on Web sites. This type of behavior undermines the reliability and security of the Internet.

Scenarios 4.3 and 4.4 fit into a second category of problematic behavior. As with the first category, the behavior is illegal, but here the core character of the criminal act predates the Internet. Scenario 4.3 describes an act of theft and extortion, and Scenario 4.4 describes a stalking. These crimes can be conceptualized without the Internet though they take a somewhat different form when the Internet is used and for this reason it seems appropriate to say that they are new species of familiar crimes.

While the first category of behavior involved attacking the Internet, in this second category the Internet facilitates and provides a new arena for engaging in behavior that would be illegal and problematic without it. Stealing electronic funds is different in certain ways from walking into a bank, pointing a gun, and asking for paper money. Likewise, cyberstalking involves different types of actions than following a person around and watching their every move in geographic space. This category includes just about any form of crime you can imagine including slander, fraud, harassment, terrorism, illegal forms of gambling, solicitation of minors, and so on, for they all can be done using the Internet.

Scenarios 4.5 and 4.6 fall into a third category of problematic behavior. This type of behavior may not rise to the level of illegality (as with the prior two categories). It may or may not rise to the level of unethical behavior. Indeed, this kind of behavior often raises the question as to whether laws should be created making the behavior illegal. Often this kind of behavior is framed as a matter civil behavior or what is sometimes called *netiquette*—a set of informal social conventions specifying how to behave when interacting on the Internet. Questions about netiquette abound. What should the conventions be? What forms of behavior should be encouraged? What forms should be discouraged? How should these conventions be communicated and entrenched?

To better understand these three categories of online behavior, it will be helpful to step back from them and ask what is unusual or special about acting and interacting on the Internet. In the next section of this chapter, I identify three features of Internet communication—global, interactive scope; anonymity; and reproducibility, that have moral significance. This analysis will provide a basis for further discussion of the three types of problematic behavior. The chapter ends with a brief review of the policy alternatives available for addressing problematic behavior on the Internet.

You may be surprised at what you will *not* find in this chapter. The Internet has generated such an endless array of ethical issues that it is impossible to cover all of them. Moreover, many of the seemingly ethical issues are descriptive or empirical rather than normative issues. For example, the Internet raises a number of questions about why individuals do what they do and about how their behavior might be controlled. Why do individuals engage in types of behavior online that they wouldn't engage in when face-to-face with others? What kinds of social relationships can and do form online? What signals do individuals respond to when they are interacting in computer-mediated environments? These questions ask for a description and/or explanation of human behavior, that is, they ask what people do and why they do it. While relevant to a discussion of ethics, these questions are not the primary focus.

Several of the ethical issues surrounding the Internet are better framed as social implications of the new medium rather than as implicitly ethical issues, and I take these issues up in Chapter 8 where I focus on social values being affected by the Internet, especially democracy and democratic values.

THREE MORALLY SIGNIFICANT CHARACTERISTICS

In Chapter 1, I argued that the ethical issues surrounding computer and information technology are new species of generic moral problems. Internet instrumented activities can be understood in just this way, as can the three categories of problematic behavior just described. Problematic behavior can be characterized in familiar moral terms such as breaking in, stealing, disrupting, being a nuisance, slander, fraud, stalking, sabotage, and so on. Nevertheless, it would be a mistake to underestimate the difference that the Internet makes. (New species have distinct features, features that other species lack.) When activities are conducted via the Internet, it becomes possible for human beings to do what they couldn't do before or to do more easily what would have been rather difficult without the Internet. So, it will be helpful to identify what is distinctive about action and interaction on the Internet.

We can begin by classifying the Internet as a means of communication, and then compare it with other forms of communication, such as face-to-face conversation, or other technology-mediated forms such as telephone, television, and radio. When this comparison is made, Internet communication is revealed to have three special features: (1) it has an unusual scope in that it provides for many-to-many communication on a global scale; (2) it facilitates a certain kind of anonymity; and (3) it has reproducibility.

Global, Many-to-Many Scope

When compared to face-to-face communication, individuals communicating on the Internet have a much broader scope or reach. In face-to-face communication, you speak to other individuals who are geographically close. Whether you stand close to the others or yell to them from a distance, your reach is limited by the structure of a human throat and the character of human ears (i.e., by the speaking and hearing capacities of humans). With the Internet, those capacities are considerably expanded; a user can (with relatively little physical effort) reach hundreds and thousands of individuals around the world. The Internet significantly extends an individual's communicative reach in relation to the effort involved.

While the breadth of reach of the Internet is unusual when compared to face-to-face communication, it is not unusual when compared to telephone communication or radio and television. Indeed, the reach of telephone communication and the reach of the Internet are the same. I will return to this point in a moment.

Without the Internet, individuals can extend the scope or reach of face-to-face communication by writing words on paper and sending them via a postal service or they can publish written words in a newspaper, magazine, or book. Letters can reach many across the globe; published words can reach thousands—even millions in some cases—of readers. By comparison with the Internet, however, these means of communication are much more difficult to use. On the Internet, you move your fingers over a keyboard and click on icons and your message can be sent to many; those many may send the message to many others, and so on. To make words written on paper reach as many people, you must after writing the words on paper, duplicate them, stuff the paper into hundreds of envelopes, address the envelopes, adhere postage, and find a postal box. Of course, you can reach more people with words written on paper when the words are published in the form of a book or magazine article. From the writer's perspective, this takes less effort because the duplication and distribution of the words is done by the publisher, but the problem here is that it is not so easy to get something published. Moreover, in both these cases—sending words written on paper and publishing words on paper—the time frame from writing to reaching an audience is much longer. So, relative to putting words on paper, the Internet is a much easier and faster way to reach many people.

This ability to reach many people easily and quickly is not exactly new or unique when compared to radio and television communication. Radio and television instrument human action in such a way that it has all the characteristics just attributed to the Internet. Its easy (you stand in front of a camera or a microphone), it can be fast (in real time), and it can reach huge numbers of people, people all over the world. You don't even have to write the words down (you just speak as you stand in front of the camera or microphone).

Still, there is one very significant difference between the Internet and television and radio. Television and radio are *one way,* going from the broadcast station to listeners and watchers. The Internet, on the other hand, is multidirectional; it is *interactive.* If we think of radio and television as communication from one to many, then the Internet is communication from *many to many.*

It is tempting to say, then, that interactivity is the unique characteristic of the Internet but, again, we have to remember that face-to-face communication has this interactivity. So, it is not interactivity alone that is the unusual feature of the Internet. Nor is it ease or global reach. Rather it is the combination of elements I have just discussed. The Internet provides to many individuals who are geographically distant the power to communicate easily and quickly. It provides something to individuals that was, before the Internet, only available to a few—namely those who owned or had access to radio or television stations. The Internet puts this power in the hands of many, creating the possibility of *interactive communication with speed and ease, on a global scale.* For lack of a better phrase, I am going to refer to this aspect of the Internet as its *many-to-many, global scope.*

This feature of Internet communication can be thought of in terms of power. Individuals whose actions are instrumented through the Internet have much more power than individuals acting without it. This power is dramatically illustrated in the case of a hacker launching a computer virus. With a few simple finger movements (and the necessary equipment and software), a hacker can create a virus, launch it, and wreak havoc on the lives of thousands of people. To be sure, the hacker could have done things offline that would wreak havoc on the lives of thousands of people (e.g., calling in a bomb threat to an airport, setting a fire in a densely occupied building). The Internet has created a new kind of environment in which individuals who want to wreak havoc can do so with relatively little effort (the degree of effort depends in part on the security measures that are in place). The Internet puts this power in the hands of many.

I discuss the many-to-many global scope of the Internet further in Chapter 8 where I will take up the issue of the Internet's democratic character. The fact that the Internet puts power in the hands of individuals leads some to believe that the Internet is a democratic technology.

Anonymity

A second important feature of the Internet is that it provides a certain kind of anonymity. It is tempting to say simply that one can communicate anonymously on the Internet but that, on closer reflection, is misleading. While it is true that we don't routinely see each other when we communicate on the Internet, it is also true that most of our activities on the Internet are easy to trace. Most of us use an Internet service provider at home or work and these service providers can see and track what we do. There are actions we can take to make ourselves more anonymous but these take more effort.

Anonymity is an enormously complicated notion. Consider the following situation. I get in my car and drive several hundred miles away from my home. I stop my car, enter a grocery store, and buy groceries. I could be said to be anonymous in this grocery store since no one in the store knows me. That is, no one knows my name, what kind of work I do, where I live, how I feel, and so on. If I go about the task of buying groceries quietly and pay in cash, no one may remember that I was there. Oddly, while I am anonymous in these ways, I am in full view. People in the store, if they bother to notice, can see what I look like, what I am wearing, and so on. The anonymity I have in this situation seems to have something to do with the fact that no one in the store could connect the information they acquire by looking at me, with my name and address or anything else about me. Of course, if I pay with a credit card, I have become somewhat less anonymous in the sense that there is now the possibility of connecting my public behavior with my name and address and many other facts about me. Only the store has this information and can make the connections, but it is important to remember that once the information is collected, others such as store employees and law enforcement officials can, with effort, make the connections.

Now imagine that when I drove the several hundred miles away from my home and stopped at the grocery store, I was wearing a curly purple wig and I had a cast on my leg. People who happen to be in the grocery store at the time still don't know my name, address, what I do, and so on, but they are much more likely to notice me. Indeed, if law enforcement authorities wanted evidence of my having been in the store at a certain time on a certain day, they would be more likely to find people who remembered me being there—because of the wig and the cast. So, was I anonymous this time? Was I less anonymous because I wore the wig and cast? The answer, it would seem, is a complicated "yes" and "no." While many people saw me and may remember seeing me, they won't be able to connect me with any other information about me—as with my first visit. So, I seem to have been equally anonymous on both visits to the store. On the other hand, if law enforcement officials wanted to verify that I was in that store on a certain day, at a certain time, assuming they knew what I looked like and what I was wearing, they would be much more likely to find witnesses for my second trip. Hence, it would seem I was less anonymous on the second trip.

Now consider a completely different context. When I go to the polls to vote in a local, state, or national election, I provide my name and address (to verify that I am a qualified voter) and then I sign the register. I then proceed to vote and my vote is considered "anonymous." It is anonymous in the sense that *how* I voted cannot be connected to me wherein "me" means my name, address, or appearance. Remember, however, that my vote was recorded—it was counted. So, while *how* I voted was anonymous, my *voting* was hardly anonymous in the sense that there is a record of my having signed in and my name and address are known.

The point of all of this is to show how very complicated the notion of anonymity is. There are different kinds of anonymity, and we achieve these different kinds of anonymity in different ways, in different contexts, for different purposes. Wallace (1999) has suggested that we think of anonymity in terms of whether information about us can be linked or coordinated with other information. In different contexts, information of one kind can be linked with information of another kind and the more links that can be made, the less anonymous we are. Notice that in the voting case, my name and address are known but this information (presumably) can't be linked with how I voted. In the grocery store case, information about my appearance and my name and address and what I bought is not easy to link if I pay in cash and stay inconspicuous. If I pay with a credit card and wear a wig, it is easier to link information.

With this in mind, let us return to Internet communication. The inclination to say that we have anonymity on the Internet seems to arise from comparisons we make with other forms of communication *and* the features we are accustomed to linking. Perhaps the most salient feature of communication on the Internet is that we do not *see* each other directly. In a sense, we see traces of each other mediated by computer technology. [It could be argued that we only see traces of each other in face-to-face communication (our bodies, not our souls), but let's not worry about that here.] The point is that we are used to using information about appearance (what someone looks like, what their voice sounds like, etc.) and we are used to linking this information with other information we acquire about individuals. We rely on this linking of information for continuity (i.e., to know when it's the same person we encountered before), and for filling in our understanding of individuals as whole persons.

So, while it is misleading to say simply that communication on the Internet is anonymous, it does seem accurate to say that the Internet facilitates a certain kind of anonymity. All that is meant by this is that certain kinds of information about a person are not available when an individual communicates via the

Internet; the person's physical appearance and the sound of their voice are not available. Innovations in computer and information technology have already increased access to this kind of information (e.g., equipment facilitating visual and voice connections), and this innovation is likely to continue. Even without this innovation, it seems possible, if not likely, that individuals will become more and more comfortable with the kind of access to one another that is available on the Internet, just as we have become comfortable with telephone communication.

Future innovations aside, related to anonymity is the availability of pseudonymity on the Internet. On the Internet, individuals can create alternative personas and this makes it very difficult for others to connect information about a person. Pseudonmymity is also possible in face-to-face communication. Individuals can disguise themselves by wearing masks and distorting their voices or simply by telling lies about who they are and what they want. Nevertheless, the inaccessibility to an individual's physical appearance (including their physical location) is, for the time being, a distinct feature of the Internet. This inaccessibility is directly connected to some of the problematic behavior discussed at the beginning of this chapter. For example, the kind of stalking described in Scenario 4.4 could not have occurred were Dellapenta's physical characteristics available to those with whom he was communicating. At least, those in the chatrooms would have seen that he was not a woman and someone might have recognized him from other contacts.

Both offline and online it is possible (though not legal) to take control of someone else's identity. It is possible for Smith to use Jones' Internet address; Smith can copy Jones' words and claim them as his own; Smith can copy Jones' words, change them, and say they are from Jones; and so on. The offline parallels are not hard to find; individuals can take credit for work that someone else did; individuals can use stolen credit cards; reporters can distort what individuals say; and so on.

In everyday life we rely on seeing people directly, and this seems to be an "ultimate test" of identity. The importance of seeing a physical person should not surprise us for it acknowledges that human beings are ultimately physical bodies (though, of course, this is not all we are). In the future, screen-image to screen-image communication will provide us with something close to this ultimate test; however, screen images will never be as reliable as seeing someone "in-person" because screen images are mediated by technology. There will always be the possibility of intervention, a technically manipulated or fabricated screen image.

The kind of anonymity that is available on the Internet has to do, then, with inaccessibility to the physical attributes of persons with whom one communicates. This is a certain kind of anonymity and not, by any means, absolute anonymity. The unavailability of information about physical appearance often means that information about a person cannot be linked to them while they are communicating on the Internet.

Ironically, while the unavailability of information about physical appearance provides a certain kind of anonymity to individuals communicating with one another, in other respects, individuals have less anonymity online than off. Internet service providers (ISPs) or others who monitor and track activities on the Internet can access most activities. They can trace and recreate everything that was done in their system. This capacity allows those who maintain the system and law enforcement officials (with a warrant) to track down hackers and other lawbreakers. Those who have Web sites can also keep track of those who access their Web site with cookies or special cursors (*Wall Street Journal*, 1999). Our behavior is available to ISPs, law enforcement officials and marketers, as well as others with the appropriate technology (e.g., hackers with sniffers). So, while the Internet may "feel" anonymous to users because of the unavailability of physical appearance and location of users, in other ways users are less anonymous on the Internet than in face-to-face communication. Individual behavior on the Internet is parallel to the behavior I described earlier—driving several hundred miles from my home and entering a grocery store. Both are, in different senses, in full view. In both cases, no one is likely to take notice of you, unless, of course, you behave in a peculiar way or do something illegal. Then, in both cases, your behavior may be scrutinized very carefully.

There is, perhaps, one important difference. If your illegal or peculiar behavior is traced on the Internet, the trace will end at a computer and telecommunications connection. There is yet another step to reach a person. This gap, a disconnection between computer/computer account and person, leaves open the possibility that someone else other than the owner used the computer to do whatever was done. It might be argued, then, that because of the disconnection between a computer and a person, there is always a modicum of more anonymity on the Internet than in physical space.

In any case, the kind and degree of anonymity we have on the Internet is a function of the link-ability of information about individuals who are acting and interacting. This is important from an ethical perspective because it affects accountability and trust. I will say more about this later, but for now it is enough to say that certain kinds of anonymity make accountability for your actions difficult to achieve and may diminish trust in the information that is exchanged. Trust can be difficult to achieve when individuals are not sure of the identity of the persons with whom they are communicating.

Reproducibility

A third important feature of the Internet is reproducibility. Reproducibility is not confined to the Internet; it is a feature of computer and information technology generally. Electronic information exists in a form that makes it easy to copy and there is no loss of value in the process of reproduction; copied data or software is perfectly usable. Moreover, there may be no evidence that the data or software was copied. The owner or creator of the data may have no reason to believe it has been copied. This makes electronic information significantly different from other kinds of things. The difference becomes most clear when the act of stealing a physical object such as a car is compared with the act of stealing electronic data. In the case of the car, the owner no longer has the car and can see that it is gone. In the case of the electronic data, the owner still has the data and may have no indication that a copy was made.

I will focus a good deal on this aspect of computer technology in Chapters 5 and 6. Because of reproducibility, every action, transaction, or event that takes place in the Internet can be recorded and this leads to a wide range of privacy and surveillance issues which are discussed in Chapter 5. The focus in Chapter 6 is on property rights in software and it is the reproducibility of electronic information that has challenged our traditional notions of property.

When you speak to someone face-to-face, words are uttered, the listener hears and understands the words, and then the words are gone (or, at most, they are locked in the speaker's and the listener's memories). This is not so in Internet communication. The words are there until someone or some event deletes them. Even after they have been deleted from one machine (say, your office computer), they may continue to exist in another machine (say, the server). Depending on how or where words have been sent, they may be available to others who can copy and send them to others, ad infinitum.

Comparing Internet communication with face-to-face communication suggests that reproducibility is the default position in Internet communication. If you do nothing, your communication continues to be available. You have to make an effort to delete it. In face-to-face communication, the default position is just the opposite: Someone can make efforts and record what is said, but if no one makes the effort, the words are gone forever.

Reproducibility is connected to both the global, many-to-many scope and to anonymity insofar as it enhances both of these. The fact that information endures adds to the increased scope and power of actions in the Internet; information endures in time as well as extending in space. Reproducibility also facilitates the disconnection between words and a person making it possible for one person to copy the words of another and change them or keep them the same and attribute them to another. As such, reproducibility facilitates anonymity and pseudonymity, and both together raise serious issues with regard to the integrity of information. How do we know that these words came from this person? The person could have copied them from the Web or someone else could be sending the words and saying that they are from so-and-so.

Reproducibility has moral implications because it goes counter to our traditional notions of property and personal privacy. Our notions of property are associated with the idea of control; an owner can control the use of her property. Our notions of privacy are based on a physical world in which actions are performed and then they are gone; they are irretrievable. (Tape recorders and cameras have also challenged this idea.) In the case of the Internet, the medium in which an action occurs makes reproduction and observation easier than in ordinary space. Though it depends on how the system is set up, effort is generally necessary to delete an action in the Internet; whereas, in ordinary space, effort is necessary to record it.

Ethical Significance

These three features of communication on the Internet lead, either directly or indirectly, to a wide range of ethical issues. The global, many-to-many scope of the Internet, as mentioned earlier, means that individuals have a good deal of power at their fingertips. It means that individuals can—with very little effort, while sitting in front of a computer connected to the Internet—do things to one another that would be very difficult (though not impossible) to do otherwise. As described earlier, individuals can disrupt, steal, cause property damage, snoop, harass, stalk, extort, and defame from greater distances and in new ways.

Ironically this new power has enormous benefits for bringing people together and for making geographic space and distance less and less important in everyday life. The benefits include giving individuals access to huge quantities of diverse information, facilitating communication, facilitating a global economy, and more. Nevertheless, the benefits do not come without drawbacks and one of the drawbacks is that this power also goes to those who will use it for heinous purposes.

Anonymity also has benefits and drawbacks. The kind of anonymity available on the Internet means that individuals do not have to risk being seen (at least not in the ordinary sense of being seen) as they act and interact. As already discussed, anonymity seems to give individuals a sense of invisibility and that sense of invisibility seems to free many to engage in behavior that they might not otherwise engage in. This can be beneficial in some contexts, dangerous in others. For example, in contexts in which race, gender, or physical appearance may get in the way of fair treatment, anonymity may serve as an equalizer. Consider academic courses taught through the Internet. Race, gender, and physical appearance are removed as factors affecting student-to-student interactions as well as the teacher's evaluations of students. Anonymity may, also, facilitate participation in certain activities where individuals might otherwise be reluctant. Consider discussions among rape victims or battered wives or ex-criminals. Individuals may be more willing to take part in these discussions under the shroud of anonymity; participation may provide individuals with valuable information or much needed emotional release. Even in less sensitive contexts, individuals may be more likely to say what they think when they have a degree of anonymity. In formal situations such as in the workplace, individuals may think more creatively and provide better feedback to authorities when they have the shroud of anonymity. Moreover, we should not forget the value of anonymity, as suggested earlier, in democratic elections. Democracy requires that citizens be free to vote as they see fit without fear of repercussions; anonymity creates this condition.

Nevertheless, anonymity leads to serious problems for accountability and for the integrity of information. It is difficult to catch criminals who act under the shroud of anonymity. And anonymity contributes to the lack of integrity of electronic information. We are inundated with information on the Internet, and forced, thereby, to make choices about what to rely on when we form opinions and make decisions. One of the ways we do this offline is by developing a history of experiences with various sources of information. Over the course of time, based on our experiences, we come to trust some sources more than others, or to trust certain sources for certain purposes (e.g., certain newspapers, certain individuals, or certain writers). This is more difficult to do online. Perhaps the best illustration of this is information one acquires in chatrooms on the Internet. It is difficult (though not impossible) to be certain of the identities of the persons with whom you are chatting. The same person may be contributing information under multiple identities; it is possible for different individuals to use the same identity; participants may have vested interests in the information being discussed (e.g., a participant may be an employee of the company/product being discussed). If you don't know the sources of the information you receive, it is difficult to develop a history of experiences with a source, and it is difficult to gage the trustworthiness of the information.

Reproducibility exacerbates the problems arising from global reach and anonymity adding some problems of its own. Privacy and property rights issues arise from reproducibility. Reproducibility facilitates global reach in the sense that it allows words and documents to be forwarded to an almost infinite number of sites. Reproducibility adds to the problems of accountability and integrity of information arising from anonymity. For example, when I receive papers from students in a class, how can I be sure that students wrote these words? Reproducibility makes it easy to download words from the Web. How can you be sure a message is intact as sent by its claimed author? Someone else may have written the message and signed someone else's name. Or someone may have captured the words of the sender, altered them, and then forwarded them.

These three features of Internet communication—global, many to many scope, anonymity, and reproducibility—create a host of potential benefits as well as problems. The remainder of this chapter is about some of the problems, but the important challenge of the Internet is to maximize the enormous positive potential of this technology while limiting the possibilities for abuse. Among other things, the challenge is to address the problems of crime and abuse on the Internet while at the same time using strategies that do not diminish the power that the technology gives to individuals. The challenge is, perhaps, best illustrated by the dilemma that arises around surveillance. To catch criminals on the Internet, it is important to be able to trace the site of activities. Yet, this very capability poses a threat to individual privacy. Just how to achieve the proper balance of protecting privacy but not tying the hands of law enforcement is a major challenge.

HACKING AND HACKER ETHICS

With this understanding of the special features of action and interaction on the Internet, we can return to the three types of problematic behavior identified at the beginning of this chapter. As mentioned, I am going to use the term *hacker* to refer to a person who engages in behavior that attacks the Internet and *hacking* to refer to the activity. In doing this, I will deviate from older usage of these terms. When hacker and hacking were first coined, hacker referred to a computer enthusiast and hacking referred to the feats such enthusiasts were able to accomplish. Hackers were individuals who loved computers and would spend hours and hours figuring out how to do clever things with them. Usually hackers were young men who had acquired a good deal of knowledge about computers, and they shared this knowledge with one another through the first electronic bulletin boards. Often hackers organized computer clubs and user groups, circulated newsletters, and even had conventions.

Only later did the term *hacker* acquire negative connotations. Hacker began to be used to refer to those who used computers for illegal actions, especially gaining unauthorized access to computer systems, and stealing (and then sharing) proprietary software. Resisting this change in usage, many old-line computer enthusiasts pushed for a distinction between *crackers* and *hackerrs*. Hacker, they hoped would continue to have its original, heroic meaning, while cracker would refer to those who engage in illegal activities—cracking into systems.

This distinction has not, however, taken hold. Hacker and hacking are now routinely used to refer to those who gain unauthorized access and accomplish other disruptive feats. Still, such a wide variety of illegal activities now occur on the Internet that it seems most useful to reserve the term hacking for only a subset of these. I propose to use the term hacking to refer to the subset of illegal behaviors that involve unauthorized access and aim at disruption and damage. Such acts undermine the security and the integrity of the Internet. On this definition, such acts as intentionally sending viruses or worms that damage computer systems, denial of service attacks, and unauthorized taking control of a Web site all count as hacking.

From an ethical perspective, hacking is not particularly interesting. In most cases, hacking is illegal and the harmfulness of the activity is apparent. Most Internet users want a system that is reliable; works without interruption; has privacy and integrity; and doesn't require a lot of effort or resources to make secure. Thus, from the perspective of most Internet users, hackers are a nuisance or worse. They snoop around trying to get access to systems they are not authorized to access; they plant viruses and worms bringing systems down and making them unreliable; they copy and distribute proprietary software; they cause expensive denial of service delays. They force everyone to invest more and more effort and resources in security.

To be sure, there are interesting sociological and psychological questions to be asked about hackers and why they hack. For example, why is it mostly male teenagers who hack? Why do they believe they can get away without being detected even though the technology is now highly traceable? Why is it that individuals who probably wouldn't break into a store on the street are willing to try to break into a computer system? While these are fascinating questions, from an ethical perspective the behavior is transparently undesirable and, therefore, not at all controversial or difficult. Hacking behavior generally doesn't pose difficult or complicated ethical challenges or dilemmas.

The situation was not always like this. In the early days of computing, the situation was different. Computers were just beginning to be used more and more, and the technology to connect computers to one another via telecommunications lines had just become available. At this time, there were no laws specifying what could or couldn't be done via remote access. There weren't laws specifically prohibiting unauthorized access; the idea of designing a worm or virus to infect a computer system had not yet occurred, let alone been prohibited. To use Moor's idea (Moor, 1985) described in Chapter 1, there were a multitude of policy vacuums.

In those days, the ethical questions were pressing because the policy vacuums had to be filled and there were substantial ethical questions about what rules would be fair and would lead to the best consequences. Perhaps the most pressing issue had to do with the ownership of software. I discuss this matter more fully in Chapter 6, but it is important to mention here because many of the first computer enthusiasts had an alternative vision of the potential of computers. They saw in the reproducibility of computer information and software, the enormous potential to spread information and knowledge across the globe. They saw the parallel between computing and the printing press and envisioned how computing could exponentially extend the spread of knowledge. The fact that electronic information could be reproduced without loss to the original and without loss to the original holder of the information meant the availability of information at essentially no cost. This was a vision of *sharing* of knowledge, not one of property and commercialization. Many enthusiasts resisted the idea of making software into intellectual property. They argued that information should be free (i.e., un-ownable).

Unfortunately, this vision of the potential of computer and information technology has largely been lost. Instead, it is now taken for granted that most information is (or could be or should be) proprietary. Acts of accessing, replicating, and distributing information without permission are immediately seen as privacy- or property-rights violations. Compared to the early days of computing, a good deal of legislation—specifying what is and is not allowed on the

Internet—now exists. Most of the policy vacuums have been filled. Thus, the arguments that hackers used to give in their defense now seem somewhat anachronistic. Still, the arguments in defense of hacking are enlightening and for this reason, I will discuss several of them briefly.

The arguments that hackers gave in their defense in the early days of computing can be sorted into four arguments. I have already suggested the first argument; it is the argument to the effect that all information should be free. I will not go into this argument since I discuss it in Chapter 6 and because so much is now already proprietary.

The second argument is that break-ins illustrate security problems to those who can do something about them. Remember the Robert Morris case at the beginning of this chapter. Morris claimed that he was trying to expose a flaw in the system. He had tried other means to get the problem fixed but system administrators had not listened to him. Hence, he defended his action on grounds that he was doing a service to computer system administrators and users by demonstrating the seriousness of the problem. In fact, he confessed that he didn't mean to do as much damage as he had done; the worm got out of control.

The argument, in effect, claims that hacking does some good. Hacking illustrates the weaknesses—the vulnerabilities—of computer systems to those who can repair them, before more serious damage is done.

Under careful scrutiny, this argument falters. It suggests that hacking into a system should be understood as an act of whistle-blowing. Individuals "blow the whistle" on illegal or dangerous activities so as to draw attention to a situation, to prevent harm and get the situation fixed. The literature on whistle-blowing suggests that whistle-blowers should always try first to fix the problem through internal channels because it is better to get a bad situation fixed with the least risk or danger (to those who are in danger as well as to the whistle-blower). Yes, we can imagine cases in which an individual is frustrated in her attempts to get a flaw fixed and we can imagine cases in which the flaw is serious enough for severe action (consider the case of Carl Babbage in Chapter 3). Still, such cases are going to be rare, not the typical motive for hacking in or using a virus.

Arguing by analogy, Spafford gives a convincing counter to the whistle-blowing argument. Spafford suggests that the hacker defense amounts to saying that "vigilantes have the right to attempt to break into the homes in my neighborhood on a continuing basis to demonstrate that they are susceptible to burglars" (Spafford, 1992). Since we would never accept this argument made in defense of burglars, we should not accept it for hacking. Spafford also points out that online break-ins, even when done to call attention to flaws in security, wastes time and money, and pressures individuals and companies to invest in security. Many do not have the resources to fix systems or implement tighter security, yet the "vigilante behavior" forces upgrades.

An analogy with automobile security seems relevant here. Thirty years ago, depending on where you lived, many individuals were able to leave their automobiles on city streets without locking them and without fear of the car being stolen. Now, in many parts of the world, owners not only must lock their automobiles, they must invest in elaborate security devices to protect against stealing. Indeed, automobile manufacturers now routinely include such devices on cars. All the resources put into automobile security (the owner's money, the police force's time, automobile manufacturers' expertise) could have been invested elsewhere, if so many individuals were not trying to steal automobiles.

Analogously, those who attempt to gain unauthorized access, plant viruses, make denial of service attacks, and so on, compel the investment of time, energy, and other resources into making the Internet secure, when these resources could be used to improve the Internet in other ways. It is important to see that this applies as much to the energies and resources of the designers and manufacturers of computer and information technology as to service providers and individual users.

This defense of hacking does not, then, seem to have force. It is unquestionably a good thing for those who become aware of flaws in the security of computer systems to inform computer administrators and urge them to fix these flaws. We can even imagine cases in which the flaws in security are extremely serious and an individual's reports of the threat to security fall on deaf ears. It is difficult, nevertheless, to imagine a case that justifies using viruses, denial of service attacks, or accessing private files as a means to get the problem fixed.

Another argument, used in defense of gaining unauthorized access to computer systems, is that breaking into a computer system does no harm as long as the hacker changes nothing. And, if the hacker learns something about how computer systems operate, then, something is gained at no loss to anyone.

A little thought reveals the weakness of the first part of this argument, for individuals can be harmed simply by the unauthorized entry. After all, nonphysical harm is harm nonetheless. If individuals have proprietary rights and rights to privacy, then they are harmed when these rights are violated, just as individuals are harmed when they are deprived of their right to vote or their right to due process. Moreover, hackers can do physical harm. For example, hackers could gain access to computer systems used in hospitals where patients are at risk or systems running industrial processes where workers are at physical risk from dangerous chemicals or explosions. Suppose a hacker were to access and tamper with the computer system used to match donated organs with those in need of organs. Here time is absolutely critical. A slow down in the system caused by tampering could make the difference between life and death.

So, the hacker defense that they are doing no harm and actually learning about computer systems is not convincing. Hacking can be dangerous and can put people at unnecessary risk.

To be sure, hackers may learn about computing and computer systems from their hacking activities. It may be argued in particular that hacking is a good way to learn about how to design computer systems to make them more secure. This argument is complex and tricky. The fact that one learns from an activity does not justify it. Giving electric shocks to learners when they make mistakes may promote learning, but this does not make it a good teaching method. Allowing children to stick things in electric outlets might result in their learning the dangers of the outlets, but there are less dangerous ways to teach this lesson. So, just because hackers learn from hacking does not make it a good thing.

Hacking is not the only way to learn about computing or computer security. Aside from the standard ways one learns in the classroom (by reading, listening to a teacher, doing problems), one can imagine a variety of creative ways to teach people about computers and computer security. These might include challenging games or tournaments that encourage learners to be creative and clever.

To justify hacking as a means to learning about computing and computer security, an argument would have to show not just that hackers learn but that hacking is the only way or the best way to learn. Showing that hacking is the "best way" would have to show that the improvement in knowledge and skill was so great as to counterbalance the risks and dangers to those who might be harmed by the hacking. In other words, if hacking promotes learning, the good of the learning would have to be weighed against the negative consequences of this method of learning. So, this defense of hacking is also not convincing.

Finally, hackers used to argue that they would help keep Big Brother at bay.[1] This argument may be more understandable after reading Chapter 5 and comprehending the threats to privacy that have arisen because of the use of computer and information technology. The thrust of the argument is that computers and information technology are being used to collect information about individuals and to do things to individuals that they don't want done. Hackers have the computer savvy to find out what is going on and tell us about it. They can assure us that covert illegalities and abuse will not go undetected. In short, the argument suggests that hackers are good vigilantes. Imagine government agencies gathering information they are not authorized or justified in gathering. Imagine companies maintaining secret databases of information that is prohibited by law from being collected or used. Hackers provide protection against this. By gaining unauthorized access to government and commercial systems, they can see when abuse is occurring and alert the public.

The argument is correct in suggesting that the public needs protection against abuses of information and Big Brother. Still, are hackers the best agents

---

[1] For those unfamiliar with the phrase "Big Brother," it comes from the novel *1984* by George Orwell. "Big Brother" refers to the government that watched over every move of every citizen.

for this kind of protection? Would the cost of tolerating hackers be worth what we gain in protection? Do hackers solve the problem or make it worse?

We have many options to monitor for such things as information abuse and government surveillance. We could create a national data protection commission that would have the authority to monitor information practices, propose legislation, and prosecute violators. Commission or no commission, we could develop better laws and clearer guidelines for information practices. We could assign special obligations to computer professionals calling upon them to report any information they acquire about data abuse and/or illegal surveillance. We could encourage users to report suspicious behavior. In short, there are a variety of strategies that could be adopted to protect the public from Big Brother.

While toleration of hackers is one such strategy, it is not the most attractive. The problem is that the public would get rid of one problem by creating another. We might reduce the threat of data abuse and covert surveillance by government and by commercial interests, but in exchange we would be at the mercy of vigilantes. The vigilantes might decide to take a look at our files or explore our computer systems, in the name of protection. Suffice it to say that we would have exchanged the rule of law and protection by formal authorities, for rule by vigilantes.

So, hacking is not justified. It causes harm; it violates legitimate privacy and property rights; it often deprives users of access to their own computer systems and to the Internet; and, it compels investment in security when the invested resources might have been used for other activities. The arguments in defense of hacking are not convincing. Hacking is unethical and has rightly been made illegal.

Nevertheless, a note of caution is in order lest some of the arguments made by hackers be too quickly dismissed. Several of the arguments point to potentials of the Internet that are being neglected—to the detriment of the Internet. Implicit in the hacker arguments is a concern to take advantage of the enormous potential of the Internet for spreading and sharing information. The reproducibility of the Internet makes it possible for information to be reproduced at negligible cost; in theory this means information and knowledge could be spread across the globe at little cost. On the other hand, this potential is undermined by extensive property rights that restrict distribution of information. Hackers seem aware of this, as well as of the vulnerability of computer systems to attack and failure. This vulnerability is often under-appreciated when important information and activities are put online without adequate security. Finally, hackers' concerns about Big Brother are worthy of consideration. As you will see in Chapter 5, privacy on the Internet is rapidly shrinking.

So, while hacking is disruptive, dangerous, and unjustified, discussion provoked by hackers and hacking—of what should be allowed and not allowed on the Internet—should not be squelched too quickly. Hacking represents a countercurrent in the development of the Internet, and to take advantage of the enormous potential of the Internet, it behooves us to listen to countercurrents.

NEW SPECIES OF OLD CRIME

The second category of behavior identified at the beginning of this chapter is criminal behavior *not* aimed at attacking the Internet. The crimes included here predate the Internet; they all have offline equivalents, though they take a somewhat different form when performed on the Internet. Scenario 4.3 is a case of theft and extortion; Scenario 4.4 is a case of stalking. In these crimes, the Internet is merely the tool for doing what could be done without it.

All else being equal, to say that certain types of behavior are crimes is also to say that they are unethical but it is important to remember that some actions are unethical only because they are illegal and other actions are unethical independent of their legal status. Killing, rape, making someone your slave, and many types of lying are examples of the latter. These actions would be unethical even if they were not illegal. In a similar vein, while some types of behavior made possible by the Internet require complex, controversial policy decisions to designate them as illegal, the moral character of others types of Internet behavior is transparent. In the latter cases, the process of extending laws from the offline environment to the Internet is straightforward. For example, in Scenario 4.4, the harm to the victim aimed at by the stalker (as well as the deception involved) makes it easy to see that the behavior is unethical and should be illegal. An Internet in which this type of behavior was tolerated would be a dangerous place. Similarly, with Scenario 4.3 it is easy to understand why laws against theft and extortion have been extended from the offline environment to the Internet. Extortion is extortion whether done with a computer and electronic numbers or done with guns, telephone calls, and threats of physical harm.

So, much of the unethical behavior on the Internet is not controversial and not all that complicated. The same goes for much of the criminal behavior on the Internet. It can be examined and questioned, but the justification for considering it unethical and making it illegal on the Internet is the same as the justification for considering it unethical and making it illegal offline.

Criminal behavior of this kind illustrates the nature of computer ethics as described in Chapter 1. The crimes involve physical movements different from their offline equivalents. Maxis, in Scenario 4.3 did not break into file cabinets to get the credit card numbers; he did not have to take possession of plastic (hard) credit cards. The stalker in Scenario 4.4 did not have to follow his victim around in geographic space. The new instrumentation (computers, software, the Internet) makes it possible for human beings to do things in new ways. It is tempting to say that the new technology makes it possible for human beings to do things they couldn't do before (and there certainly is a sense in which this is true), but what the new instrumentation does is more complex. The Internet allows these perpetrators to act on common criminal motives, aimed at familiar forms of harm, but to do this via new forms of physical and technological behavior.

Before computers and the Internet, extortionists and stalkers did not have the advantage of the special features of the Internet—broad, interactive scope, anonymity, and reproducibility. Both the extortionist and the stalker are able to perform their crimes without leaving their homes—by sitting in front of computer screens and moving their fingers. The extortionist takes advantage of the reproducibility of the technology; he makes copies of the credit card numbers with ease and without the company knowing the numbers have been taken (copied). The stalker takes advantage of the anonymity and pseudonymity of the Internet by using his victims' identity and exploiting the fact that his physical appearance is not available to others.

So, the Internet creates a new instrumentation for familiar or common crimes. This is not all it does, but it does not exactly thrust us into entirely unfamiliar moral territory; rather the new instrumentation allows us to do things in new ways and calls on us to think about what the new capabilities mean for our moral ideas, our moral values, and principles.

NETIQUETTE

A third category of behavior on the Internet has to do with informal conventions that promote *effective* or *civil* or *pleasant* interaction online. This type of behavior is often referred to as *netiquette*. Netiquette can be defined as "the dos and don'ts of online communication" or as "informal rules of the road" or "common courtesy online." Violations of netiquette may be considered unethical but they are not illegal. Insofar as netiquette encourages people to behave in civil and cooperative ways, it serves to fend off regulation of the Internet; that is, if Internet users followed netiquette, there would be less of a need for legislation.

Not surprisingly, you will find plenty of information on netiquette on the Internet. If, for example, you go to Dark Mountain's Netiquette Guide (www.darkmountain.com/netiquette/index.shtml), you will find information about how to behave when it comes to: bandwidth; e-mail, chatrooms, and BBSs; groups; international interaction; and, virus alerts, chain letters, and hoaxes. In its most general statement of netiquette, Dark Mountain lists three simple rules: be polite, be patient, and don't break any laws. Notice that these three rules are good rules for interacting offline as well as online. This is no accident. Most traditional, informal rules for polite and respectful behavior are general enough so that they apply to a broad variety of situations. Because of this generality, the rules can be applied to behavior on the Internet.

Scenario 4.5 depicts a flaming and Scenario 4.6 describes one of the first incidents of spamming to draw the attention of thousands of Internet users. These are both violations of netiquette.

A flame is an inflammatory or insulting message sent via e-mail or in other forms of online communication such as chatrooms. The Dark Mountain Web site explains what one should do when one receives flames:

The best move is to just throw them in the trash. If, however, you feel the flame is definitely worth a response, your reply will be starting a Flame War. A Flame War consists of one or more people who keep sending each other Flames (offensive e-mails). How does it end you ask? As soon as one person gets tired of responding to the other, the War is over!

Though we don't call it "flaming," notice that behavior similar to flaming takes place offline when individuals yell and scream at each other and complain about how they have behaved. Indeed, the similarities and differences between flaming and offline yelling and screaming are interesting because they illustrate some of the effects of the special features of the Internet. The reproducibility of the Internet extends the scope of a yelling and screaming incident insofar as it allows messages to be distributed across the globe; the participants in a flame war can be geographically disbursed. By contrast a yelling and screaming incident in geographic space seems to have a more limited scope—limited by the hearing and seeing range of humans. On the other hand, neither form of yelling and screaming is *necessarily* larger or smaller than the other; a yelling and screaming incident in geographic space can turn into a riot involving thousands of people, and an online flame can extend to only two or three people.

Because the participants in an offline yelling and screaming incident have to be physically close to one another (so that the insults and screams can be heard), such conflicts have the potential to escalate into physical violence. In the case of flaming, however, there is no such possibility since the participants don't have access to each other's bodies. This seems an important difference between flaming and its offline equivalent. On the other hand, there seems to be no difference when it comes to the harm that intimidating, demeaning, or insulting words can do. Words can have a traumatic effect whether delivered electronically or face-to-face. Nevertheless, there is the possibility in a Flame War that the insults and screams come from individuals who are anonymous or pseudonymous. This could make for a subtle difference in the effect of the words except that the type and degree of anonymity can vary from flame to flame and from offline incident to offline incident. In other words, participants in a Flame War can know each other very well and participants in an offline yelling and screaming war can be strangers.

Spam, as described in Scenario 4.6, is unsolicited bulk e-mail. It is the e-mail equivalent of junk mail. Spam is considered by many Internet users to be so annoying and disruptive that efforts are being made to make spam illegal. The U.S. Congress has tried to pass several pieces of legislation banning spam, but, as of this moment, all the attempts have been unsuccessful.

The fact that legislation is pending suggests that netiquette has not been effective; that is, netiquette has not taken hold enough to prevent Internet users from sending spam. In the incident described in Scenario 4.6, the perpetrators could not resist the temptation to send spam because the potential rewards—in terms of increased business—were just too great. Here we have a case where the scope of the Internet and the ease of reaching thousands and thousands of people provides an enormous potential for marketing. Yet while spam has this enormous marketing potential, it also has the potential to clog up mailboxes across the globe, and to use up bandwidth and slow down traffic. Nevertheless, since it is so easy to send, social conventions (netiquette) are insufficient to control its use.

While I have only briefly discussed netiquette, its importance for the smooth functioning of the Internet should not be underestimated. Law comes into play when informal conventions fail, but law alone is not sufficient to regulate human behavior. Much, if not most, of the civility and ordered character of social life comes from individuals being socialized and habituated to behave in certain ways and not just from the existence of law and the threat of punishment. Netiquette promotes this informal aspect of social life, and as such, is an important mechanism for shaping behavior on the Internet.

POLICY APPROACHES

I turn now to a brief survey of policy approaches to shaping behavior on the Internet. At the broadest level, there are two general approaches, the technological and the social. Even public policy makers often do not explicitly recognize technology as a mechanism for social control, but it is. Think of the way traffic lights shape behavior or think of security tools that prevent breaking into files. Technology has a powerful influence on how individuals behave: Where one lives is a function of access to automobiles and/or mass transit systems; the food we eat is a function of agricultural and transportation technology. Technology facilitates certain kinds of behavior and constrains or impedes other kinds of behavior. So, technology can be and is used to shape behavior on the Internet. Indeed, the three features of the Internet that I have discussed throughout this chapter are functions of computer and information technology and they shape the kind of interactions individuals have with one another.

Cryptography is currently being used to develop technological devices that will affect some of the problematic behavior described in this chapter. It will (and already has) made hacking and other crimes more difficult to commit online. Cryptography is being used both to protect transactions from hackers and for authentication of identity. Of course, cryptography also has the potential to make law enforcement more difficult when it is used by criminals and terrorists.

Technology is likely to play a key role in shaping problematic behavior on the Internet. In fact, Lawrence Lessig in his recent book, *Code* (2000) argues that regulation of Internet will be done through code. The Internet is designed in code.

Human behavior is not just shaped by technology. It is shaped by a wide variety of human and social systems and practices. Individuals are socialized and educated; laws tell them what they can and can't do; businesses, workplaces, neighborhoods, and so on are set up in ways that facilitate and constrain behavior in many ways. Behavior on the Internet can be and is shaped by legislation, education, attitudes, social conventions, and social practices. Legislation is perhaps the most visible and obvious of the social mechanisms used to shape human behavior. It is a key tool for responding to socially undesirable human behavior, and so it is not surprising that there are now an abundance of laws regulating behavior on the Internet. In Chapter 8, I discuss how the challenge for the future is to create global laws because of the global scale of the Internet.

By contrast with law which is intentional, explicit, and formal, social attitudes are extremely influential and they are all too often informally, unintentionally, and implicitly conveyed. The college teacher, for example, who challenges students to find a way around a new security system may be unaware of conveying a sense that it is fun and not a serious offense to try to break into a computer system. The secondary school teacher who accepts pirated software from a student condones unauthorized copying when he or she accepts the copy. A news reporter may glamorize a hacker as a hero "sticking it to" a big, faceless corporation.

Education is another form of the social approach to controlling behavior on the Internet. Because of the special features of the Internet, it is particularly important that Internet users are educated to understand the connection between their behavior online and its impact on other users. Anonymity seems to undermine the sense of impact of one's behavior on others. For example, the connection between the act of sending a virus and the impact on individual lives should be salient in the minds of all Internet users. It may be naive to believe that this alone will stop hackers, but it would help in decreasing some thoughtless and careless behavior.

A range of types of education are possible: formal and informal programs in K-12 education as well as college. College students majoring in computer science are especially important because they are acquiring the expertise often required for undesirable behavior. Legislators, lawyers, and judges need to understand computer and information technology well enough to respond appropriately to various cases and issues as they arise.

The list can go on. The more integrated the Internet becomes, the more important it is that every user understand both how the Internet works and what their own behavior does.

CONCLUSION

So many of the activities of daily life are being moved to the Internet that it is only slightly far-fetched to say that human life is being recreated in a new medium. The new medium has special features and I have identified global, interactive scope, anonymity, and reproducibility as morally significant features. Among other things, these special features of the Internet lead to several types of problematic behavior. I distinguished three such types: hacking, new versions of familiar crimes, and violations of netiquette. The challenge of the Internet is to take advantage of the new possibilities it offers and to develop it in ways that serve humanity well. This requires shaping human behavior. There are a variety of mechanisms for shaping and controlling behavior on the Internet, not the least of which is the design of the technology. All of these approaches should be used and coordinated. None of them alone will do the job.

STUDY QUESTIONS

1. What are the three categories of problematic behavior on the Internet according to the author? Give examples of each.
2. What are the morally significant characteristics of communication on the Internet? Explain each and describe how they are problematic.
3. How was the term *hacker* originally used? How is it generally used now?
4. What are the four arguments that can be given in defense of hacking?
5. What are the counters to each of these arguments?
6. Is there a morally significant difference between those crimes committed on the Internet that can also be committed without the Internet?
7. What is Netiquette?
8. What is flaming?
9. What is spaming?
10. What types of policy approaches can be taken to control behavior on the Internet? Which approach(s) do you think will be most effective?

SUGGESTED FURTHER READING

BAIRD, ROBERT, REAGAN RAMSOWER, and STUART E. ROSENBAUM, *Cyberethics, Social and Moral Issues in the Computer Age* (Amherst, NY: Prometheus Books, 2000).

DENNINGS, DOROTHY E. and PETER J. DENNING, eds., *Internet Beseiged: Countering Cyberspace Scofflaws* (New York: ACM Press, 1998).

GRAHAM, GORDON, *The Internet: A Philosophical Inquiry* (London: Routledge, 1999).

CHAPTER 5

Privacy

SCENARIO 5.1 **Fund-raising and potential donors.**

Jan Perez began college as a computer science major. She loves computers and has always been very good at figuring out how to do things on the Internet and the Web. However, after a year and a half of college, Jan decides that as much as she likes computing, she doesn't want to major in it; she chooses, instead, a major that is more likely to lead to a career involving contact and interaction with people. She also wants something that involves public service or promoting good causes.

After college, Jan is delighted to find that the development office of a large, private university wants to hire her. She accepts the job enthusiastically, thinking she will do some good by raising money for a great university.

Jan's supervisor is extremely pleased to find out how much Jan knows about computers and the Internet. Within a few months of starting the job, Jan is asked to find out all she can about a Frank Doe. Mr. Doe has never been approached by the university; Jan's supervisor only recently heard from another donor that Mr. Doe has a very positive impression of the university and has the capacity to make a major contribution.

The fund-raising unit needs to know how wealthy Mr. Doe is to determine what kind of contribution to ask for. They need to know about his life and interests to know which of their projects he might want to support. And, they need to know about him personally so they can approach him, put him at ease, and not offend him in any way. Jan is given some suggestions about where to look, but she is also told to find out whatever she can.

Using the Internet, Jan does the following:

1. She searches a variety of public databases which give her information about his real estate holdings, his memberships on the boards of public corporations, a list of corporations for which he is a major stockholder.
2. She searches other databases to find out if he has made contributions to political parties or campaigns.
3. She searches archives of newspapers to see if Mr. Doe has ever been written about in the news.

4. She searches other databases to see if he has had any encounters with law enforcement agencies.

5. She searches other databases to find out what religious organizations he supports.

6. She contacts credit agencies and requests his credit history.

7. Jan wonders if Amazon.com would tell her what types of books, if any, Mr. Doe purchases.

8. Jan wonders which Internet service provider Mr. Doe uses; she contemplates what she could learn about Mr. Doe if his service provider would tell her about his online activities. For example, he may keep a portfolio of stock holdings in his account.

9. Mr. Doe is a local resident. Jan's supervisor mentions in passing that Mr. Doe, she has been told, uses the university's medical complex for all his medical treatment. Jan decides to see whether she can access patient files at the university medical complex. Much to her surprise, she is able to access Mr. Doe's insurance records and this tells her that in the last several years, he has been receiving frequent treatment for a kidney ailment. She wonders if this will make him interested in contributing to the hospital or for kidney research.

At the end of several weeks of research, Jan has an enormous amount of information about Mr. Doe. As she acquired each bit of information from a separate database, there didn't seem anything wrong with doing that; now, however, the cumulative effect of putting all of this information together makes Jan feel uncomfortable. She wonders if this is right. She feels a bit like a voyeur or stalker.

Has Jan done anything wrong?

SCENARIO 5.2 Taking data home.

Max Brown works in the Department of Alcoholism and Drug Abuse of a northeastern state. The agency administers programs for individuals with alcohol and drug problems and maintains huge databases of information on the clients who use their services. Max has been asked to take a look at the track records of the treatment programs. He is to put together a report that contains information about such factors as number of clients seen in each program each month for the past five years, length of each client's treatment, number of clients who return after completion of a program, criminal histories of clients, and so on.

To put together this report, Max has been given access to all files in the agency's mainframe computer. It takes Max several weeks to find the information he needs because it is located in a variety of places in the system. As he finds information, he downloads it to the computer in his office; that is, he copies the information from the mainframe onto the hard disk of his office microcomputer.

Under pressure to get the report finished by the deadline, Max finds that he is continuously distracted at work. He decides that he will have to work at home over the weekend to finish on time. This will not be a problem. He copies the information (containing, among other things, personal information on clients) onto several disks and takes them home. He finishes the report over the weekend. To be safe, he leaves a copy of the report on his home computer as well as copying it onto a disk which he takes up to work.

Was Max wrong in moving personal information from the mainframe to his office computer? in moving the information from his office computer to a disk? To his home computer? in leaving the information on his computer at home? What could happen as a result of Max's treatment of the data? Should the agency for which Max works have a policy on use of personal information stored in its system? What might such a policy specify?

SCENARIO 5.3 Workplace monitoring.

Estelle Cavello was recently hired to supervise a large unit of a medical insurance company. Estelle will be in charge of a unit responsible for processing insurance claims. When she was hired, the vice president made it clear to Estelle that he expects her to significantly increase the efficiency of the unit. The company has targets for the number of claims that should be processed by each unit and Estelle's unit has never been able to meet its target.

One of the first things Estelle does when she starts this job is to install a software system that will allow her to monitor the work of each and every claims processor. The software allows Estelle to record the number of keystrokes made per minute on any terminal in the unit. It also allows her to bring the work of others up on her computer screen so that she can watch individual work as it is being done. As well, Estelle can access copies of each employee's work at the end of each day. She can find out how much time each worker spent with the terminal off; she can see what correspondence the person prepared; she can review e-mail that the worker sent or received; and so on.

Should Estelle use this software to monitor her employees?

SCENARIO 5.4 Data mining.

Ravi Singh works for one of the major credit card companies in their data-processing center. The company is continuously developing new products to offer to customers and add revenue to the corporation. He is an avid reader of computer magazines and recently has been reading about data-mining tools that are now available for a reasonable cost. Ravi goes to his supervisor with the suggestion that their unit purchase one of these tools and use it to find out more about their customers. The information may be telling in terms of customer interest and capability.

The supervisor likes the idea. After exploring the systems that are available, the unit purchases one and Ravi is assigned to explore patterns in the database of information on the company's customers and their purchasing habits.

Ravi discovers that certain zip codes are highly correlated with loan defaults. These zip codes must be in low-income areas for the mined and analysed data indicate that the company could reduce its losses significantly by refusing to extend credit to anyone living in twenty-five zip codes, while at the same time not significantly reducing their revenues. In other words, on average losses due to default generated by individuals in those zip codes were greater than revenue generated.

Ravi continues with his data mining. Next he discoverers a correlation between those who use their credit cards to make contributions to Hindu charitable organizations and those who charge over $40,000 a year on their credit cards. This information seems important. If the company made a special effort to solicit Hindu's as customers, it might be able to increase its revenues significantly.

Ravi goes to his supervisor with the suggestion that they adopt these strategies. Has Ravi done anything wrong? If his company adopts these strategies, have they done anything wrong?

These scenarios depict just a few of the ways that information can be created, gathered, moved, and used with computer technology. Of all the social and ethical concerns surrounding computer technology, the threat to personal privacy was probably the first to capture public attention. And this issue persists in drawing public concern and leading to action by policy makers. One hears about it frequently in the popular media; major studies continue to be undertaken; new books continue to be written; and new legislation continues to be passed to regulate electronic information. It will be helpful to begin by laying out just why and how computer technology facilitates information gathering and seems to threaten personal privacy.

IS THERE ANYTHING NEW HERE?

In Chapter 1, I suggested that computer and information technology, like other new technologies, creates new possibilities; it creates possibilities for behavior and activities that were not possible before the technology. Public concern about computers and privacy arises for precisely this reason. Computers make it possible (and in many cases, cheap and easy) to gather detailed information about individuals to an extent never possible before. Federal, state, and local government agencies now maintain extensive records of individual behavior including such things as any interactions with criminal justice agencies, income taxes, employment history for social security, use of human services agencies, motor vehicle registration, and so on. As well, private organizations maintain extensive databases of information on individual purchases, airline travel, credit worthiness, health records, telephone or cellular phone usage, employment, and so on.

We have the technological capacity for the kind of massive, continuous surveillance of individuals that was envisioned in such frightening early twentieth-
century science fiction works as George Orwell's *1984* (1949) and Zamyatin's *We*
(1920). The only differences between what is now possible and what was envisioned then is that much of the surveillance of individuals that takes place now is
done by private institutions (marketing firms, insurance companies, credit
agencies), *and* much of the surveillance now is via electronic records instead of
by direct human observation or through cameras.

Indeed, many authors now suggest that we are building a world that is, in
effect, a "panopticon." *Panopticon* is the word Jeremy Bentham used in 1787 to
describe his idea for the design of prisons. In the panopticon, prison cells
would be arranged in a circle and the side of each cell facing the inside of the
circle would be all glass. The guard tower is placed in the center of the circle,
from which every cell is in full view. Everything going on in each cell can be
observed. The effect is not two-way; that is, the prisoners cannot see the guard
in the tower. The idea of the panopticon was picked up by Michel Foucault in
1975 and brought to wider public attention (Bozovic, 1995). Bentham and Foucault recognized the power of surveillance to affect the behavior of individuals. In the panopticon, a prison guard need not even be there at every moment;
when prisoners believe they are being watched, they adjust their behavior.
When individuals believe they are being watched, they are compelled to think
of themselves as the observer might think of them. This shapes how individuals
see themselves and leads them to behave differently than they might if they
weren't being observed. ← control

Many authors have expressed concern that the degree of information gathering that now takes place in our society is having or will have a similar effect.
We are building a panopticon in which everything we do is observed and could
come back to haunt us.

Of course, we can try to be skeptical about the similarities between the
panopticon prison and our world today; we can try to be critical of the parallel. Indeed, we can ask whether there is anything fundamentally different
about today as compared to fifty years ago or a century ago. Record-keeping is
far from a new phenomenon. Government agencies and private corporations
have been keeping records for thousands of years and using this information in
variety of ways. So, is there anything different about the kind or degree of privacy that we have today as compared to fifty or a hundred years ago?

Computer technology has changed record-keeping activities in a number
of undeniable and powerful ways. First, the *scale of information gathering* has
changed. Second, the *kind of information* that can be gathered has changed.
And, third, the *scale of exchange* of information has changed enormously.

In the precomputer, "paper-and-ink" world, the mere fact that records
were paper and stored in file cabinets, imposed some limitations on the
amount of data gathered, who had access, how long records were retained, and
so on. Electronic records do not have these limitations. We can collect, store,

Why ICT had impact

manipulate, exchange, and retain practically infinite quantities of data. The point is that technology no longer limits what can be done; now only time and money and, perhaps, human capabilities impose limits on the quantity of information that can be gathered and processed.

The kind of information that it is now possible to collect and use is also new. Think about the workplace monitoring scenario at the beginning of this chapter. Employers can keep records of every keystroke an employee makes. Before computers, finger movements of this kind would not have been thought to be important, let alone the kind of thing that could be recorded. Employers can monitor their employees' uses of the Web, their participation in chat rooms, not to mention their e-mail.

One particularly important new form of information is referred to as transaction generated information (TGI). TGI includes purchases made with a credit card, telephone calls, entry and exit from intelligent highways, and so on. As you move about in the world, your activities (transactions) are automatically recorded.

You might argue that TGI does not exactly create a panoptic world because there is no one guard tower at the center of it all. There is no single government or private organization accumulating all of the information. TGI gathering seems to be fragmented and, therefore, seems not to pose the threat of Big Brother. *cannot control info*

Indeed, in the very early days of computing, especially in the 1960s and 1970s, many social commentators expressed concern about the information gathering potential of computer technology and these fears were articulated as fears of Big Brother—fears that all the information would be funneled to a highly centralized U.S. government. The fear was that electronic information gathering practices would give too much power to government. It would create a potentially totalitarian government, a surveillance society. Those fears wained in part because legislation was passed that restricted government information gathering. *what precautions are in place to put in at ease that this won't happen?*

Fear also weakened because computer technology changed. It became smaller and cheaper, and, consequently, became available much more widely. On the one hand, this diffused fear of Big Brother because it promised computer power in the hands of "many" rather than just big government. At the same time, however, smaller computers in the hands of many companies and individuals facilitated the exchange of information to an extent previously unimaginable. Typically information of one kind will be gathered and stored separately from information of another kind; for example, marketing firms will gather and store information on buying habits, one government agency will record income tax information, another government agency will record criminal justice activities, and so on.

With computer technology, however, it is technically possible to combine all this information. In the private sector this is done routinely. Think of the fund-raising example at the beginning of this chapter. Within government this

You give it to one, you give it to all

happens less frequently because the Privacy Act of 1974 restricted data matching. Nevertheless, it does happen. Matches have been made, for example: between federal employee records and records of the Aid to Families with Dependent Children program, to investigate fraud; and between IRS records of taxpayer addresses and lists of individuals born in 1963 (supplied by the Selective Service System), to locate violators of the draft registration law (Shattuck, 1984). Matching of records can produce a profile of an individual which, before computers, would only have been available to those who knew the individual intimately.

The restriction on matching mentioned in the Privacy Act of 1974 did not apply to private organization, just to the federal government. What was called "matching" in the 1970s is today called data mining and is quite common in private organizations. Indeed, you can now purchase data-mining tools, sometimes called knowledge discovery instruments (kdi) that help find patterns of behavior among groups of individuals. Their use is described in Scenario 5.4.

Add to these changes in the scale and kind of information gathered with computer technology, a further element. Because computerized information is electronic, it is easy to copy and distribute. Before computers were connected by telephone lines, information could be fairly easily copied using tapes or disks. Now that computers are connected via telecommunication lines, information can go anywhere in the world where there are telephone lines. Hence, the extent to which information can be exchanged is now practically limitless. Once information about an individual is recorded in a machine or on a disk, it can be easily transferred to another machine or disk. It can be bought and sold, given away, traded, and even stolen. The information can spread instantaneously from one company to another, from one sector to another, and from one country to another.

The Max Brown case (Scenario 5.2) is illustrative here. He takes sensitive data home on a disk. From a technical point of view, he could have simply accessed the data from home. But in either case, the data moves around. Once it moves out of its source, it is very difficult to keep track of all the places it might exist, be it on disks or hard drives.

Movement of data happens when you subscribe to a magazine and your name and address are sold to a marketing firm. The marketing firm infers from the subscription that you have certain tastes and begins sending you a variety of opportunities to buy the things you like. Forester and Morrison (1990) report the case of a women who took her landlord to court after he refused to do anything about the pest problem in her apartment. He did not show up for court but evicted her shortly after the court date. When she went looking for another apartment, she found that she was repeatedly turned down by landlords. She would look at an apartment, notify the landlord that she wanted it, and within a few days hear back that the apartment was already rented to someone else. It turned out that a database of names of individuals who take landlords to court is maintained and the information is sold to landlords. Needless to say, landlords don't want to rent to individuals who may take them to court.

As far as the technology goes, the distribution of information can take place with or without the knowledge of the person whom the information is about, and it can take place intentionally as well as unintentionally. There is an unintentional distribution when records are provided that contain more information than is requested. As well, when information is stolen, the exchange is unintentional from the point of view of the agency that gathered or maintained the records. Think again of the Max Brown scenario; Brown's wife, children, or friends might (while using his home computer) inadvertently access the data on individuals in the state's treatment programs and see the names of clients in the state programs.

If all of this were not cause enough for concern, there is more. Information stored in a computer can be erroneous, and, at the same time, can be readily distributed. The effect of a small error can be magnified enormously. Information can be erroneous due to unintentional human error or because someone has intentionally altered it to harm a competitor or enhance their own records. It is important to remember that databases of information are not always as secure as we would like them to be. When computers are connected via telecommunications lines, the possibilities of data being tampered with or stolen are increased. You have already read about hackers in Chapter 4.

Suppose John A. Smith's file is inadvertently combined with John B. Smith's. John A. Smith is turned down for a loan on the basis of erroneous information since John A. has *never* failed to pay his debts, has a good job, and has a sizeable holding of stocks, but John B. has a low-paying job, declared bankruptcy three years ago, and is once again deeply in debt. John A. is wronged when he is turned down for a loan. Moreover, suppose that after a series of inquires and complaints by John A., the error is identified, and John A.'s file is corrected. (This is not always as easy as it sounds. Companies are often very slow in responding to complaints about errors in records.) John A. asks his bank to send for the updated report, and the bank changes its mind about the loan when it sees the accurate information. It would appear that the injury to John A. has been remedied. Not necessarily. The inaccurate information may have been given to other companies before it was corrected, and they, in turn, may have given it to others. As a result, it may be difficult, if not impossible, to track down all the databases in which the error is now stored. It may be impossible to completely expunge the erroneous information from John A.'s records. *greased*

When information is stored in a computer, there is little incentive to get rid of it; hence, information may stay with an individual for a long period of time. Information stored in a computer takes up very little space and is easy to maintain and transfer. Because of this, details can be carried in a record forever. Something insignificant that happened to an individual when he was 10 years old may easily follow him through life because the information has been recorded once and there is little motivation to delete it. In the past, the inconvenience of paper served to some degree as an inhibitor to keeping and exchanging apparently useless information.[1]

Because it is so easy to keep information, some fear that individuals will get categorized and stigmatized at early stages in their lives. One way to see this is to imagine what it would be like if elementary and secondary school records were put into a national database where prospective employers, government agencies, or insurance companies could get access. We might find decisions being made about us on the basis of testing done when we were in elementary school or on the basis of disciplinary incidents in our teenage years.

When decision makers are faced with making decisions about individuals, they want data. They want data both to insure a good decision and to justify their decision to others. When they must choose between making a decision on the basis of little or no data, and making it on the basis of lots of data known to be unreliable, many prefer the latter. Hence, information tends to get used if it is available even though it may not be relevant or reliable.

In summary, while record-keeping is, by no means, a new activity, it appears that computer and information technology has changed record-keeping activities in the following ways: (1) it has made a *new scale* of information gathering possible; (2) it has made *new kinds* of information possible, especially transaction generated information; (3) it has made *a new scale of* information *distribution and exchange* possible; (4) the *effect* of erroneous information can be *magnified;* and (5) information about events in one's life may *endure* much longer than ever before. These five changes make the case for the claim that the world we live in is more like a panopticon than ever before.

As an aside here, you may be tempted to say that computers are not really the problem or the cause of the problem. It is individuals and organizations that are creating, gathering, exchanging, and using information. Computers, according to this line of argument, are simply tools: If there is a problem, the problem is the people who use computers, not the computers themselves.

While there is some truth to this, it is important to remember that computer technology facilitates certain kinds of activities. Computer technology makes it possible for individuals to do things they could not do before. Individuals and organizations are more likely to engage in activities when they are possible (not to speak of easy and inexpensive). For example, in Scenario 5.4, Estelle would not have monitored employees to the extent she did or in quite the way that she did if computers and the monitoring software were not available. Individuals choose actions because they find themselves in a world which has certain possibilities; in a world with different possibilities, they would behave differently. Insofar as computer technology changes what it is possible for

---

[1] Ironically, it can work the other way as well. Sometimes, that is, changes in technology may result in data being forgotten. In other words, where paper records stored in boxes in an archive may be obtained (even with difficulty), data stored on an old computer may be much more difficult to access because the technology is obsolete.

human beings to do, it can be a major factor in determining what people do and the kind of society in which we live.

UNDERSTANDING THE "COMPUTERS AND PRIVACY" ISSUE

Uses of Information

Information about individuals would not exist if organizations did not have an interest in using it. Information is created, collected, and exchanged because organizations can use it to further their interests and activities. Information about individuals is used to make decisions about those individuals, and often the decisions profoundly affect the lives of those individuals whom the information is about. Information about you, stored in a database, may be used to decide whether or not you will be hired by a company; whether or not you will be given a loan; whether or not you will be called to the police station for interrogation, arrest, or prosecution; whether or not you will receive education, housing, social security, unemployment compensation, and so on.

The computers and privacy issue is often framed as an issue that calls for a balancing of the needs of those who use information about individuals (typically government agencies and private institutions) *against* the needs or rights of those individuals whom the information is about. Later in this chapter, I will argue against this framing of the issue on grounds that it is biased in favor of information gathering, but for the moment it is important to understand why organizations want information.

In general, those who want information about individuals want it because they believe that it will help them to make better decisions. Several examples quickly illustrate this point. Banks believe that the more information they have about an individual, the better they will be able to make judgments about that individual's ability to pay back a loan or about the size of the credit line the individual can handle. The FBI's National Crime Information Center (NCIC) provides criminal histories of individuals to all the states. Law enforcement agencies justify the existence of this database on grounds that the more information they have about individuals, the better they will be able to identify and capture criminals. We might also bring in examples from the insurance industry where decisions are made about which individuals to insure at what rate, or from the Department of Health and Human Services where decisions are made about who qualifies for various welfare and medical benefits. And, of course, don't forget the fund-raising organization, data-mining and workplace monitoring scenarios at the beginning of this chapter. In theory, the more and better the information these organizations have, the better their decision making will be.

Companies also claim that they need information about their customers to serve them better. If a company like Amazon.com keeps track of the books that you buy, it can infer from this information what new books you are likely to be interested in. When they send you information on these new books, they claim they are providing a service to you (even if it is one that you didn't ask for and one that happens also to serve their interest in selling more books). If an advertising firm knows what I buy at the grocery store, it can use that information to send me coupons for items I am likely to buy. If television stations know what I watch on television and when I change the channel, they can use that information to develop programming more suited to my tastes. If marketing companies know about my income level and my tastes in clothes, food, sports, and music, they can send me catalogues or special offers for products and services that fit my precise tastes.

In the standard understanding of the computers and privacy issue we have public and private institutions that want information about individuals. They make a powerful case for how this information improves their decision making and helps them to do their job better and more efficiently. In theory, all of that means better serving us, as consumers and citizens. It means, for example, better law enforcement; more efficient government; better, more customized services; and so on.

Personal privacy is generally put on the other side of the balancing scales. The issue is framed so that we have to balance all the good things that are achieved through information gathering and exchange *against* the desire or need for personal privacy. Some even claim that we have a right to personal privacy for if that were true, the scales would weigh heavily on the side of personal privacy. From a legal and constitutional point of view, however, we have, at most, a limited and complex right to privacy.

This framing of the issue seems to be skewed heavily in favor of information gathering and exchange. The only way to counter the powerful case made on behalf of information gathering and exchange is, it would seem, to make a more powerful case for protecting and ensuring privacy in the lives of individuals. Either we must show that there is a grave risk or danger to these information-gathering activities—a danger so great that it counterbalances the benefits of the activity. Or we must show that there is a greater benefit to be gained from constraining these activities. To put this another way, once the benefits of information gathering and exchange are on the table, the burden of proof is on privacy advocates to show either that there is something harmful about information gathering and exchange or that there is some benefit to be gained from constraining information gathering. Either way, there is a daunting hurdle to overcome.

Many of us feel uncomfortable with the amount of information that is gathered about us. We do not like not knowing who has what information about us and how it is being used. Why are we so uncomfortable? What do we fear? Part of the fear is, no doubt, related to our mistrust of large, faceless organizations, and part of it is related to mistrust of government. The challenge is to translate this discomfort and fear into an argument that counterbalances the benefits of information gathering.

Odd as it may seem, the case for protecting personal privacy has not been easy to make. From the point of view of public policy, arguments on behalf of personal privacy have not "won the day." I am going to discuss a number of ways that the case for individual privacy can be and has been made, but I am also going to argue for a somewhat different framing of the issue. At least part of the problem, I believe, lies in framing the issue as a matter of balancing the interests of private and public institutions against the interests of individuals. We ought, instead, to recognize that privacy is both an individual and a social good, one that goes to the heart of the kind of beings we are and important to the realization of a democratic society.

Personal Privacy

Two big questions have dominated the philosophical literature on privacy: What is it and why is it valuable? Needless to say, the two questions are intertwined. Neither has been easy to answer. The term *privacy* seems to be used to refer to a wide range of social practices and domains, for example, what we do in the privacy of our own homes, domains of life in which the government should not interfere, things about ourselves that we tell only our closest friends. Privacy seems, also, to overlap other concepts such as freedom or liberty, seclusion, autonomy, secrecy, controlling information about ourselves. So, privacy is a complex and, in many respects, elusive concept. A variety of arguments have been put forward to explain the value of personal privacy.

As we review several of these, it will be helpful to keep in mind a distinction between privacy as an instrumental good and privacy as an intrinsic good. When privacy is presented as being valuable because it leads to something else, then it is cast as an instrumental good. In such arguments, privacy is presented as a means to an end. Its value lies in its connection to something else. On the other hand, when privacy is presented as good in itself, it is presented as a value in and of itself. As you might predict, the latter argument is harder to make for it requires showing that privacy has value even when it leads to nothing else or even when it may lead to negative consequences.

The most important arguments on behalf of privacy as an instrumental good have focused either on its being necessary for special relationships or on its being necessary for democracy. Charles Fried (1968), for example, argued that we have to have privacy to have relationships of intimacy and trust. In a society in which individuals were always being observed (as in the panopticon), he argued, friendship, intimacy, and trust could not develop. If we want such relationships, we must create domains of privacy. Others argue that privacy is necessary for democracy. Here the important idea is that if individuals are constantly being observed, they will not be able to exercise the kind of independent thinking that is essential for democracy to work.

The arguments on behalf of privacy as an instrumental good begin to cross over into privacy as an intrinsic good when they suggest a connection between privacy and autonomy. You'll remember from the discussion of Kantian theory that autonomy is not just one among many values; autonomy is fundamental to what it means to be human, to our value as human beings. If privacy is essential to autonomy, then the loss of privacy would be a threat to our most fundamental values. But the connection between privacy and autonomy is often presented not exactly as a means-ends relationship. Rather the suggestion is that autonomy is inconceivable without privacy.

It will take us too far afield to explore all of these arguments. In what follows, I am going to explore several of the most salient arguments on behalf of privacy, and I will move from a focus on privacy as an individual good to privacy as a *social good*.

Information Mediates Relationships

To begin with what seems most clear, information about an individual seems to be a fundamental precondition for establishing a relationship with that individual. Moreover, the information determines the character of the relationship. James Rachels (1975) has argued that people need to control information about themselves in order to maintain a diversity of relationships. His insight is that individuals maintain a variety of relationships (e.g., with parents, spouses, employers, friends, casual acquaintances, and so on), and each of these relationships is different because of the different information that each party has. Think, for example, about what your best friend knows about you as compared with what your teacher, your employer, or your dentist knows about you. These diverse relationships are a function of differing information.

Take your relationship with your dentist. Suppose she has been your dentist for five years but she knows relatively little about you, except, of course, for what she knows about your teeth. Now suppose you need extensive work done on your teeth, and you begin to go to her office regularly at a time of the day when she is not rushed. You strike up conversations about your various interests. Each time you talk to her, she learns more about you and you learn more about her. Suppose you discover you have several hobbies and sports interests in common. She suggests that if you schedule your appointment next week so you are her last appointment, you could go out and play tennis afterward. The story can go on about how this relationship might develop from one of patient-professional, to good friends, perhaps to one of intimate friends. The changes in the relationship will in large measure be a function of the amount and kind of information you acquire about one another.

Rachels uses this insight to argue that privacy is important because it allows us to maintain a diversity of relationships. If everything were open to all (that is, if everyone knew the same things about you), then diversity would not be possible. You would have similar relationships with everyone.

Rachels seems right about the way information affects relationships. We control relationships by controlling the information that others have about us.

When we lose control over information, we lose significant control over how others perceive and treat us. However, while Rachels seems right about this, his analysis does not quite get at what is worrisome about all the information gathering that is facilitated by computer technology. That is, the information gathering and exchange that goes on via computer technology does not seem, on the face of it, to threaten the diversity of personal relationships each of us has. For example, despite the fact that huge quantities of data now exist about my purchases, phone calls, medical condition, work history, and so on, I am able to maintain a diversity of personal relationships. Rachels seems slightly off target in putting the emphasis on the diversity of relationships, rather than simply on the loss of control of relationships that comes with loss of control of information. Perhaps, this is not surprising given that Rachels focused on personal relationships rather than relationships between individuals and organizations.

What happens when you lose control of information is better thought of on the model of an everyday case in which gossip generates some (false) information about you and the information is spread from one person to another. You are interested in being viewed and treated in a certain way and you know the information (true or false) will affect the way people see you and treat you. Once the information begins to move from person to person, you have no way of knowing who has heard it. If it is false information, you have no way contacting everyone and correcting their repository of information about you. Even if the information is true, there may be individuals that will treat you unfairly on the basis of this information and yet since you don't know who has it, you can't protect yourself. So, loss of control of information reduces your ability to establish and influence the relationships you have and the character of those relationships.

Individual-Organization Relationships

In trying to understand the threat to privacy posed by the new type and scale of personal information gathering made possible by computer technology, the relationships most at issue are those between *individuals and formal organizations.*[2] In these relationships what is important to the individual is that the individual have some power or control in establishing or shaping the relationship (not that he or she has a diversity of such relationships). Information about us is what allows an organization such as a marketing firm, a credit card company, or a law enforcement agency to establish a relationship with us. And, information determines how we are treated in that relationship. One is sent an offer to sign up for a credit card when the credit card company gets your name and address

---

[2] Of course, information stored in databases could affect personal relationships and gossip can spread on the Internet, but most large-scale, massive databases are maintained by formal organizations who make powerful decisions about individuals.

and finds out how much you earn and/or own. How much credit is extended depends on the information. Similarly, a relationship between you and your local police force is created when the police force receives information about you; the nature of the relationship depends on the information received.

Currently, organizations may establish (or try to establish) a relationship with you without any action on your part. That is, you may subscribe to a magazine or open a bank account and establish a relationship with one organization, but when that organization sells information about you, another organization creates a file on you and begins to evaluate you for their purposes.

As an aside, let me point out that the twentieth century was a period of enormous growth in the size of public and private organizations (facilitated in part by the development of computer and information technology). This growth is likely to continue in the twenty-first century on a global scale. What this trend means is that instead of interacting with small, local, family-owned businesses wherein one might know or come to know the decision makers personally, most of us now (and in the future will) interact mostly with large national or international organizations operating with complex rules and regulations. Indeed, it is often a computer that makes the decision about our credit line or loan application. We may shop at grocery stores, department stores, or franchises that are local units of national companies. We may purchase items from catalogues or on the Internet and have no idea where the offices of the company are located. We may deal with banks that are national or international, go to large impersonal agencies for government services such as driver's licenses or building permits, attend colleges of 2,000 to 40,000 students, and so on. While our dealings with these organizations may have the most powerful effects on our lives, we may know little about these organizations and the people who own or manage them. Yet they will have (or have access to) an enormous amount of information about us—be it accurate or relevant. And unless we make an exerted effort, we are not likely to know what information they have about us to use when making decisions.

Everything that I have said here was recognized in the 1977 report of the Privacy Protection Study Commission when computer technology was in its early stages of development (i.e., when record-keeping practices were relatively primitive as compared with today's practices). Contrasting face-to-face relationships with relationships to record-keeping organizations, the report explains:

> What two people divulge about themselves when they meet for the first time depends on how much personal revelation they believe the situation warrants and how much confidence each has that the other will not misinterpret or misuse what is said. If they meet again, and particularly if they develop a relationship, their self-revelation may expand both in scope and detail. All the while, however, each is in a position to correct any misrepresentation that may develop and to judge whether the other is likely to misuse the personal revelations or pass them on to others without asking permission. Should either suspect that the other has violated the trust on which the candor of their communication depends, he can sever the relationship altogether, or alter its terms, perhaps by refusing thereafter to

discuss certain topics or to reveal certain details about himself. Face-to-face encounters of this type, and the human relationships that result from them, are the
threads from which the fabric of society is woven. The situations in which they
arise are inherently social, not private, in that the disclosure of information about
oneself is expected.

An individual's relationship with a record-keeping organization has some of
the features of his face-to-face relationships with other individuals. It, too, arises
in an inherently social context, depends on the individual's willingness to divulge
information about himself or to allow others to do so, and often carries some ex-
pectation as to its practical consequences. Beyond that, however, the resemblance
quickly fades.

By and large it is the organization's sole prerogative to decide what information the individual shall divulge for its records or allow others to divulge about
him and the pace at which he must divulge it. If the record-keeping organization
is a private-sector one, the individual theoretically can take his business elsewhere
if he objects to the divulgences required of him. Yet in a society in which time is
often at a premium, in which organizations performing similar functions tend to
ask similar questions, and in which organizational record-keeping practices and the
differences among them are poorly perceived or understood, the individual often
has little real opportunity to pick and choose. Moreover, if the record-keeping organization is a public-sector one, the individual may have no alternative but to yield
whatever information is demanded of him.

So, private and public organizations are powerful actors in the everyday
lives of most individuals in our society, and yet it would seem that individuals
have very little power in those relationships. One major factor making this possible is that these organizations can acquire, use, and exchange information
about us, without our knowledge or consent.

To summarize: Individuals control what relationships they have and the
nature of those relationships by controlling the flow of information to others;
when individuals have no control over information that others have about
them, there is a significant reduction in their autonomy.

While this seems a powerful argument, as I mentioned earlier, it has not
"won the day" in public policy debates. Part of the reason is historical and political. While I will not go into detail, it is worth noting that in the late 1970s
when major privacy legislation was being contemplated, American lawmakers
adopted an approach that (1) emphasized protection from government record-
keeping, leaving private organizations to self-regulate with an informal code
of fair information practices, and (2) was piecemeal rather than comprehensive. That is, each domain of activity has its own legislation. At a critical point
in legislative history, lawmakers let go of the idea of a privacy protection commission that would have monitored database creation and use. Instead, in the
United States we have separate legislation protecting our credit records, our
educational records, and so on for medical records, video rentals, employment
records, and so on.

Privacy legislation will be discussed more later; for now, the important
point is that the American approach has been piecemeal. Within each domain,
when the issue is framed as a trade-off between a social good to be achieved

versus a loss of control of information by individuals, the trade-off seems worth making. Better law enforcement seems to justify giving up some control of information about ourselves. A reduction in the number of loan defaults that may lead to lower costs of borrowing makes giving more information to credit agencies seem worthy. Less expensive government (reduced taxes) may seem to justify allowing the government to sell information from our drivers' licenses. And so on.

REFRAMING THE COMPUTERS AND PRIVACY ISSUE— PRIVACY AS A SOCIAL GOOD

A major part of the problem seems to come from the combination of taking a piecemeal approach and then framing the computers and privacy issue as one involving a trade-off between social goods, such as law enforcement and government efficiency, and the interests of individuals in controlling information about themselves. Instead of thinking comprehensively about what record-keeping and exchanging practices would be best for our society, the problem has been framed as one in which interests are pitted against one another and business and government seem to be pitted against individuals. This is odd when one remembers that ultimately business and government are justified in terms of their service to individuals as consumers and citizens.

In her 1995 book, *Legislating Privacy,* Priscilla M. Regan examined three privacy policy debates that took place in the United States in recent years—information privacy, communications privacy, and psychological privacy. She concludes that when individual privacy is pitted against social goods such as law enforcement or government efficiency, personal privacy loses. Regan suggests that privacy should be seen not as an individual good but rather as a social good. As an important social good, privacy would be on par with other social goods such as law enforcement or government efficiency. Instead of a social good outweighing an individual good, it would be clear that we have two social goods at stake. In reframing the issue in this way, privacy would be more likely to be treated as equally important, if not more important, than other social goods.

How, then, can the case be made for privacy as a social good? Earlier I argued that loss of control of information about us significantly reduces our autonomy—our power in relationships with formal organizations. Now I want to push this line of thinking even further. Instead of emphasizing loss of control, however, I want to return to the idea of the panopticon. If most everything that we do is recorded, then it would seem that the world that we live in is fundamentally changed from the world that existed in the past. And with this change comes an extremely important loss of freedom. We are unable to go places or do things without a record being created. The act of making a phone call is now the act of making a phone call *and* creating a record. We no longer have the option of making a phone call and not creating a record. Therefore, we have lost a degree of freedom. The loss of this freedom might be justified if you are in prison after having been fairly prosecuted and found guilty. But it hardly seems justified if you have done nothing wrong.

Even more important are the changes that take place in individuals as a result of constant surveillance. When a person is being watched, they tend to take on the perspective of the observer. When you know that decisions will be made about you on the basis of your activities (e.g., your educational records, work records, political activities, criminal activities), you think about that fact before you act. You take on the view of the private and public institutions that will make decisions about you. This can have a powerful effect both on how individuals behave and on how they see themselves. Individuals may come more and more to view themselves as they are viewed by those who watch them.

You may think of this as a good thing insofar as it means more social control and perhaps fewer crimes, fewer loan defaults, people working harder, and so on. The consequences of this kind of social control are, however, insidious. For one thing, it means that formal organizations exert an enormous amount of social control that may or may not be justified. Individuals may be inhibited about what they buy at the grocery store when they learn that their purchases are being recorded and analyzed. Remember that freedom is one of the most fundamental aspects of democracy. Yet freedom is eroded (or at least threatened) when every move is recorded. The result may be individuals who are ill-equipped to live in a democracy.

Consider how Jeffrey Reiman (1995), drawing on other authors, describes the situation:

> To the extent that a person experiences himself as subject to public observation, he naturally experiences himself as subject to public review. As a consequence, he will tend to act in ways that are publicly acceptable. People who are shaped to act in ways that are publicly acceptable will tend to act in safe ways, to hold and express and manifest the most widely-accepted views, indeed, the lowest-common denominator of conventionality. . . . Trained by society to act conventionally at all times, people will come so to think and so to feel. . . . As the inner life that is subject to social convention grows, the still deeper inner life that is separate from social convention contracts and, given little opportunity to develop, remains primitive. . . . You lose both the practice of making your own sense out of the your deepest and most puzzling longings, and the potential for self-discovery and creativity that lurk within a rich inner life. . . . To say that people who suffer this loss will be easy to oppress doesn't say enough. They won't have to be oppressed, since there won't be anything in them that is tempted to drift from the beaten path.

The idea of democracy is the idea of citizens having the freedom to exercise their autonomy and in so doing to develop their capacities to do things that have not been thought of and to be critical. All of this makes for a citizenship that is active and pushing the world forward progressively. But if the consequences of trying something new, expressing a new idea, acting unconventionally are too negative, then there is no doubt that few citizens will take the risks. Democracy will diminish.

When the argument for privacy is framed in this way, privacy is shown to be something which is not just an individual good that can be diminished for the sake of a social good; rather, it is shown to be a social good in its own right and more important than other social goods such as efficiency and better consumer services.

Possible Counterarguments

The case for privacy seems powerful and suggests that there are serious dangers with the amount and kind of data gathering that now goes on in the United States. However, before we turn our attention to privacy legislation, some readers may still not be convinced that there is much of a problem. Lets consider what the skeptics might say to the analysis of privacy I just presented:

1. Someone might argue that the situation is not so bad, that individuals who have done nothing wrong, have nothing to fear. If you haven't broken the law, if you are doing a good job at work, if you are paying your bills, and so on, then you have nothing to worry about. This argument might even go as far as to say that privacy only protects people who have something to hide.

Unfortunately, this argument does not work on several grounds. First, erroneous information can dramatically affect your life. Suppose you are traveling away from your home and the police begin chasing your car. They point guns and rifles at you and force you to get out of your car. They frisk you. If you panic and respond suspiciously, you could be beaten or killed. The police officers believe you are driving a stolen vehicle and disregard your explanation and evidence that the car is *yours,* that it *had* been stolen, but was found last week and returned to you by the police in the city where you live. When you reported the car stolen, the information was put into a database available to patrol cars in several bordering states. Evidently, however, the information that the car was found never made its way into the database. It takes police officers a day to confirm the error, while you are sitting in jail. Even though you have done nothing wrong, you have been harmed as a result of inaccurate information in a database. So, it is *not* true to say that as long as you have done nothing wrong, you have nothing to worry about.

Second, organizations, be they private or public, corporations, nonprofits or government, can use criteria in their decision making that are inappropriate and discriminatory. Imagine databases containing information about the race, religion, ethnic background, or political affiliations of individuals. Such databases could be sold to decision makers and used by them even though the information is irrelevant and often illegal for decision makers to use. As a result, you, who have done nothing wrong, could be turned down for insurance, for a job, not given a loan, and so on.

Finally, remember the subtle change in the behavior of individuals when they know they are being watched. Social pressure leads to conformity and when information on all your activities is being gathered, the pressure to conform is great. Remember also that some of the most important progressive changes that have shaped our society (from the American Revolution, to women's suffrage, to civil rights legislation), have been led by individuals who were willing to non-conform. The less privacy we have, the harder it will be to bring about social change.

So, the computers and personal privacy issue cannot be written off as only of concern to those who have something to hide. The way in which personal information is gathered, exchanged, and used in our society affects all of us.

2. A second possible counter to the account of personal privacy given above is to argue that individuals in our society do have some power to control their relationships with private and public organizations. Many individuals, it might be argued, have simply opted to give up their privacy. After all, each of us could refuse to give out information about ourselves.

This argument contains an ounce of truth, but hides a much more complicated situation. In particular, it hides the fact that the price of privacy in our society has become extremely high. Yes, I can choose not to use credit cards (using only cash) so that there is no information gathered about my buying activities. I can choose not to subscribe to magazines so that no company ever identifies my interests and sells my name and address to a marketing firm. I can choose not to buy a home until I have saved enough to pay for it in cash (that way I don't have to ask a bank for a mortgage loan and tell them all the facts about my financial standing). I can choose to pay for all my medical care myself to avoid records being created by a health insurance company. I can choose not to have an account with an Internet access provider or if I do have such an account, I could choose never to access information on the Web so that there would be no records of what I had viewed. These choices will reduce the amount of information that private organizations have about me. Notice, however, that I will have to give up a great deal; I have to pay a high price for my privacy.

When it comes to public organizations, what I have to give up in order to get privacy is even more precious. Citizens are entitled to many benefits such as social security, medicare, driver's licenses, as well as having rights to due process, protection from law enforcement agencies, and so on. However, the moment I request these entitlements, information is created about me and stored in a computer. The information becomes a matter of public record. For example, in many localities when one purchases or sells property, the transaction becomes a matter of public record, and may subsequently be published in a local newspaper. Soon after I perform such a transaction, I will begin to get an onslaught of telephone calls and mail offering me services appropriate to new homeowners. As well, the information may now be matched with other records on me in other government agencies. Remember also the case of the database of tenants who sued their landlords. To avoid my name being put into such a database, I would have to give up my right to take my landlord to court; in other words, I would have to give up participating in a process which protects my rights as a citizen.

So, while there are many things an individual can do to protect his or her personal privacy, the cost is extremely high and goes counter to the idea of living in a free society. It doesn't seem fair or accurate to argue that individuals have freely chosen to give up their privacy.

Finally, someone might still insist that we have nothing to worry about because we are protected by a wide array of legislation against abuses of information. Indeed, it may be argued that the government has decided to allow these information gathering and exchange practices to go on because it has deemed that these are in our best interests. Moreover, you could argue that we have voluntarily given up our privacy by supporting legislators who believe we prefer less privacy to better law enforcement and more efficient organizations.

This is a more complicated argument because it raises the question of how information gathering practices have evolved to where they are today; and, it raises the question of whether the legislation we have today is enough. Let us now turn our attention to the legislative background of the current situation.

LEGISLATIVE BACKGROUND

How, you may ask, have we gotten here? Why is our personal privacy so poorly protected? Does it have to be this way? Is it this way in other countries? What can we do to change things? Answers to these questions are crucial to understanding what any of us should do (as citizens, consumers, or computer professionals) to bring about change. I will only be able to begin to answer these questions here.

I have already mentioned that the American approach to privacy protection has been piecemeal. We have a patchwork of legislation dealing separately with personal information in different domains or sectors. Federal laws that cover the collection and use of personal and consumer data include the Fair Credit Reporting Act (1992), the Electronic Communications Privacy Act (1986), the Family and Educational Privacy Act (1974), the Privacy Act (1974), the Video Privacy Protection Act (1988), the Telephone Customer's Protection Act, and the Driver's Privacy Protection Act (1994) to mention a few. In addition to federal statutes, each state has its own array of laws protecting various aspects of privacy and various types of records. On the Web site of the Electronic Privacy Information Center (www.epic.org), you will find a checklist for each state indicating which type of records are protected by some form of state legislation. The list of possible privacy-related topics that a state law might address includes: arrest records, bank records, cable television, credit, criminal justice, government data banks, employment, insurance, mailing lists, medical records, polygraphing, school records, social security numbers, tax records, and more.

Up until the mid-1980s, most American statutes had been modeled after the Privacy Act of 1974 and it in turn had been modeled after the "Code of Fair Information Practices." The "Code of Fair Information Practices" was developed and recommended for implementation in the 1973 Report of the Secretary of Health, Education, and Welfare's Advisory Committee on Automated Personal Data Systems (titled "Records, Computers and the Rights of Citizens"). The Code was never made into law, but in the 1970s and early 1980s it was treated as a standard. In addition to being a model for legislation, businesses treated it as an informal standard to which they must adhere both to protect them from suits by individuals and to fend off government regulation. While the influence of the Code can still be seen in legislation, it no longer seems to be the standard.

The Code consists of five principles:

1. There must be no personal data record-keeping system whose very existence is secret.
2. There must be a way for an individual to find out what information about him or her is in a record and how it is used.
3. There must be a way for an individual to prevent information about him or her that was obtained for one purpose from being used or made available for other purposes without his or her consent.
4. There must be a way for an individual to correct or amend a record of identifiable information about him or her.
5. Any organization creating, maintaining, using, or disseminating records of identifiable personal data must assure the reliability of the data for their intended use and must take precautions to prevent misuse of data.

As just mentioned, for the most part, these principles seem to continue to be recognized, though with several important exceptions. First, information collected for one purpose seems now routinely to be used for other purposes. Think of the fund-raising scenario at the beginning of the chapter. Or think of information that is gathered on your Web navigation activities. Or think of data mining. You may think of these activities as innocuous since your personal identity is not attached to this information. Still the point is that information is being used for purposes other than those for which it was gathered.

Another area of slippage in the intention of the Code is the right that it gives you to access information about you in a database. While this right exists in principle, how would an individual go about checking information about him or her. It would seem that it would be impossible to do this given the number of databases that now exist and given the extent to which information is now routinely exchanged.

GLOBAL PERSPECTIVE

In the twenty-first century, information gathering and exchange is likely to take on a new scale because of the Internet. Oddly this expansion has the potential to improve privacy protection, though it could also go the other way. Expanding use of the Internet means a powerful expansion in the scale of information gathering and exchange, but it also means that control of information gathering has to occur at the global level. Information about individuals will flow across national borders more and more so that whatever approach an individual nation state takes to privacy, there will be pressure on it to harmonize its information policy with protection provided in other countries. Otherwise, individuals will have no guarantees once information is collected. So, for example, if you are a citizen of an European Union country, information about you gathered by one organization cannot be used by another. However, if the first organization sends the information to the United States, there is no telling what will happen to it. Unless, we have policies that recognize the laws of other countries or we have common policies, privacy protection is uncertain.

The European Union has developed a policy that applies to all the member-countries. It looks very much like the code of fair information practices. While it is a long document, consider the provisions in Chapter II, Section I entitled "Principles Relating to Data Quality":[3]

1. Member States shall provide that personal data must be:
   (a) processed fairly and lawfully;
   (b) collected for specified, explicit, and legitimate purposes and not further processed in a way incompatible with those purposes. Further processing of data for historical, statistical or scientific purposes shall not be considered as incompatible provided that Member States provide appropriate safeguards;
   (c) adequate, relevant, and not excessive in relation to the purposes for which they are collected and/or for which they are further processed;
   (d) accurate and, where necessary, kept up to date; every reasonable step must be taken to ensure that data which are inaccurate or incomplete, having regard to the purposes for which they were collected or for which they are further processed, are erased or rectified;
   (e) kept in a form which permits identification of data subjects for no longer than is necessary for the purposes for which the data were collected or for which they are further processed. Member Sates shall lay down appropriate safeguards for personal data stored for longer periods for historical, statistical or scientific use.

Privacy protection in the United States could be improved if the United States were compelled to harmonize its laws with those of the EU, but it is also

---

[3] For the full text of the directive, see: www.privacy.org/pi/intl_orgs/ec/final_EU_Data_Protection.html

possible that EU protection will give way to the U.S. model. Harmonization of privacy policies throughout the world is a process you should watch closely in the coming years.

PROPOSALS FOR BETTER PRIVACY PROTECTION

In the remainder of this chapter, a variety of ways to bring about change will be briefly discussed. For a problem so deeply embedded in the fabric of our society, it would seem that a many-pronged approach will be necessary. Change will not be easy to bring about.

Broad Conceptual Changes and Legislative Initiatives

There are a number of broad conceptual changes that would have a powerful impact on public policy with regard to personal privacy. One mentioned earlier is to think of privacy as a social good at the heart of liberal democratic societies and hence to be given much more weight in balancing of social goods. To make this shift is to move from seeing privacy as simply something individuals want for their personal protection, but not worth the cost in terms of inefficiency to recognizing privacy's role in democracy and, hence, recognizing that it is worth what it may cost in terms of less efficient institutions.

As mentioned before, the United States has taken a piecemeal, ad hoc approach to information privacy with each sector being dealt with separately. Significant improvement could be had by taking a comprehensive approach and developing legislation that lays out the parameters for public and private information gathering. Such legislation should be made with an eye to global exchange of information.

Issues in the private sector are especially worrisome in the United States because they are not covered by the constitutional tradition. Our legal notions of privacy can be traced back to two of the Amendments to the Constitution. The first amendment addresses freedom of speech and the press, while the fourth amendment proscribes unreasonable search and seizure, and insures security in person, houses, papers, and effects. These two amendments deal, respectively, with the relationship between the government and the press, and the government and the individual. Our American forefathers were concerned about protecting us from the power of government (as they should have been). They did not envision the enormous power that private organizations might have over the lives of individuals. Corporations are treated, in law, as persons in need of protection from government, rather than as powerful actors that need to be constrained in their dealings with individuals. We need to consider broad changes that would address this gap in our tradition.

We might be better served if we treated personal information as part of the infrastructure of our society. Infrastructure activities are those that facilitate commerce and affect so many aspects of our lives that they serve us better when managed outside the marketplace. We ought, at least, to explore whether we might be better served by a system in which personal information were *not* treated as a commodity to be bought and sold, but instead managed as part of a public utility. This way of thinking about information might lead us to adopt a system similar to those that have been adopted in some European countries. Sweden, for example, has a system in which a Data Inspection Board (DIB) has the responsibility for licensing all automated personal information systems in both the public and private sectors. The DIB has the authority to control the collection and dissemination of personal data and has the power to investigate complaints, to inspect information systems, and to require information from organizations. It is responsible for designing detailed rules for particular systems and users, including what information may be collected, and the uses and disclosures of this information (OTA, 1986).

Computer Professionals

Computer professionals can play an important role, individually and collectively. First and foremost, individual professionals must not wash their hands of privacy issues. For example, a computer professional can point out privacy matters to clients or employers when building databases containing sensitive information. Whether or not computer professionals should refuse to build systems which they judge to be insecure is a tough question, but certainly one that ought to be considered an appropriate question for a "professional."

Individually and collectively, computer professionals can inform the public and public policy makers about privacy/security issues, and they can take positions on privacy legislation as it pertains to electronic records. As mentioned in Chapter 3, computer professionals are often in the best position because of their technical expertise, to evaluate the security of databases, and the potential uses and abuses of information.

The original ACM Code of Professional Conduct (passed by the ACM Council in 1973) specified that: An ACM member, whenever dealing with data concerning individuals, shall always consider the principle of the individuals' privacy and seek the following:

- To minimize the data collected.
- To limit authorized access to the data.
- To provide proper security for the data.
- To determine the required retention period of the data.
- To ensure proper disposal of the data.

These principles were not included in the 1992 ACM Code but they continue to be useful general guidelines for computer professionals.

One of the General Moral Imperatives of the 1992 ACM Code of Ethics and Professional Conduct is that an ACM member will "Respect the privacy of others." The Guidelines explain that: "It is the responsibility of professionals to maintain the privacy and integrity of data describing individuals. This includes taking precautions to ensure the accuracy of data, as well as protecting it from unauthorized access or accidental disclosure to inappropriate individuals."

Technology

Related to the contribution of computer professionals is the potential of technology to protect rather than erode privacy. Privacy enhancing technologies (sometimes referred to as PETs) are now being developed, though I think it is too soon to tell whether they will succeed. Computer scientists and engineers have been working on and have developed IT tools that allow one to navigate the Web with anonymity; to send e-mail anonymously through anonymous remailers; or to detect the privacy level of Web sites before one accesses them. More generally crytographic techniques are being developed with various schemes that could allow one to make various transactions such as banking, purchasing, and so on, with confidentiality or to authenticate mail of various kinds.

Institutional Policies

Where no law applies or the law is unclear, private and public organizations can do a great deal to protect privacy by adopting internal policies with regard to the handling of personal information. Computer professionals working in such organizations can recommend and support such policies. For example, banks, insurance companies, registrars' offices of universities, marketing agencies, and credit agencies should have rules for employees dealing with personal information. They ought to impose sanctions against those who fail to comply. It is not uncommon now to hear of employees who casually reveal interesting information about individuals that they discover while handling their records at work. Remember the case of Max Brown in the scenario at the beginning of this chapter. Perhaps his agency should have had a policy prohibiting employees from moving personal information out of an agency computer without special authorization.

Personal Actions

As suggested above, it will not be easy, and may be quite costly, for individuals to achieve a significant degree of personal privacy in our society. Gary Marx (1991) has provided a list of steps that individuals can take. His list includes the following: (1) Don't give out any more information than is necessary; (2) don't say things over a cellular or cordless phone that you would mind having overheard by strangers; (3) ask your bank to sign an agreement that it will not release information about your accounts to anyone lacking legal authorization and that in the event of legal authorization, it will contact you within two days; (4) obtain copies of your credit, health, and other records and

check for accuracy and currency; (5) if you are refused credit, a
an apartment, ask why (there may be a file with inaccurate, incon
evant information); (6) remember that when you respond to tele
to-door surveys, the information will go into a databank; and (
when you purchase a product or service and file a warranty card or participate
in a rebate program, your name may well be sold to a mailing-list company.

CONCLUSION

Privacy is, perhaps, the most important of the ethical issues surrounding computer and information technology. I have tried to show this by making clear the importance of privacy to democratic society and the subtle ways in which our lives are changed when we are being watched. Individuals who walk through life knowing that each step creates a record that may or may not end up in a database somewhere are very different from individuals who walk through life feeling free and confident that they live in a open society in which the rules are known and fair.

Protecting personal privacy is not easy and is not likely to get easier. The most effective approach to privacy protection is a many-pronged approach. One thing is for sure, the use of personal information is not going to diminish of its own accord. Information about individuals is extremely valuable both in the private and in the public sector. This issue is not going to go away until we do something about it.

STUDY QUESTIONS

1. Is there anything new about the current computers and privacy issue?
2. How has computer and information technology changed information gathering practices?
3. What is the panopticon? How is it a metaphor for the future?
4. Why is information about individuals so important to organizations? Give examples of the uses of personal information by private and public organizations
5. What arguments can be given for the importance of personal privacy?
6. How does information mediate relationships? relationships with organizations?
7. The author offers an alternative to framing the computers and privacy issue as a tension between individual interests in privacy and the social value of information. What is the alternative?
8. Describe cases in which individuals would be harmed by inaccurate and/or irrelevant information.
9. Why does the author claim that current information gathering practices make personal privacy too costly to individuals?

/. Describe three policy approaches to protecting personal privacy. What are the advantages and disadvantages of each?

11. How does globalization of the economy impact information gathering practices?

SUGGESTED FURTHER READING

Agre, Philip E., and Marc Rotenberg, *Technology and Privacy: The New Landscape* (Cambridge, MA: MIT Press, 1997).

Bennett, Colin J., and Rebecca Grant, *Visions of Privacy, Policy Choices for the Digital Age* (Toronto, Ontario: University of Toronto Press, 1999).

De Cew, Judith Wagner, *In Pursuit of Privacy, Law, Ethics, and the Rise of Technology* (Ithaca, New York: Cornell University Press, 1997).

Regan, Priscilla M., *Legislating Privacy, Technology, Social Values and Public Policy* (Chapel Hill: University of North Carolina Press, 1995).

Smith, Robert Ellis, "Compilation of State and Federal Privacy Laws," *Privacy Journal* (2000).

WEB SITES

For the Electronic Privacy Information Center, see: www.epic.org
For Privacy International, see: www.privacyinternational.org/

CHAPTER 6

Property Rights in Computer Software

SCENARIO 6.1 **Obtaining pirated software abroad.**

Carol works as a computer consultant for a large consulting company. She loves her job because it allows her to continuously learn about new IT applications and she uses many of these applications to do her work. Carol has vacation time coming and she and her husband decide to spend two weeks visiting a country in Southeast Asia. While there, Carol and her husband decide to check out the computer stores to see what sort of software and hardware is available. While rummaging in one store, Carol finds an office suite package. It includes a spreadsheet, a word processor, presentation applications, and more. Indeed, it looks identical to a package made by a well-known American company, a package that she has been thinking about buying. The price in the U.S. is around $1,200 which is why she has been reluctant to buy it, but here the package costs the equivalent of $50. She has heard that countries like the one she is in do not honor U.S. copyrights. She notices that the written documentation looks like a duplicated copy; it doesn't look like it has been professionally printed. The deal is just too good to resist. She buys the software!

As she prepares for the airplane trip home, she wonders where she should put the package. She's not sure what will happen if custom officials notice it as she re-enters the United States.

Has Carol done anything wrong? Would it be unfair if U.S. custom officials stopped Carol and confiscated the software package?

SCENARIO 6.2 **Stealing the idea.**

Imagine that it is 1980. Use of computers is growing and there are a wide variety of computers and operating systems available. Bingo Software Systems has an idea for a new operating system that, it believes, will be significantly better than anything that has yet been produced. Bingo is a small company employing twenty people. It obtains venture capital and spends three years developing the operating system. Over the course of the three years, Bingo invests approximately two million dollars in development of the system. When completed, the new system is successfully marketed for about a year, and Bingo recovers about 25 percent of its investment. However, after the first year, several things happen that substantially cut into sales. First, a competing company, Pirate Pete's Software, starts to sell a system very similar to Bingo's, but Pirate Pete's system has several features not available in Bingo's system. It appears that Pirate Pete's Software has examined the system developed by Bingo, adopted the same general approach, possibly copied much of the code, and, in any case, produced a modified and improved version. Second, copying of Bingo's system is rampant. Customers, primarily small businesses, appear to be buying one copy of Bingo's system, and then making multiple copies for internal use. It appears that they are giving copies to other businesses as well. As a result, there is a significant reduction in demand for Bingo's system. Bingo is unable to recover the full costs of developing the system and goes into bankruptcy.

Is this situation unfair? Has Pirate Pete's Software wronged Bingo Software Systems?

SCENARIO 6.3   **Improving software.**

Earl Eniac spends a year developing a virus tester. He finally has it developed to a point where he is pleased with it. It detects all the viruses he has ever encountered and repairs them. Earl makes the tester available from his Web site; anyone who wants it can download it for free. He also publishes an article in a computer journal describing how it works. Jake Jasper downloads a copy from the Web site, reads the article, and figures out how the virus tester works. He thinks it is a clever, creative, and useful piece of software. He also sees how several small changes could be made to the tester, changes that would make it even better. Since the copy that Jake downloaded from the Web allows him access to the source code, Jake makes these changes to the program. He then sends the revised program to Earl with an explanation of what he has done. Jake makes the improved version available from his Web site where he also describes what he has done, giving credit to Earl for the original.

Has Earl or Jake done anything wrong?

In this chapter, we turn our attention to a set of issues that arise because of the very nature of computer and information technology. In one sense, computers are simply machines. They are on par with other devices that we use to get things done—lawnmowers, washing machines, and automobiles. Many of these machines now contain computerized parts, but the point is that all machines are similar insofar as they are created by manipulating materials and laws of nature (e.g., laws of physics). In another sense, however, computer and information technology is different, and its distinctiveness becomes apparent when it comes to issues of ownership and property rights.

While it is difficult to pinpoint, the distinguishing feature of computer and information technology has to do with its intangibility and its reproducibility (discussed in Chapter 4). The standard way to conceptualize computer technology is to think of computers as a combination of hardware and software. *Hardware* refers to the machine, a malleable machine with practically infinite possible configurations. *Software* refers, essentially, to a set of instructions for the machine. Software controls and configures the machine. When software is put into a computer, it causes switches to be set and determines what the computer can and cannot do. The software sets up the computer so that it responds in determinate ways when users press keys or input programs.

Note that while this understanding of computers (as a combination of hardware and software) is fairly standard, the technology has evolved in ways that blur the distinction between hardware and software. For example, devices can be created by taking what is essentially a software program and etching it into a silicon chip. The microchip that is created is a hybrid between software and hardware.

When software was first created, it was considered a new type of entity. Nothing with the characteristics of software had existed before computers.[1] And, it is the ownership of this new entity that has posed daunting ethical and legal issues. To be sure, there have been and continue to be ownership issues with regard to computer hardware, but software has posed the most difficult challenge.

Software has created ethical and legal issues both at the macro or public policy level and at the micro or individual level. The broadest macro level issues have to do with whether or not, and what aspects of, computer software should be owned. In other words, what aspects, if any, of computer software should be legally protected as private property. The most compelling micro level issues have to do with whether it is wrong for an individual to make a seemingly illegal copy of computer software. For example, is it wrong for Mary in Scenario 1.1 (in Chapter 1) to copy the penny stock software? Or is it wrong for Carol in Scenario 6.1 to buy software that violates a copyright?

In the analysis that follows, I address both the legal and the moral issues and I address both descriptive and normative questions (i.e., what does current law specify and what should the law be in this domain). When it comes to the law, my focus is primarily on U.S. law though many countries of the world have similar copyright and patent laws.

The legal and moral issues are inextricably tied together in a number of ways. If laws set up unfair arrangements, then the moral critique of those arrangements is relevant to the interpretation of the law. Deciding what the

---

[1] Parallels have been made between software and the scrolls used in player pianos and between software and the keys used to set the functions of weaving looms. However, software is different from each of these in its form—digitalized instructions causing electronic switches to be set.

laws should be in a domain such as software ownership is in part a moral matter. For example, Scenario 6.2 suggests a problem in the legal protection provided to those who want to develop software, and this is also a moral matter in that it concerns the fairness of the situation and the social consequences of the situation. In an important sense, the law sets the rules of the game of software development, and the game ought to be fair in addition to producing good consequences. In addition to legal issues often being moral issues, moral issues often hinge on what the law is. For example, in Scenario 1.1, to determine whether Mary did something wrong, one important consideration is whether she broke the law. All else being equal, citizens have an obligation to obey the law. In Scenario 6.1, this question is more complicated since Carol is visiting another country in which the laws differ from those of her own country.

I begin this chapter by describing the legal mechanisms that are now available to those who develop and want to claim property rights in computer software. The question driving this description—a question on the minds of many in the software industry—is whether current legal tools are adequate for computer software. To fully understand the problems with software ownership, it is essential to take a broad philosophical perspective and consider the most basic question: Should computer software be owned at all? Should it be treated as property? You may find this question odd since so much is already owned in the domain of computing, by copyright or patent. Nevertheless, answering this philosophical question is important both for understanding why we have the laws that we currently have and for contemplating whether and how these laws might be changed in the future.

Software property rights continue to be uncertain in many areas and property rights claims are continuously being contested. The courts and law journals are filled with case after case in which this or that aspect of computing is being claimed as a property right—an encryption schema, a knowledge-discovery tool, a new operating system, a new digital-imaging technique, and so on. Moreover, the Internet has added several new dimensions to this already complex area. Search engines, privacy-enhancing tools, virus detectors, and other software systems are continuously being invented to implement activities on the Internet. In addition and consequently, international, cross-border property rights issues are intensified. While there have always been international law issues concerning property created in one country moving to another, the Internet has made these issues more intense and more pressing because it is so easy to send copyrighted materials and patented processes across national boundaries. International law must be brought to bear to determine the legal standing of something copyrighted or patented in one country when it moves to another country (Burk, 1994). International law is enormously complex, and there is no universally recognized power or authority to enforce international laws. The World Trade Organization is currently in the process of developing policies to cover intellectual property issues in international trade.

The property rights issues surrounding computer software are in many ways the most intriguing. Unfortunately, however, because there are so many issues, this chapter remains at the broadest level. The aim is to understand the foundations of property rights and then to explore how foundational principles apply to computer software. This analysis can easily be supplemented with current cases found in law journals, on the Web, or in newspapers.

After explaining the standard forms of legal protection currently available to software developers and identifying their limitations, I focus on the philosophical and moral foundations of property. I argue here that the moral arguments do not show that computer software *must* be treated as property. At least, neither utilitarian nor natural rights arguments establish that societies without intellectual property are unjust or immoral societies. Intellectual property rights are socially created rights and a variety of social arrangements are possible that are morally acceptable. Building on this analysis, I conclude the chapter with a discussion of the micro level question: Is it wrong for an individual to make a copy of proprietary software? Here I argue that it is wrong to make a copy because it is illegal, but not because there is some prelegal immorality involved in the act.

DEFINITIONS

To understand the software ownership issue, it is essential to understand what software is, and this requires understanding the distinction between algorithms, object programs (and code), and source programs (and code). As described earlier, software sets switches in computers and configures the computer in a specific way. Software sets up—programs—a computer so that it can receive and respond to commands given to it by a user or another program. What a particular program does to a computer can be described in three different ways: as an algorithm, in source code, and in object code.   Though dated in the computer languages and technology to which it refers, Gemignani's 1980 explanation remains one of the most lucid:

> Programs are responses to problems to be solved. First, the problem in issue must be clearly formulated. Then a solution must be outlined. To be amenable to implementation on a computer, the solution must be expressible in a precise way as a series of steps to be carried out, each step being itself clearly defined. This is usually set forth as a flowchart, a stylized diagram showing the steps of the algorithm and their relationship to one another. Once a flowchart has been constructed, it is used as a guide for expressing the algorithm in a "language" that the computer can "understand." This "coding" of the program is almost certain to employ a "high level" computer language, such as BASIC or FORTRAN. When the algorithm is "coded" in a high level computer language, it is called a *source program*. A source program may bear a striking resemblance to a set of instructions expressed in literary form. The source program is fed into the computer by means of an input device, such as a terminal or card reader. The source program is "translated" by the compiler, a part of

the operating systems program, into machine language, a language not at all similar to ordinary speech. The program expressed in machine language is called an *object program*. It is the object program which actuates the setting of switches which enables the computer to perform the underlying algorithm and solve the problem (Gemignani, 1980).

To update this account, we need only specify a somewhat different explanation of object and source code:

> Source code and object code refer to the "before" and "after" versions of a computer program. The source code consists of the programming statements that are created by a programmer with a text editor or a visual programming tool and then saved in a file. For example, a programmer using the C language types in a desired sequence of C language statements using a text editor and then saves them as a named file. This file is said to contain the source code. It is now ready to be compiled with a C compiler and the resulting output, the compiled file, is often referred to as object code. The object code file contains a sequence of instructions that the processor can understand but that is difficult for a human to read or modify. For this reason and because even debugged programs often need some later enhancement, the source code is the most permanent form of the program (see www.whatis.com).

As you will see later on, intellectual property laws treat each of these aspects of computer software in different ways.

THE PROBLEM

We can begin with the situation described in Scenario 6.2. Bingo Software is unable to sell its operating system software because Pirate Pete's has copied the software and made improvements on it. Pirate Pete's is able to sell its software at a markedly lower price because its development costs were so much lower than Bingo's. On the face of it, the situation seems unfair. The unfairness does not, however, arise simply from the fact that Bingo cannot recoup its investment. That happens frequently when a new business venture fails to find a sufficient market for its products. Rather the unfairness in the situation has to do with the fact that Pirate Pete's is able to use the work of Bingo without having to pay for it. Pirate Pete's is able to make a better system more cheaply by building on the work of Bingo. Bingo makes an investment in the development of a product with its money, its effort and its ingenuity, and yet gets none of the rewards. Pirate Pete's gets the reward without making the investment.

At first glance, this may seem a problem with an easy solution. All we have to do is give Bingo a legal right to own the software it creates, a legal right that excludes others from using or selling Bingo's software without Bingo's permission.

While this seems a good solution, it is much harder to implement than it seems, and there are good reasons for hesitating to give such protection. The reasons for hesitating go to the heart of intellectual property law. In both copyright and patent law, there are limitations on what can be owned (claimed). In copyright law, expressions of ideas can be owned but not the ideas themselves. In patent law, applications or implementations of ideas can be owned, but abstract ideas, mathematical algorithms, mental steps, or laws of nature cannot be owned. Similarly, philosophical theories of property recognize that property rights are problematic when they get in the way of future development, creativity, and innovation. So, before leaping to the conclusion that we should give software developers the kind of ownership they need to avoid exploitation of the kind described in Scenario 6.2, we should consider the reasons for refusing to grant such protection.

CURRENT LEGAL PROTECTION

At present, three legal mechanisms can be used by those who create software to claim ownership in and protect their creations: (1) copyright, (2) trade secrecy, and (3) patent. In the late 1970s and early 1980s, a good deal of concern was beginning to be expressed that none of these legal mechanisms adequately protected computer software. That concern has persisted. In the 1970s and 1980s, a sizable literature described the extent and impact of software piracy and illegal copying and expressed fear that software development would be significantly impeded because software developers would not be able to recover the costs of development, let alone profit from their creations. This, it was feared, would significantly dampen the incentive to create.

While there is no indication that software piracy has subsided since the early 1980s, the environment for software development has changed. Many more patents on software-related inventions have been issued, and the software industry has found ways to successfully prosecute copyright infringement claims. Still, there is dissatisfaction with the legal situation. In addition to complaints about inadequate protection for software, there are serious concerns about too much being owned. The new concern is that copyrighting and patenting constrain software development because when a company develops a new piece of software, it has to do an extensive search to find out what is already claimed. Depending on what it finds, it may have to pay enormous fees to license a process that has been patented or it may have to craft a copyright claim in contorted ways to ensure that its claim does not infringe on others. All of this creates a barrier to new invention; it slows down the process and increases the costs of getting something to the marketplace.

Copyright

In the United States, when a software developer creates an original piece of software, the developer can use copyright law to obtain a form of ownership that will exclude others from directly copying the software without permission. That is, others are not permitted to reproduce a copyrighted work, distribute copies of it, or display or perform the copyrighted work publicly, without first obtaining permission from the author (copyright holder). Until 1998, copyright protection extended for the life of the author plus 50 years. In 1998, copyright law was amended to extend the term of coverage to the life of the author plus 70 years.

Copyright protection is rooted in the United States Constitution where article I section 8, clause 8 specifies that Congress shall have the power "To promote the Progress of Science and useful Arts, by securing for limited Times to Authors and Inventors the exclusive Right to their respective Writings and Discoveries." The Copyright Act protects "original works of authorship fixed in any tangible medium of expression, now known or later developed, from which they can be perceived, reproduced, or otherwise communicated, either directly or with the aid of a machine or device." (17 U.S.C. Section 102 (a) (1995))

While copyright provides a significant form of protection to authors, when it comes to computer software, the protection is limited and poses complex issues of interpretation. At the heart of copyright law is a distinction between ideas and expression. An idea cannot be copyrighted; the expression of an idea can be. The distinction between idea and expression makes sense when it comes to literary works. An author cannot own the ideas in his or her writing but can copyright the writing as a unique expression of those ideas. With this form of protection, authors are able to stop others from copying their writings without permission, and this makes it possible for authors to make money from the sale and distribution of their writings.

To be sure, copyright protection can be problematic for literary works. Claims to a number of famous literary works have been contested and authors have learned the hard way that the line between idea and expression is not so easy to draw. However, when it comes to computer software, the problems are even more complex because copyright does not seem to protect the most valuable part of software.

Generally, algorithms are thought to be the ideas expressed in a program and, hence, they are not copyrightable. When expressed as source and/or object code, however, programs are copyrightable. Both the source program and the object program are understood, in copyright law, to be "literary works," that is, formal expressions of ideas. The problem is that it is often sufficient for a competitor to study the software and with minor effort, and without directly copying, create comparable, and sometimes better, software. The task of creating new source and object code may be negligible once the algorithms or the ideas or the approach taken in the software is grasped from using the program.

In practical terms, this has meant a plethora of court cases and legal decisions trying to make clear when a copyright has and has not been violated. It may be fair to say that the extension of copyright to the domain of computer and information technology has created as many questions as answers.

The problem seems to be that the distinction between idea and expression is not suitable for software. Software is like literary works in being expressive, but it is unlike literary works in that it is also useful (functional). Software behaves; it performs tasks in a determinate way. The behavior of software is valuable and that value is not protected by copyright (Davis et al., 1996). As already mentioned, competitors can "read" the software and see and understand its useful behavior, and then create an original, alternative program behaving in the same way but not copying the literal expression of the original software.

Recognition of this difference between software and literary works has led some computer scientists and legal scholars to argue for a new and specially designed form of legal protection for software. Davis et al. (1996), for example, have argued for a new framework that protects against behavior clones for a limited period of time, and calls for a system of registration of software innovations but does not rule out the use of copyright for literal code. This system, they argue, would promote disclosure and dissemination while giving innovators time to develop their market.

In the absence of a new, alternative framework for protection, legal controversy surrounding current copyright laws persists with issues of interpretation being raised in a wide variety of ways. One important area of contention has been in determining when a copyright has been infringed. Whether or not there is infringement depends on whether the idea has been expressed in a new way or merely copies the pre-existing copyrighted expression. This determination is not easy to make.

When a software developer believes that her or his copyright has been infringed, the copyright holder must take the accused infringer to court. The burden of proof is on the copyright holder to prove infringement. To prove infringement, the copyright holder must show that there is a "striking resemblance" between the copyrighted software and the infringing software, a resemblance so close that it could only be explained by copying. If the defendant can establish that he or she developed the new program on his or her own, without any knowledge of the pre-existing program, then there has been no infringement. This is important to note: Copyright does not give a monopoly of control of a literary work. If someone else independently (without any knowledge of a pre-existing work) writes something similar or even identical, there is no infringement.

Copyright infringement disputes often hinge on whether it is plausible to suppose that someone would come up with an identical program on their own or whether the resemblance between the programs is so close as to be explained only by direct copying. Although this is an extremely difficult hurdle for a copyright holder to overcome in pursuing an infringement action, copyright holders have been successful in overcoming it. Perhaps the most famous case is that of *Franklin v. Apple,* decided by the United States Supreme Court in 1984. Apple was able to show that Franklin copied Apple's operating system (the object code of their operating system) because Franklin's operating system contained line after line of identical code. Franklin had not even bothered to delete segments of code that included Apple's name.[2]

Franklin v. Apple is also important because it was the decision establishing that computer programs in object code are copyrightable. Before this case was decided, no one was sure whether object code would count as expression since object code cannot be "read" by a human. The Supreme Court decided that machine-readable code counted as "expression."

If a copyright holder goes to court to prove infringement and establishes only that there is a resemblance but not a *striking* resemblance between the copyright holder's software and the defendant's software, then the copyright holder can try to win the case in a different way. The law allows copyrighted material to be appropriated by others without permission if something significant is added to the copyrighted material, such that a new expression is produced. The law makes a distinction between improper and proper appropriation. You are entitled to draw on a copyrighted work as long as you create or add something new. While *improper appropriation* is not a precise notion, it is meant to define the line between taking another's work and building on another's work. Hence, a copyright holder can stop an infringer if the copyright holder can show that the accused relied heavily on the copyright holder's program *and* did not add anything significant to it. This shows improper appropriation.

In either case—whether using striking resemblance or improper appropriation—the copyright holder must also show that the defendant had access to the program. This casts doubt on the possibility that the defendant created the program on his or her own. As already explained, if the defendant produced a similar program on his or her own, then there is no infringement. In the case of computer software, access is often easy to prove, especially if the copyrighted software has been widely marketed. If on the other hand, the software has been kept out of the marketplace, as, for example, when a company produces software for its own internal use and later finds a competitor has identical software, access will not be so easy to prove.

Since the invention of computers and the creation of software, copyright law has been clarified in certain areas, but new issues continue to arise. While there are too many issues to cover here, several can be mentioned to illustrate the diversity and complexity of copyright disputes.

In pursuit of protection for functional software, various aspects of software have come into focus as the valuable part of the software. Both the "structure, sequence, and organization" of programs and the "look and feel" of user interfaces have been seen as potentially what should be protected by copyright. In *Whelan Associates, Inc. v. Jaslow Dental Laboratory, Inc.,* Whelan had developed a program for Jaslow (for the business activities of his dental office) with the understanding that she (Whelan) would own the rights in the program (*Whelan v. Jaslow,* 1987). A few years after the program had been completed, Jaslow decided

---

[2] This case established that copyright applies to operating systems programs as well as applications programs.

that there would be a market for a program like the one Whelan had developed for him, but in a different language and for use on a personal computer. Jaslow developed such a program. While he did not use any of the code written by Whelan, he, evidently, studied how Whelan had organized the program. Whelan sued Jaslow for copyright infringement. The court found infringement based on "comprehensive nonliteral similarity." That is, it found that "copyright protection of computer programs may extend beyond a program's literal code to its structure, sequence and organization."

Yet other more recent cases have attempted (and in many cases succeeded) in extending copyright protection to the look and feel of a program and other "nonliteral" elements of programs. These include general flow charts and "more specific organization of intermodular relationships, parameter lists, and macros" as well as program outputs such as "screen displays and user interfaces, menus, and command tree structures contained on screens" (*O. P. Solutions v. Intellectual Property Network Ltd.*, 1999). In addition, endless copyright issues have arisen around the use of images and text on the Web. Needless to say, these issues are made even more complex by the global scope of the Internet.

Copyright continues to be an important legal mechanism for protecting software, though, as you can see, it is far from an ideal form of protection for computer software.

Trade Secrecy Laws

Trade secrecy laws vary from jurisdiction to jurisdiction but in general what they do is give companies the right to keep certain kinds of information secret. The laws are aimed specifically at protecting companies from losing their competitive edge. Thus, for example, a company can keep secret the precise recipe of foods that it sells or the formula of chemicals it uses in certain processes.

Trade secrecy laws were not designed with computer technology in mind and, consequently, their applicability to the computer industry has been somewhat unclear. Nevertheless, this form of protection is used.

To hold up in court, what is claimed as a trade secret typically must (1) have novelty, (2) represent an economic investment to the claimant, (3) have involved some effort in development, and (4) the company must show that it made some effort to keep the information a secret. Software can qualify for such protection; that is, software can be novel, involve effort in development, and require significant investment. Some software companies try to keep their software secret by using nondisclosure clauses in contracts of employment and by means of licensing agreements with those who use their software. Nondisclosure clauses require employees to refrain from revealing secrets that they learn at work. An employee promises not to take copies of programs or reveal the contents of programs owned by the firm, even when he or she leaves the firm. With licensing agreements, companies do not actually sell their software but license its use. Those who want such licenses are required to agree not to do anything that will reveal the "secret." They agree, that is, not to give away or sell copies of the software that has been licensed.

In addition to employment contracts and licensing agreements, program developers have employed a variety of technical devices to protect their secrets. Such devices include limiting what is available to the user (i.e., not giving the user access to the source program), or building into the program identifying codes so that illegal copies can be traced to their source.

Though this form of protection is used by the software industry, many complain that even with improved technical devices for maintaining secrecy, the protection offered is not adequate. For one thing, the laws are not uniform throughout the United States and this makes it difficult for businesses that operate in multiple jurisdictions. Also, the protection provided is still uncertain because the laws were not designed for computer technology. Thus, companies have to take a risk that the courts will support their claims when and if they are ever tested in the courts.

Most important is the problem of meeting the requirement of maintaining secrecy. Enforcing employment agreements and licensing agreements is a tricky business. Violators can be caught taking or selling direct copies of programs, but there is nothing to stop an employee of one firm from taking the general knowledge and understanding of the principles used in a program to a new job at another firm. Likewise someone who works with licensed software may grasp general principles that can be used to create new software. So while agreements can be made, there are always ambiguities in what one agrees not to reveal.

These problems are not unique to computer software. In a competitive environment, many types of information are better kept secret. What is somewhat unusual about computer software is that often a company must reveal the secret in order to sell the software. That is, in order to provide a licensee with usable software, the software must be modifiable for the licensee's unique needs, and sometimes the only way to do this is to give the licensee access to the source code. The licensee can, then, alter the source code to fit its unique situation. Once the source program is available, the secret is less likely to remain secret, and trade secrecy laws may not apply.

In the typical case described in Scenario 6.2, trade secrecy laws would have been helpful to Bingo, but only to a point. Bingo could have kept the design of its new operating system secret during its development by means of nondisclosure clauses in employment contracts. Once the system was ready for marketing, however, keeping it a secret would have been more difficult. In showing the system to potential users, some information would be revealed, and once the system was in widespread use, Bingo's control of the situation would weaken significantly. Companies that have licenses to use the system cannot police their employees; they cannot entirely control what they see or even what they copy and the general principles used in the system would become known to many users even without malicious intent.

Many companies try to counter this problem by making all modifications to the system for each customer and doing all repairs and maintenance themselves. Provisions for this can be built into the licensing agreement, which minimizes the licensees' exposure to the source code. It works to some extent, though there are still problems in the gray areas of employment agreements and it is not at all practical for small, less complicated programs, where it is impractical for the company to modify every copy sold.

Thus, trade secrecy offers a strong form of protection insofar as it allows the owner to keep software out of the public realm. The problem is that it is often not possible to use trade secrecy because the software has to be put into the public realm in order to be sold or licensed.

Patent Protection

In principle, patent protection offers the strongest form of protection for software because a patent gives the inventor a monopoly on the use of the invention. A patent gives the patent holder both the right to exclude others from making, using or selling the invention, and the right to license others to make, use, or sell it. Even if someone else invents the same thing independently, without any knowledge of the patent holder's invention, the secondary inventor is excluded from use of the patented device without permission of the patent holder. A patent is a legitimate monopoly. Patent protection would seem to give Bingo Software, in Scenario 6.2, the power to prevent Pirate Pete's from marketing its system.

There are three types of patents: utility patents, design patents, and patents on plant forms. The primary concern here is with utility patents for utility patents hold the most promise of protecting software. Utility patents are granted for a term of seventeen years, though the term may be extended for an additional five years.

When it comes to software, the problem with patent protection is not in the kind of protection it provides, but rather the apparent inappropriateness of patents on software. The courts have been reluctant to grant patents on software, and for good reason. To understand the good reasons for not extending patent protection to software, it is helpful to consider the aims and purposes of the patent system.

The aim of the patent system is not simply to ensure that individuals reap rewards for their inventions. Rather, the ruling principle behind the patent system is the advancement of the useful arts and sciences. The objectives of the patent system are to foster invention, to promote disclosure of inventions, and to assure that ideas already in the public domain remain there for free use. The furthering of these objectives is, in turn, expected to improve the economy, increase employment, and generally make better lives for citizens.

One way to encourage invention is to have a system that rewards it. Patent protection does not guarantee that individuals will be rewarded for their inventions. It provides a form of protection that is a precondition of reward. In other words, if you have a monopoly *and* if your invention has commercial value, then you (and no one else) will be in a position to market the invention. By assuring the possibility of reaping rewards, patent protection encourages invention and innovation. Allowing inventors to profit from their inventions is a means, not an end.

The patent system recognizes that inventions brought into the public realm are beneficial not just in themselves but also because others can learn from and build on these inventions. If new ideas are kept secret, progress in the useful arts and sciences is impeded. Patent protection encourages the inventor to put her ideas into the public realm by promising her protection that she wouldn't have if she simply kept her ideas to herself. If an inventor chooses not to patent his or her invention but to keep it secret, then the inventor will not have recourse if someone else comes up with the same idea or copies the invention. There is nothing to prevent a copier from patenting and marketing the invention.

These two arguments—that patents encourage invention and encourage the bringing of inventions into the public realm—also lead, however, to important restrictions. Abstract ideas, mathematical algorithms, scientific principles, laws of nature, and mental processes cannot be patented. To give someone the exclusive right to use these kinds of things would inhibit further invention rather than fostering it because these things are the building blocks of invention. If individuals had to get permission from a patent holder to use an idea or an algorithm or a law of nature, invention would be significantly impeded. Imagine, for example, the enormous power of the person who held a patent on the law of gravitational pull or the mental steps involved in addition or multiplication!

While this restriction on what can be patented seems more than reasonable, it has caused problems for the patenting of software. A patent claim must satisfy a two-step test before a patent is granted. The claim must (1) fall within the category of permissible subject matter and (2) satisfy three separate tests: (a) it must have utility; (b) it must have novelty; and, (c) it must be non-obvious. The latter three tests are not easy to pass, but they have not been problematic for computer software. That is, many software programs are useful, novel, and not so simple as to be obvious to the average person. Rather, software has had difficulty passing the first step and qualifying as permissible subject matter.

The subject matter of a patent is limited to "a process, machine, manufacture or composition of matter or . . . an improvement thereof." Generally, software has been considered a process or part of a process:

> That a process may be patentable, irrespective of the particular form of the instrumentalities used, cannot be disputed . . . A process is a mode of treatment of certain materials to produce a given result. It is an act, or a series of acts, performed upon the subject matter to be transformed and reduced to a different state or thing. If new and useful, it is just as patentable as is a piece of machinery. (*Cochrane v. Deener*, 94 U.S. 780, 787-788:161876:17)

One difficulty in extending patent protection to software has been in specifying what subject matter is transformed by software: Data? The internal structure of the computer? And so on. However, this problem is secondary to a larger issue.

In the 1970s and 1980s, there was reluctance to grant patents on software or software-related inventions for fear that in granting patents on software, ownership of mental processes might, in effect, be granted. Each of the steps in an algorithm is an operation a human can, in principle at least, perform mentally. If a series of such steps was patented, the patent holder might be able to require that permission or a license be sought before those operations were performed mentally. Needless to say, this would significantly interfere with freedom of thought.

The fear of interfering with mental steps was fairly quickly overcome, but it was followed by concern about patent holders acquiring patent rights to computer and/or mathematical algorithms. Granting a monopoly on the use of a software invention could, it was feared, lead to a monopoly on the use of a mathematical algorithm. This is explicitly prohibited in patent law as inappropriate subject matter. The problem is, what is a software invention if not an algorithm—the order and sequence of steps to achieve a certain result. The issue goes to the heart of what exactly one owns when one has a patent on a piece of software.

Before the *Diamond v. Diehr* case was settled in 1981, very few patents had been granted on computer software (*Diamond v. Diehr*, 1981). There had been a struggle between the United States Supreme Court, the Patent Office, and the Court of Customs and Patent Appeals (CCPA), with the former two resisting granting of patents and the latter pressing to extend patent protection to software. In *Diamond v. Diehr*, the Supreme Court, on only a 5 to 4 vote, denied a patent to Diehr. Even though it was a close and disputable decision, the Patent Office and especially the CCPA interpreted the court's reasoning so as to justify granting patents on software inventions. Although only a handful of software-related patents had been granted before *Diamond v. Diehr*, many thousands have been granted since. Browning (1993) reported that over 9,000 software patents were granted between late-1960s and the end of 1992, and 1,300 were issued in 1992 alone. Statistics vary widely but one recent source reports that "The U.S. Patent and Trademark office bestows more than 20,000 software patents annually" (*Atlanta Constitution*, April 2, 2000).

As mentioned earlier, concerns are now being expressed that too much is being patented and that patents are getting in the way of development in the field. These concerns go to the heart of the patent system's aim, for they suggest that because so much is owned, innovation is now being inhibited. The subject matter limitation on what can be patented aims to insure that the building blocks of science and technology should not be owned so that continued development will flourish, yet complaints suggest just that: the building blocks may now be owned.

The situation can be described roughly as follows: Because so many patents have been granted, before putting new software on the market a software developer must do an extensive and expensive patent search. If overlapping patents are found, licenses must be secured. Even if no overlapping patents are found, there is always the risk of late-issuing patents. Patent searches are not guaranteed to identify all potential infringements because the Patent Office has a poor classification system for software. Hence, there is always the risk of lawsuit due to patent infringement. You may invest a great deal in developing a product, invest more in a patent search, and then find at the last minute that the new product infringes on something already claimed. These factors make software development a risky business and constitute barriers to the development of new software. The costs and risks are barriers especially for small entrepreneurs.

A number of important legal scholars have argued that the Patent Office and the CCPA have overextended the meaning of the Supreme Court's decision in *Diamond v. Diehr* (Samuelson, 1990). The League for Programming Freedom (LPF) (1990) proposes that we pass a law that excludes software from the domain of patents. The situation seems to call for change. Yet, at this point, change may be difficult simply because the computer industry has grown and solidified in an environment structured by these forms of protection.

Summary of Legal Mechanisms

At present, then, there are three forms of legal protection available to software developers, but there are drawbacks to the use of each. Copyright does not give software developers a monopoly on their software and does not protect the valuable part of a program, its functionality. Moreover, copyright law does not provide a stable environment for software developers in that it leaves a good deal of uncertainty about what one owns when one has a copyright on computer software. Trade secrecy (together with employment contracts and licensing agreements) protects all aspects of software by keeping the software out of the public domain. The problem here is that trade secrecy is not always useful to software developers because often they cannot market their software without revealing the secret, and once the secret is out, the law may not apply. Moreover, trade secrecy has the disadvantage that in the long run society does not receive the benefit of exposure to the ideas in the software. Patents promise the strongest form of protection, a monopoly, but the process of acquiring a patent is long, expensive, and fraught with uncertainty. Moreover, extensive use of patent protection may do as much harm as good for software development by interfering with the building blocks of innovation.

This unsatisfactory situation arises because computer software does not fit neatly into the traditional categories employed in property law. Computer software seems to defy the distinction between idea and expression and the distinction between patentable and unpatentable subject matter. Neither copyrights nor patents protect the most valuable aspect of software—the functionality and/or the algorithm. To understand the implications of this situation and look for alternative solutions, it is helpful to think about the philosophical roots of our ideas about property.

THE PHILOSOPHICAL BASIS OF PROPERTY

Property is by no means a simple notion. It is, effectively, created by laws specifying what can and cannot be owned, how things may be acquired and transferred, what owners can and cannot do with their property, and so on. Laws define what counts as property and create different kinds of property. The laws regulating ownership of an automobile, for example, are quite different from those regulating ownership of land. In the case of land, there are rules about how far the land goes down into the ground and how far up into the air space above, about what can and cannot be constructed on the land, when the land may be confiscated by the government, and so on. With automobiles, you may have to show proof of insurance in order to take possession of a car, and even if you own one, you cannot drive it on public roads unless you have a license. Thus, what it means to have property and what it means to own something are rather complex matters.

Software has challenged our traditional notions of property and ownership. American laws, at least, do not grant property rights in the most valuable aspects of software. American laws do not give software developers the kind of protection they claim to need to successfully market innovative software inventions. In debates about whether or not and how software should be protected, assumptions are implicitly made about moral (not just legal) rights in property. These assumptions need to be uncovered, articulated, and critically examined. Drawing on the analysis presented in Chapter 2, on philosophical ethics, two distinct theories of property can be articulated. One theory is consequentialist in justifying the assignment of property rights by the good consequences that result. The other theory is not Kantian though it is closer to Kant in deriving a right to property from a prior, natural right to autonomy and/or personhood. This is the labor theory of property.

It should be clear from the earlier discussion of the legal environment for software ownership that the reasoning behind both the patent and copyright systems is consequentialist. Both systems aim to encourage and facilitate creativity and innovation so that new expressions and new products and processes will be created and made available. Both systems are designed to produce the good consequences of ongoing technological progress. Nevertheless, many discussions of property rights assume that property is not a matter of social utility but a matter of natural right. For this reason, it may be helpful to begin with an examination of the natural rights approach and its implications for software ownership.

Natural Rights Arguments

Drawing on the natural rights tradition, an argument on behalf of ownership of software could be made as follows. A person has a natural right to what he or she produces and this natural right ought to be protected by law. John Locke's labor theory of property fills in this claim. According to Locke, a person acquires a right of ownership in something by mixing his or her labor with it. In a state of nature (before laws and civilized society), an individual who came upon a stretch of land and spent months cultivating the land by planting seed, tending to the plants each day, nourishing them, and protecting them from bad weather would have rights in the crops that grew. The laborer would have a right to the crops because his or her labor produced them. The crops would not have existed without this labor. More to the point, it would be wrong for someone else to come along and seize the crops without permission from the laborer. The thief, in effect, confiscates the laborer's labor.

This Lockean account is intuitively appealing. It appeals to a notion of individual sovereignty and self-ownership. Individuals own themselves or, at least, cannot be owned by another. Since one's labor is an extension of one's body, one's labor cannot be owned by another. The argument goes to the heart of the prohibition on slavery for if an individual puts her labor in something and then someone else takes it, the laborer has been rendered a slave.

Using this Lockean account, it would seem that a software developer could argue that the software he or she develops is rightfully his or her property because it was created from his or her labor. Indeed, the unfairness we sense in Scenario 6.2 derives precisely from the fact that Bingo's labor (and investment of resources acquired by prior labor) has been confiscated by Pirate Pete's. Pirate Pete's has effectively rendered Bingo its slave. This seems a powerful argument for granting some sort of property right in computer software, a property right that would prevent Pirate Pete's from confiscating Bingo's labor.

Critique of the Natural Rights Argument

Yet despite its appeal, the natural rights argument has several flaws especially when it comes to computer software. First, the argument is careless in the way it connects ownership to labor. It would seem that the connection has to be justified. Imagine a society in which individuals do not acquire rights to what they create with their labor. Imagine that no one owns the products of their labor or the products of anyone else's labor. Such a society would not, necessarily, be unjust. Yes, it would be unjust if some individuals acquired rights to what other individuals created, but if there are no property rights whatsoever, then it would seem there is no injustice. Individuals would know that when they mixed their labor with something, they lose their labor. Robert Nozick makes this point, questioning the connection between labor and ownership in his book, *Anarchy, State and Utopia* (1974):

Why does mixing one's labor with something make one the owner of it? Perhaps because one owns one's labor, and so one comes to own a previously unowned thing that becomes permeated with what one owns. Ownership seeps over into the rest. But why isn't mixing what I own with what I don't own a way of losing what I own rather than a way of gaining what I don't? If I own a can of tomato juice and spill it in the sea so that its molecules (made radioactive, so I can check this) mingle evenly throughout the sea, do I thereby come to own the sea, or have I foolishly dissipated my tomato juice? (Nozick, pp. 174–175)

While Nozick simply asks a question, the question reveals the possibility of a disconnection between labor and property. It shows that there is not a natural connection between your labor and rights to those things created by your labor. A just world in which individuals do not own the products of their labor is plausible.

Nozick's point does not apply in a world in which some property rights are recognized. It does not eliminate the injustice of one person becoming the owner of something created by the labor of another. In other words, there may be nothing unjust about a world in which no one has property rights to anything, but in a world in which there is property, it is wrong for one person to take another's labor. In the latter case, the laborer is rendered a slave. So, Locke's labor theory seems valid in a world of property rights even though we may not need property rights to have a just society. Putting this in terms of Scenario 6.2, if Pirate Pete's copied the software developed by Bingo and then let others copy the software ad infinitum and if there were no laws prohibiting this, there is no natural injustice. However, if Pirate Pete copies Bingo's software, declares the software their property (according to law), and sells the software to others, Pirate Pete's has confiscated Bingo's labor and this seems unfair. So, Locke's labor theory does have implications for the ownership of software.

A second counter to the labor theory directly attacks the confiscation issue. We have to distinguish tangible and nontangible property. Even if the labor theory applies to tangible property (e.g., crops, land, machines), it does not apply to intellectual or nontangible things. In the case of intellectual things such as ideas, musical tunes, and mental steps, more than one person can have or use these things at the same time. If someone comes along and takes or eats the crops that I have grown, I lose the products of my labor altogether. On the other hand, if I labor in creating a song or formalizing an abstract idea such as the Pythagorean theorem and someone hears the song (even memorizes it) or comprehends the idea (and can remember it and use it), I do not lose the song or the theorem. I can continue to have and use these things while others have and use them. So, in the case of intellectual, nontangible creations, the labor expended in creating the thing is not confiscated when another takes the thing. The laborer still has the products of his or her labor.

This is precisely what is at issue with software. Software is intelligible as a nontangible entity. The software developer can describe how the software works and what it does. Another person can comprehend the idea of the software, even its functionality, and then use this understanding to write original software (source code) that does what was described. Moreover, once a piece of software is developed, many others can make identical copies of the software and yet not deprive the developer of the software.

At the beginning of this chapter and earlier in this book, I mentioned that the reproducibility of computer software has challenged traditional moral and legal notions. In the context of property rights, it should now be clear that this feature of software is both old and new. It is not new in that all forms of intellectual property are reproducible. You and I and many others can all, at the same time, possess a poem written by someone else; that is, we can posses it in the sense of knowing it and being able to recite it. Nontangible things such as ideas, expressions of ideas, mental steps, and music can be possessed and used by many simultaneously, and without interfering with possession by others, including the creator. Yet, while software is not unique in being reproducible, it does have distinct features. Software is a new species of nontangible, reproducible entity. No prior nontangible entity, for example, was capable of transforming the internal structure of an electronic machine into a powerful information-processing device.

Because of the reproducibility of computer software, the labor theory of property cannot be used to justify the assignment of property rights to software developers. If I create a complex piece of software and you copy it and use it, I am *not* deprived of the product of my labor. It is worth noting here that the reproducibility of software is often commended for having this quality in that it offers the potential for broad, democratic distribution.

It is also worth noting that from a natural rights point of view, there seems nothing immoral about a society in which there are no intellectual property rights. Justice prevails if all citizens of such a society know that they cannot own their intellectual creations and can have free access to the intellectual creations of others. Such a society would be open to the criticism that its system does not maximize good consequences, but that is a matter I will take up in a moment.

Even though Locke's labor theory does not provide a justification for property rights in computer software, our analysis of the theory's application to software has cleared the way to the heart of the software ownership issue. Once we concede that software developers do not lose the products of their labor when others copy their software, the core issue becomes clear. While software developers do not lose their software, they do lose something very valuable; they lose *the capacity to sell (and make money from) their creations*. While Bingo in Scenario 6.2 is not deprived of the software it created when Pirate Pete's copies it, Bingo is deprived of the capacity to make money from the software it created. Pirate Pete's is able to sell the product of Bingo's labor (and more) at a lower price. Why would anyone buy something they can acquire at less cost?

What software developers want is not just a right to own (in the sense of possess and use) the products of their labor. They want a right that gives them the capacity to sell and, if successful at selling, make a profit from their creation.[3] This is a claim to an *economic* right, that is a right within an economic system.

Establishing a right to the capacity to sell something requires more than showing that one has labored over the thing. Economic rights are social, not moral or natural rights. Economic rights are created by means of laws that regulate the marketplace. Such laws specify what can and cannot be put into the stream of commerce, under what conditions, meeting what standards, and so on. In the United States, for example, certain drugs are prohibited from being put into the stream of commerce except under very narrowly circumscribed conditions. Similarly, human organs may not be bought and sold in the United States. Another interesting example, counter to the labor theory, is children. Children are, in part at least, the products of their parents' labor, but parents lose all rights to their children when they become adults. Even while they are children, they cannot be sold by their parents. In any case, the point is that a right to sell something is derivative from a complex set of rules structuring commercial activity.

Both the failure of the natural rights argument and the recognition that the right at issue is an economic right, point in the direction of the software ownership issue being best understood in a consequentialist framework. That is, determining whether or not software developers should have a right to sell and profit from their creations is best understood as a matter of consequences, the good and/or bad consequences that will result from granting or not granting such a right. Indeed, the earlier discussion of copyright and patent law provided just such a rationale in that both those systems are aimed at good consequences, namely, progress in the technological arts and sciences. However, before we move to the consequentialist framework, there is one additional natural rights argument worth putting on the table. This is an argument against the ownership of software.

Against Software Ownership

Some of the early legal literature and several early court cases concerning the ownership of software focused on the idea that a patent on a program might violate "the doctrine of mental steps." This doctrine states that a series of mental operations, like addition or subtraction, cannot be owned. Concern was expressed by lawyers that ownership of software might violate this doctrine because computers perform, or at least duplicate, mental steps. It was recognized

---

[3] I say right to the *capacity* to profit because we couldn't have a right to profit—the creation might not be successful in the marketplace—we can at most have a right to put some thing into the marketplace in a form such that if consumers bought it, it could be profitable.

that in a computer, these operations are performed very quickly so that in a short time, an enormous number of steps are taken. Nevertheless, the operations performed are in principle capable of being performed by a person. If this is so, then ownership of programs could lead to interference with freedom of thought. Those who were granted patents on programs might surreptitiously acquire a monopoly on mental operations. Even though unintended, the fear was that as patent holders used their patents to stop infringements, the effect might be that the patent holder would come to be seen as the owner of the performance of certain mental steps. In other words, down the road of a series of court cases, there might be a case in which performance of mental operations in a person's mind could be ruled an infringement.

Insofar as this fear is accurate, it is a natural rights argument against ownership of computer software. In the language of natural rights, a person has a natural right to freedom of thought. Ownership of software could seriously interfere with freedom of thought. So, ownership of software should not be allowed.

While this argument does not seem to come into play in the legal arguments made today, it is an important potential implication of software ownership to keep in mind. It may well come into play in the future as expert systems and artificial intelligence become more and more sophisticated. That is, property rights in such systems could be contested on grounds that they will interfere with human thinking.

The natural rights arguments for and against ownership of software have been mentioned here because they are so often implicit in discussions of proprietary rights in software. They are also important to keep in mind because they illustrate some of the special fascination with computer and information technology. Many of the tasks now performed by computer and information technology were thought, before the twentieth century, to be the unique province of human beings. Today, a variety of artificial agents are already available and being developed with ever-increasing sophistication. There are good reasons for not allowing the ownership of thought processes, yet machines that think (in some sense of that term) are now a reality. Hence, concerns about the ownership of mental operations should not be dismissed as trivial.

CONSEQUENTIALIST ARGUMENTS

As already indicated, the arguments for ownership of software seem best framed as arguments for a social and economic right to the capacity to sell, and potentially make money from, the development of computer software. Moreover, the arguments for such a right are best framed in terms of consequences. Turning now to the consequentialist framework, the argument for ownership has two parts: bad consequences result from no ownership, and good consequences result from ownership.

Bad Consequences from No Ownership

Those who favor ownership of software are quick to point to the negative effect of no ownership, namely that individuals and companies will not invest their time, energy, and resources to develop and market software. Innovation and development will be impeded, even brought to a standstill. Why develop a new program if the moment you introduce it, others will copy it, produce it more cheaply, and yours will not sell? If we, as a society, want software developed, we will have to give those who develop it the protection they need. Otherwise, society will lose. The great promise of computer and information technology will not be realized. So the argument goes.

This is an important and powerful argument. In short, the argument claims that software will not be developed unless there is an incentive to create it, and it presumes that the only incentive to develop software is to make money. If there is no potential to make money from software development, there will be no software development. Again, so the argument goes.

While the argument is strong, it is important to recognize that it is not quite as powerful or accurate as it may seem. Software development would not come to a complete standstill if there were no ownership because making money is not the only incentive to create software. For one thing, individuals create software because they enjoying creating it and because they need software for various purposes. Once a person creates a piece of software, the person can simply give it to whoever wants it. The creator can make it available on the Web. Such software is sometimes referred to as *freeware*. Freeware is an example of software being created independent of any money-making incentive or any property rights.

Moreover, instead of using making money as the primary incentive for software development, a credit system could be instituted. In a credit system, individuals register their creations and, thereby, claim credit for having created something. If others like what has been created, this adds to the good reputation and pride of the creator. A type of credit system is used in science for scientific discoveries and scientific publications. When individuals publish the results of their research, they are given credit and recognition for their work. In the case of software development, an informal credit system seems already to exist in the sense that many individuals in the field know who developed what and they admire individuals for their accomplishments. Also there are hackers who create software just to show that they can do it or to show that something can be done.

Admittedly, credit may not motivate everyone and it may not create enough of an incentive to promote the development of many expensive and elaborate systems. Still, the point is that making money is not the only incentive for software development and software development would not come to a standstill if software were declared un-ownable.

Indeed, if the focus of attention were more on creating a system that would encourage the development of software, it would seem that private ownership of software would be only one of many alternatives. *Shareware* is another example of an alternative system. Shareware is software that is initially made available free of charge. Users are encouraged to make copies; shareware can generally be downloaded from the Web. Users are then encouraged to voluntarily pay a small price if they like the software. Sometimes instead of charging for the software itself, the developer will offer to support the software and provide printed documentation to those who register and pay a fee.[4]

In addition to credit and shareware, other possible systems for encouraging software development were seriously considered in the early days of computing. Perhaps the most interesting idea was to make software available free of charge and focus the market on hardware. Computers are useless without software, so hardware companies would be compelled to create good software in order to make their computers marketable. In this environment, there would be an incentive to create software, and the incentive would persist since the better the software available for a type of computer, the better the computer is likely to do in the marketplace.

I am not arguing that any of these alternatives would *necessarily* be better than what we have now. I mention them only to show that software development would not come to a standstill were software to be declared un-ownable. How much and what kind of software would be developed in an environment of no ownership would depend on what alternatives were adopted, if any, to promote software development.

Good Consequences from Ownership

Even though the bad consequences argument is not as strong as it may seem, when it is coupled with the argument pointing to the good consequences from ownership of software, the case is quite persuasive. The argument for the good consequences of ownership has already been given in the discussion of copyright, patent, and trade secrecy. The rationale for creating these forms of legal protection for inventions, expressions, and processes is that giving these protections—these property rights—will encourage invention, innovation, new products, and creative expression. All three systems of law aim at promoting development in the technological arts and sciences. The copyright and patent systems also recognize the value of encouraging inventors and authors to put their creations into the public domain, where others can learn from and build on them, facilitating further invention.

Patent and copyright law have long traditions and there is lots of evidence to suggest that the technological arts and sciences have, in fact, progressed as a result of inventors and authors using these forms of legal protection. Nevertheless, when it comes to software, caution is in order.

---

[4] Perhaps, the best example of successful shareware is the Linux operating system.

Remember that both the patent and copyright systems limit what can and cannot be owned. Both recognize that the very thing we want to encourage—development in the technological arts and sciences—will be impeded if we fail to limit ownership. To avoid this, copyrights are granted only on the expression of ideas, not the ideas themselves, and patents are granted only on applications of ideas and laws of nature, not the ideas or natural phenomena themselves. It is understood that progress in the technological arts and sciences will be impeded if the building blocks of science and technology are owned. Hence, while the good consequences of ownership make a powerful case for creating and protecting property rights in computer software, the case is qualified. Software should be protected but *not* at the cost of giving away the building blocks of science and technology. We should be careful to maintain an environment that is good for future development.

CONCLUSIONS FROM THE PHILOSOPHICAL ANALYSIS OF PROPERTY

This leaves us with the dilemma facing judges, lawyers, software developers, and policy makers. How can a line be drawn between ownable and un-ownable aspects of software such that software developers can own that which is valuable from a marketplace perspective and yet not own that which will interfere with future development in the field? This is no easy dilemma.

As mentioned earlier, several legal scholars and computer scientists believe that an alternative form of legal ownership should be created just for computer software. While this alternative holds great promise, policy makers are resistant to abandoning traditional forms of property. Copyrights and patents seem to have survived the test of time and appear to have successfully served countries that have adopted these forms of property.

Whether or not a new form of protection should be created for computer software is an important question, but an answer to this question would require a more thorough analysis of current case law than is possible here. The aim here was to provide a broad perspective on the issue. I leave it to readers to more fully explore the current copyright and patent case law to determine whether these legal tools are capable of being interpreted and used in a way that will resolve the dilemma of software ownership. Are they capable, that is, of being interpreted in a way that will give software developers the kind of protection they need while at the same time leaving the building blocks for future development un-ownable?

What is clear from the preceding analysis is that software property rights are best understood in a consequentialist framework (and not a natural rights framework). The consequentialist framework puts the focus on deciding ownership issues in terms of effects on continued creativity and development in the field of software. This framework suggests that the courts will have to continue to draw a delicate line between what should be ownable and what should not be ownable when it comes to software, along the lines already delineated in patent and copyright law.

IS IT WRONG TO COPY PROPRIETARY SOFTWARE?

Whatever conclusion you draw from the previous discussion, currently there is legal protection for computer software in the United States and many other countries of the world. Software is proprietary; individuals and companies can obtain copyrights and patents on the software they develop or keep software they have developed as a trade secret. Software can be put into the stream of commerce and bought and sold. This means that a person who makes a copy of proprietary software without purchasing the software (or in one way or another obtaining permission from the copyright or patent holder) is breaking the law. A person who makes an illegal copy of software violates the legal right of the patent or copyright holder. The question I now turn to is the question whether such an action is morally wrong. Is it wrong for an individual to make a copy of proprietary software?

First, a clarification: making a back-up copy (for your own protection) of software you have purchased is, generally, not illegal. This is not the type of action that will be examined here.

Second, while the issue to be taken up here is an individual moral issue, the individual at issue could be a collective unit such as a company or agency. From a moral perspective, it makes no difference whether the copier is an individual human being or a collective entity such as a company. Scenario 6.1 depicts Mary copying software that John has purchased. A comparable act occurs when a company buys a software package (and does not obtain a license for multiple copies) and makes multiple copies for use within the company.

Making copies of proprietary software is not uncommon. It seems that many individuals intuitively feel that such behavior is not wrong or not seriously wrong. Indeed, it seems that individuals who would not break any other law will make illegal copies of software. Perhaps, this is not so hard to understand. Making a copy of a piece of software is easy and produces no visible harm. It is not like taking a car or a television where taking possession means depriving the owner of their object. In fact, the illegality of the act of copying is quite subtle. In Scenario 6.1 when Mary copies software purchased by John, there is no question that John owns the software. However, when John bought the software, he only bought the right to possess and use it. He didn't buy the right to make copies for use by others. John owns the software but in a very different way than he owns his car and his bicycle or other tangible possessions.

Consider that the intuitive feeling that copying a piece of software is not harmful can be formulated into an argument for the moral permissibility of software copying. The argument can be made as a two-pronged argument:

Software copying is not wrong because (1) there is nothing intrinsically wrong with copying, and (2) it does no harm.

The first claim, (1), is true in the sense that if there were no laws against copying, the act of copying would not be wrong. Earlier I argued that intellectual property rights are not natural but a matter of social utility, and that argument seems to support this idea that copying is not intrinsically wrong. In a state of nature, the act of copying would have no moral significance. Only when there are laws against it does copying have moral significance.

The second claim, (2), is that the act of copying is not wrong because it does no harm. Here also the claim seems to be true if it refers to the actions of individuals in a state of nature. The act of copying does no harm in the sense that in a state of nature it does no physical harm and it doesn't deprive the possessor of his or her possession.

Nevertheless, both of these arguments have limited application. In societies with laws—laws creating legal rights to certain things, when a person's legal rights are violated, the person is harmed. The person is deprived of something they are legally entitled to—be it life, a vote in an election, possession of a material object, or control of intellectual property. In a society with legal rights to computer software, the act of copying software without permission of the copyright or patent holder, is illegal and harms the owner of the software by depriving the owner of his or her legal right to control use of that software. It deprives the software owner of the right to require payment in exchange for the use of the software. This is not physical harm but it is harm nevertheless. Those who continue to think that this isn't harm should consider the case of Bingo in Scenario 6.2.

So, while the intuitive feeling that software copying is not wrong can be understood, software copying is wrong in a world in which there are property rights in computer software. The argument here is interesting and can be further elaborated.

SOFTWARE COPYING IS IMMORAL BECAUSE IT IS ILLEGAL

The argument just given claims that software copying is immoral *because it is illegal*. There are cases in which the illegality of an act and its immorality are independent. For example, the act of intentionally killing another person would be immoral even if it were not illegal. Software copying is not like this; it is *not* immoral independent of it being illegal. As conceded earlier, there is nothing intrinsically immoral about the act of software copying. Rather the immorality of software copying derives from its illegality. Once a system of property laws has been created, individuals who live under those laws have certain rights, and those who break the laws violate the rights of property holders.

You might be resistant to this line of thinking because you think the laws protecting software ownership are bad laws. Given the discussion in previous sections, you might be worried that I am putting too much weight on the illegality of software copying. After all, you might argue, the laws creating property rights in computer software are not very good. They don't succeed in protecting software developers very well; they don't take advantage of the potential of software; and they lead to bad consequences when they grant ownership of the building blocks of software development.

The problem with this argument is that it implies that it is permissible to break laws whenever they are bad. While there may be cases in which individuals are justified in breaking a bad law, it overstates the case to claim that it is permissible to break any law one deems not good.

There is a rich philosophical literature on why citizens have an obligation to obey the law and when citizens are justified in breaking the law. The literature recognizes that there are conditions in which individuals are justified in breaking the law, but the conditions are limited. The literature suggests that citizens have what is called a *prima facie* obligation to obey the laws of a relatively just state. Prima facie means "all else being equal" or "unless there are overriding reasons." A prima facie obligation can be overridden by higher order obligations or by special circumstances that justify a different course of action. Higher order obligations will override when, for example, obeying the law will lead to greater harm than disobeying. For example, the law prohibiting automobiles from being driven on the left side of the road (as is the case in many countries) is a good law, but a driver would be justified in breaking this law in order to avoid an accident. On this account of a citizen's obligation to obey the laws of a relatively just state, one has an obligation to obey property laws unless there are overriding reasons for breaking them.

Most cases of software copying do not seem to fall into this category. Most of those who make illegal copies of computer software do so because it is so easy and because they don't want to pay for the software. They don't copy software because an overriding moral reason takes priority over adhering to the law.

You might try to frame software copying as an act of civil disobedience. In the United States and many other countries there is a tradition of recognizing some acts of disobedience to law as morally justified. However, acts of civil disobedience are generally justified on grounds that it would be immoral to obey such laws. Obedience to the law would compel one to act immorally or to support immoral institutions.

It would take us too far afield to explore all the possibilities here but let me suggest some of the obstacles to making the case. To make the case, you would have to show (a) that the system of property rights for software is not just a bad system, but is an unjust system. And you would have to show (b) that adhering to those laws compels you to perform immoral acts or support unjust institutions. Making the case for (a) will not be easy. The critique would have to show either that all copyright and patent laws are unjust *or* that these laws when extended to software are unjust *or* that these laws when interpreted in a certain way (for example, giving Microsoft control of so much of the market) are unjust.

If you can make the case for (a), then (b) will become more plausible. That is, if the system of property rights in computer software is unjust, then it is plausible that adhering to such laws might compel to you act immorally. But this will not be an easy case to make since adhering to the law simply means refraining from copying. In other words, you would have to show that refraining from software copying is an immoral act or supports an immoral institution. This seems somewhat far fetched but several authors have tried to make this sort of argument. That is, several authors have argued that there are some circumstances in which *not* copying is wrong.

Richard Stallman (1995) and Helen Nissenbaum (1994) both point to situations in which a friend is having a great deal of trouble trying to do something with information technology and you have software that will solve the friend's problems. Both make the point that not helping your friend when you know how to help and when you have the means to help seems wrong.

Stallman and Nissenbaum both emphasize that the system of ownership we now have discourages and disables altruism. Neither author seems to recognize the harm done to the copyright or patent holder when the copy is made. In fact, the situation described seems to set up a dilemma in which one can choose one harm over another—violate the right of the software owner or fail to help your friend. This seems to push us back to the idea of overriding circumstances. There probably are some circumstances in which making a copy of proprietary software will be justified to prevent some harm greater than the violation of the software owner's property rights. However, those cases are not the typical case of software copying.

The case for the moral permissibility of software copying would be stronger if the system of software ownership were shown to be unjust or if all property rights were shown to be unjust. Stallman seems to hold the latter view. He seems to believe that all property rights promote selfishness and discourage altruism. He might well be right about this. However, if he is right, why pick on software copying as if it were a special case of justified property rights violation?

I am quite willing to grant that there may be situations in which software copying is justified, namely when some serious harm can only be prevented by making an illegal copy of a piece of proprietary software and using it. In most cases, however, the claims of the software owner would seem to be much stronger than the claims of someone who needs a copy to make their life easier.

In order to fully understand my argument, it will be helpful to use an analogy. Suppose I own a private swimming pool and I make a living by allowing others to use the pool for a fee during certain hours of the day. The pool is closed on certain days and open only for certain hours of other days. You figure out how to break into the pool undetected, and you break in and swim when the pool is closed and I am not around. The act of swimming is not intrinsically wrong, and swimming in the pool does no visible or physical harm to me, or to anyone else.

Nevertheless, you are using my property without my permission. It would hardly seem a justification for ignoring my property rights if you claimed that you were hot and the swim in my pool made your life more tolerable and less onerous. Your argument would be no more convincing if you pointed out that you were not depriving me of revenues from renting the pool since you swam when the pool was closed. Note the parallel to justifying software copying on grounds that it does no harm, makes the copier's life better, and doesn't deprive the owner of revenue since you wouldn't have bought the software anyway.

Now, the argument would still not be convincing if instead of seeking your own comfort, you sought the comfort of your friend. Suppose, that is, that you had a friend who was suffering greatly from the heat and so you, having the knowledge of how to break into the pool, broke in, in the name of altruism, and allowed your friend to swim while you watched to make sure I didn't appear. In your defense, you argue that it would have been selfish for you not to use your knowledge to help out your friend. Your act was altruistic.

There are circumstances under which your illegal entry into my pool would be justified. For example, if I had given permission to someone to swim in the pool while it was closed to the public and that person, swimming alone, began to drown. You were innocently walking by and saw the person drowning. You broke in and jumped into the pool in order to save the drowning swimmer. Here the circumstances justify your violating my property rights.

There seems no moral difference between breaking into the pool and making a copy of a proprietary piece of software. Both acts violate the legal rights of the owner—legal rights created by reasonably good laws. I grant that these laws prevent others from acting altruistically. I concede that private property in general is individualistic, exclusionary, and even selfish. Nonetheless, it is prima facie wrong to make an illegal copy of proprietary software because to do so is to deprive the owner of their legal right, and this is to harm them.

CONCLUSION

The issues discussed in this chapter are both fascinating and important. Our ideas about property are tied to deeply ingrained notions of rights, fairness, and economic justice. Law and public policy on the ownership of various aspects of computer software structure the environment for software development, so it is important to evaluate these laws to insure the future development of computer and information technology.

The issue of the permissibility of making personal copies of proprietary software is also fascinating and important but for different reasons. Here we are forced to clarify what makes an action right or wrong. We are forced to come to grips with our moral intuitions and to extend these to entities with unique characteristics.

The thrust of this chapter has been to move discussion of property rights in computer software away from the idea that property rights are given in nature, and towards the idea that we can and should develop property rights that serve us well in the long run.

STUDY QUESTIONS

1. Describe the difference between hardware and software.
2. What are the differences among object programs, source programs, and algorithms?
3. Explain the kind of protection offered by copyright, trade secrecy, and patents. What are the advantages and disadvantages of each for developers of computer software?
4. What is meant by improper appropriation in copyright law?
5. Why is it sometimes difficult for employees to keep company information secret?
6. What is Locke's *labor theory* of property? Why doesn't it necessarily apply to ownership of computer software?
7. What natural rights arguments can be made for and against ownership of software?
8. What are the consequentialist arguments for and against ownership of software?
9. What would happen to software development if software were declared unownable?
10. What arguments support the claim that software copying is immoral? What arguments support the claim that software copying is not immoral?
11. The author argues that software copying is immoral because it is illegal. How does she arrive at this conclusion? Are there limits to the applicability of this argument?

SUGGESTED FURTHER READING

BURK, DAN L., "Transborder Intellectual Property Issues on the Electronic Frontier," *Stanford Law & Policy Review,* vol. 6, no. 1 (1994), pp. 9–16.

DAVIS, RANDALL, PAMELA SAMUELSON, MITCHELL KAPOR, and JEROME REICHMAN, "A New View of Intellectual Property and Software," *Communications of the ACM,* vol. 39, no. 3 (March 1996), pp. 21–30.

U.S. Congress, Office of Technology Assessment, *Finding a Balance: Computer Software, Intellectual Property, and the Challenge of Technological Change,* OTA-TCT-527 (Washington, DC: U.S. Government Printing Office, May 1992).

WEB SITES

For materials on the Web, try the Lexis-Nexis search engine.

CHAPTER 7

Accountability and Computer and Information Technology

A virtual rape.

It happened in the living room in LambdaMOO. LambdaMOO is a multiuser designed (MUD) object-oriented program, a complex database maintained inside Xerox Corporation in Palo Alto and open to public access via the Internet. The program allows users to create and design the interaction space and context; a user can describe his or her own character any way he or she likes and can build new objects, including rooms and furniture. While users interact with one another as the characters that they have created, they see a stream of dialogues and stage descriptions.

One night a character, Bungle, entered LambdaMOO. Bungle had designed a subprogram, Voodoo doll, which could attribute actions to other characters. Using the Voodoo doll subprogram, Bungle took control of two other characters, Legba and Starspinner, and proceeded to ascribe sadistic actions to them, including eating pubic hair and sodomizing one of the victims. Legba and Starspinner were helpless throughout the entire incident. The episode ended when another character, Zippy, used a subprogram to freeze Bungle's commands.

The virtual rape caused enormous ripples across the community of LambdaMOOers. One of the victims, Legba, wanted Bungle to be "toaded"—that is, to have his account removed from LambdaMOO. Opinion was divided over what should be done to Bungle. On the evening of the third day after the incident, the users gathered in LambdaMOO to discuss Bungle's fate. There were four arguments: (1) The techno libertarians argued that rape in cyberspace was a technical inevitability and that a solution would be to use defensive software tools to filter out the offender's words. (2) The legalists argued that Bungle could not legitimately be "toaded" since the MOO had no explicit rules at all; they proposed the establishment of rules and virtual institutions to exercise the control required. (3) The third group of users believed that only the programmers, or wizards as they are known in MOO, have the power to implement rules. (4) The anarchists, on the other hand, wanted to see the matter resolved without the establishment of social control. There was no agreement between these groups. To Bungle, who joined midway through the conference, the event was simply a sequence of events in virtual reality that had no consequences for his real life existence.

After weighing the arguments, one of the programmers, the Wizard Joe-Feedback, decided to "toad" Bungle and banish him from the MOO. As a result of this incident, the database system was redesigned so that the programmers could make changes based on an action or a petition of the majority of the LambdaMOO community. Eight months and 11 ballots later, widespread participation produced a system of checks and capabilities to guard against the type of violence that had occurred. As for Bungle, he is believed to be reincarnated as the character, Dr Jest.

Did Bungle do anything wrong? Is he responsible for his behavior? Should he have suffered any consequences for his behavior? Should he have suffered any "real-world" consequences?

Written by Marc Quek Pang, based on "A Rape in Cyberspace" by Julian Dibbell, *Village Voice* (December 21, 1993), pp. 36–42.

SCENARIO 7.2   Using decision-making systems.

Kimiko Syun works for an investment company that manages several pension funds. Kimiko has been managing pension accounts for ten years and has been increasingly successful. She is now in charge of one of the company's largest accounts, the pension fund of a major automotive company.

When Kimiko first started working at this company, it purchased an expert system to aid in investment decisions. The system has been upgraded several times and each upgrade has provided more complex analysis and more useful data. Kimiko can input current figures for key economic indicators, and the system produces a set of recommendations. This week Kimiko is quite nervous about the stock market. All the indicators she has come to trust point in the direction of a serious and long-term downswing, so she believes it would be best to reduce the pension fund's holdings in stocks. However, the expert system recommends just the opposite. She rechecks the figures she has put into the system, but the output continues to recommend that the percentage of holdings in stocks be increased to 80 percent of the portfolio.

Kimiko does not understand the reasoning that is built into the expert system; hence, she does not know whether to act on the system's recommendation. It is possible that the system can detect features of the current situation that she doesn't see, but it is also possible that the system is malfunctioning. If she goes with the advice of the expert system, the account could lose heavily, so much so that income to retirees would have to be adjusted downward. On the other hand, if she goes against the expert system and she is wrong, the account could be jeopardized and she would be in serious trouble for diverging from the recommendation of the expert system. What should she do?

SCENARIO 7.3   Service provider liability for bulletin boards.

Milo Simpson is a freelance journalist. He uses the Internet in several ways to keep up to date on the topics on which he writes. He subscribes to a computer service that sends him articles and news reports on topics that he specifies; he subscribes to several list serves and bulletin boards on these topics; and he participates in chatrooms devoted to these topics. Participants in the bulletin boards post information and ideas, comment on one another's ideas, reference articles, and so on; participants in the chatroom discuss topics in real time.

Milo has been away on an assignment for the past month and upon his return he reviews what the service has sent; then he reviews postings on the bulletin board about South American politics, a field in which he has a growing reputation. As he reads through various comments, he is outraged to find that one of the postings attacks him, claiming that he is involved in illegal drug operations, and suggesting that his stories are filled with lies to protect others who are involved.

After the shock subsides, Milo writes up a denial of the accusations and posts it on the bulletin board. Milo knows, however, that even with this denial, the accusations have damaged his reputation. He decides to contact his ISP (Internet Service Provider) since the bulletin board is on the ISP system. Since the defamatory comment came from someone who was obviously using a pseudonym, he asks the ISP to give him the name and (hard) address of the person who posted the comment. The ISP refuses to give out this information citing a policy they have posted that protects user identity.

Since the accusations are completely false, Milo wants to sue for defamation of character. Since he can't obtain the identity of the individual, he decides to sue the ISP. After all, the ISP could have monitored postings on the bulletin board and filtered out irresponsible and defamatory comments. Should the ISP be liable for the contents of its bulletin boards?

SCENARIO 7.4   The Y2K problem.

By now it is history, but during the 1990s there was great fear and apprehension that many vital activities dependent on computer technology would come to a standstill when clocks turned from December 31, 1999 to January 1, 2000. Billions of dollars were spent as computer professionals working around the world in business and government scrambled to fix the problem referred to as the "year 2000 problem" or the "Y2K problem."

The problem arose because well into the 1980s computer manufacturers were producing systems with internal calendars that had space for only two digits in the year designation. The early designers of computers had chosen to save space in the storage capacity of computers by assuming the "19" in all date-entries. Forty-five would mean 1945; 82 would mean 1982; and so on. However, as the year 2000 approached, it became clear that unless something was done, computers would interpret 00 to mean 1900 and this would wreak havoc on many computer systems.

This is how one computer professional explains what happened:

> There are many reasons why programmers, including me, chose to represent years by using just two digits. . . . Decades ago digital real estate was scarce: computer memory was expensive, and typical punch cards were only 80 columns wide. People also rationalized the shortcut by citing the efficiency of reduced keystrokes. Of course, the absence of standards played an enabling role, and many of us truly believed (incorrectly so) that the software we were writing would long be retired before the new millennium. Thanks to sheer inertia and lingering Tea Party logic (Why store more than two digits when the century stays the same for such a long time together?), the practice continued long after computer memory and cost constraints were legitimate concerns. (de Jager, 1999)

As January 1, 2000 approached, there was fear that the following sorts of things would happen: in determining retirement benefits, medical treatment, and the like, the calculation of someone's age would be rendered a negative; products with a limited lifespan would be rejected for being too old; credit card transactions for cards with expiration dates in "00" would be rejected because the card was long expired, and so on. Since computers are used in so many contexts, the list of possible catastrophes is endless. What would happen to electric power grids, traffic lights, payroll systems, railroad crossings, inventory controls, elevators, medical monitoring equipment, and so on? These are all calendar-dependent computerized activities, and since computers are all connected to one another, even those computers that had been fixed or upgraded might be affected when they interacted with systems that hadn't been fixed.

The public reaction to the problem included disbelief and outrage. How could such a thing happen? Were computer professionals asleep at the wheel? Was this a ploy to get companies and individuals to hire computer professionals to fix the problem and to invest in new equipment? The reaction raised complex issues of accountability. Who was responsible for the situation? Why didn't computer manufacturers and software designers have more foresight? Why wasn't more done sooner to fix the problem? Who should pay for the costs of fixing the problem?

January 1, 2000 has now passed and we all know the ending to this story. No major catastrophe occurred. Some systems did have problems, but the effect was not widespread. For most people, the day passed uneventfully. Nevertheless, the accountability questions linger. How could computer professionals have made such a simple mistake? Why did they continue to build systems with the two-digit year field well into the 1980s? Who is responsible for this? What should be done to them?

Computer and information systems are powerful technologies and can have powerful effects. When the technology fails, serious harm can result: Human beings can be physically or psychologically harmed, money can be lost, reputations destroyed, and so on. Often when negative effects occur (or are anticipated to occur, as with the Y2K problem), we want to know *why* the negative effects have occurred and we want something to be done. Since technology is a human contrivance, failures are not written off as natural or uncontrollable phenomena; failures are not treated simply as "acts of God." What went wrong? Why did it go wrong? Who was at fault? Who will pay for the damages?

Issues of accountability and responsibility surround computer and information technology. Responsibility issues have explicitly or implicitly been mentioned in all chapters of this book, but especially in Chapters 3 through 6. In Chapter 3 on Professional Ethics, several of the duties (responsibilities) of computer professionals were identified and discussed. In Chapter 4 on the Internet, the global scope, anonymity, and reproducibility of the Internet all were shown to affect accountability. These features make it possible for individuals to more easily do what would be extremely difficult without the technology. However, these features also make it difficult to hold individuals accountable for their behavior. In Chapters 5 and 6, while responsibility issues were not explicitly mentioned, they lurked in the background. Protecting personal privacy and assigning and protecting property rights both involve assigning responsibility and then holding institutions and individuals accountable when they violate personal privacy and property rights.

Scenarios 7.1 to 7.4 illustrate yet other accountability issues. Scenario 7.1 illustrates a puzzle created about responsibility for behavior in a virtual environment. Using his programming skills, Bungle violently attacked and raped fictitious characters. Because his behavior involved programming and took place in a virtual environment, participants in the MUD were confronted with an unusual responsibility issue. The question was not whether Bungle was causally responsible for the untoward event; he was. The hard question was what exactly he did wrong given that no real person was violated. And then there is the question how, if at all, his behavior should be viewed and responded to. He took control of other characters which seems a violation of an implied, though not a formalized, rule of the MUD. He inflicted violence on fictitious characters in the game, though game participants felt that they had been violated. What exactly did Bungle do wrong? How should he be treated?

Scenario 7.2 raises a very different kind of accountability issue, an issue having to do with increasing use of computer systems in decision making. Kimiko's situation suggests a possible negative accountability-effect arising from reliance on computer systems. Can Kimiko be held responsible for what happens to the pension plan money if she is expected to use a computer model that she doesn't, and perhaps can't, understand? Can or should computer decision systems (or their designers) be held legally responsible for failures due to poorly designed computer systems? Should we be allowed to sue if a computer decision system makes an error in recommending how we invest our money or how we do our income tax or how much credit we get?

Scenario 7.3 raises another kind of accountability issue. Should Internet Service Providers be responsible for the content of their bulletin boards? Their chatrooms? Their Web sites? If not, who should be responsible? And Scenario 7.4 raises yet another kind of accountability issue. Who is, or should be held, responsible for all the expenses that companies incurred in fixing the Y2K problem? Was anyone at fault for creating the problem? Or for not addressing it sooner?

These issues can be sorted in a variety of ways. For example, we could categorize the issues in terms of the type of technology that is at issue. Somewhat different issues arise when there is a problem with hardware, software, data, the Internet, and with different types of software—graphical interfaces, database management systems, security systems, or different uses of the Internet. We could sort the issues in terms of the laws or parts of the legal system with which they could be addressed. If there is a flaw in a product, one set of laws and legal precedents is brought to bear. If there is a flaw in provision of services due to incompetence or negligence, then another set of laws and legal precedents is relevant. If there is an issue of defamation, failure to fulfill the terms of a contract, or something else, then yet other parts of the law may come into play.

Instead of opting for one of these approaches over another, this chapter provides a mixture of approaches. The aim is to address several different kinds of issues so as to provide an understanding of why computer and information technology gives rise to accountability issues as well as an understanding of the range and complexity of the issues.

The chapter begins with a discussion of the different meanings and uses of terms such as responsibility, accountability, liability, and blame. With clarity on how these terms are used, the focus turns to the legal environment for the buying and selling of computer technology and services. The chapter then turns to responsibility issues that are somewhat special to computer and information technology: the Y2K problem, diffusion of responsibility, and Internet issues.

DIFFERENT SENSES OF RESPONSIBILITY

The terms accountable, responsible, responsibility, liable, and liability are sometimes used interchangeably and other times in quite different ways. I use *accountable* as the broadest of these terms. To say that someone is accountable is to say that the person (which could be a collective unit such as a government agency or a legal person such as a corporation) is the appropriate agent to respond (i.e., to give an account) for an event or incident or situation. Just what the person is accountable to do depends on a variety of factors that will become clearer later on. Sometimes being accountable means that a person is accountable to give a report of what happened; other times the person is accountable to go to jail or pay compensation; yet other times the person is accountable in the sense that they should bear guilt and remorse for the situation.

At least four different uses of responsibility can be distinguished. The first I refer to as *role-responsibility*. Here *responsibility* is interchangeable with *duty* and refers to what individuals are expected to do in virtue of one of their social roles. We have duties in virtue of being an employee, a parent, a citizen, a friend, a member of a church, a member of an occupation—lawyer, doctor, police officer, and so on. In Chapter 3, I discussed the role-responsibilities of computer professionals.

In many contexts, we assume that individuals have certain role-responsibilities without thinking much about them and without explicitly articulating them, until someone fails to fulfill one of these responsibilities. So, for example, in Scenario 7.1 most participants in the LamdaMOO seemed to assume that each participant had a duty to play by the rules, and while not explicitly specified, most participants seemed to assume that playing by the rules meant not taking control of another person's character. This is not surprising for it is generally difficult to specify all the ramifications of the duties associated with a role; they are often subtly part of a shared social-cultural understanding of social roles. Consider, for example, the duties you have to your parents by virtue of being a child or the duties you have to a brother or sister, or the duties you have by virtue of being a citizen of a country. These roles entail responsibilities that may not come into play until a special situation arises (e.g., your parent becomes ill, your brother goes bankrupt, war is declared).

A second, important use of *responsible* is *causal responsibility*. Sometimes when we say that an individual is responsible for an untoward event, we mean that the individual did something (or failed to do something) that caused the untoward event. The person is responsible here simply in the sense of being the cause. In Scenario 7.2, if Kimiko Syun put 80 percent of the pension fund money into stocks and a major downturn in the stock market were to occur, she would be causally responsible for the money being invested in the stock market at the time of the downturn. Though it is a complex matter to determine causal responsibility, Kimiko's action could be picked out as the causal event leading to major losses in the pension fund.

Consider a simpler case. Suppose that there is an automobile accident. John was driving one of the vehicles involved and he failed to yield at a stop sign. We might say, then, that John *is responsible for* the accident because his behavior (failing to yield at a stop sign) caused it. So, John (like Kimiko) is responsible in the sense that his behavior caused the event.

Causal responsibility can be attributed to nonhuman events as well as persons. Suppose, for example, that a house is severely damaged in a storm. We might say the strong winds were *responsible for* the roof being blown off the house. The strong winds are picked out as the cause of the damage.

Attributions of causal responsibility often seem simple when they are very complex. In most situations, an event or effect is the result of a multitude of factors but a single factor is picked out as "the cause." Suppose, for example, that there is a forest fire and fire fighters trace the fire back to a campfire in a particular campsite and Elena was the last to use that campsite. We would say, "Elena is *responsible for* the forest fire; she failed to adequately put out her campfire." Of course, a variety of factors may have contributed to the fire. Oxygen was present, the trees were dry because of a drought, air temperature was extremely high, the campfire was close to the trees, and so on. The fire would not have started had any of these conditions been different. Yet we pick out Elena's behavior as the non-normal and, therefore, causal factor.

Related to causality, a third use of *responsible* and *responsibility* is equivalent to blameworthy. Blameworthiness is generally connected to doing something wrong or being at fault. That is, the attribution of responsibility is made on the basis of a judgment that a person did something wrong and his or her wrong-doing led to an untoward event or circumstance. In the previous examples, the actions of John and Elena are picked out as the non-normal, and therefore, causal factors because they did something blameworthy. John failed to stop at a stop sign; Elena failed to put out the campfire. On the other hand, while Kimiko's behavior was causally responsible for the pension fund money being in the stock market at the time of the downturn, she may not be considered blameworthy. If the model recommended this action or if her actions were reasonably justified, she may have done nothing wrong. She would be considered responsible in the sense of having *caused the situation*, but she would not be responsible in the sense of *blameworthy*.

Individuals are often considered blameworthy when they fail to fulfill a role-responsibility. A programmer who releases software with many bugs is blameworthy for failing to do his or her job properly. Campers have a duty to completely put out their campfires. Individuals can be absolved of blameworthiness if their failure is due to extenuating circumstances. For example, parents are generally considered blameworthy if their children are malnourished; however, if the parents and child live in a poverty-stricken country, the blame will be put elsewhere. If John tried to stop at the stop sign but was unable to do so because his brakes failed, he would not be considered blameworthy (unless, of course, he had been negligent in not having the brakes inspected by the legally required date).

Finally, individuals can be considered responsible in the sense of being liable. *Liability* is most often used to refer to the way certain situations are treated legally. To be legally liable is to be the person who, according to law, must pay damages or compensate when certain events occur. A good example of legal liability is that associated with home ownership. If someone is working at your house and they slip and hurt themselves, you are responsible, in the sense of liable, for any harm done to the person. You could be liable to pay for their treatment, their pain and suffering, and any loss of wages due to the injury. You are considered liable because the accident occurred on your property. Of course, you may not be blameworthy, and you may not be responsible in the causal sense.

Legal liability is often, though not always, tied to one of the other senses of responsibility. One may be legally liable for failure to fulfill a role-responsibility, for being the cause of an untoward event and for being blameworthy (especially when the blameworthy action is a causal factor in an untoward event).

Consider a computer case where all four types of responsibility come into play. Software vendors have a duty to be honest about the products they sell. Suppose a vendor is irresponsible with regard to this role-responsibility and when selling a software package to Customer X, the vendor lies about what the software package can do. Customer X has her employees install the package; they use it for a while and then it crashes. The crash permanently destroys data and disrupts Customer X's business for several weeks causing considerable losses in revenue. The software vendor may be responsible in the sense of *liable* to refund the price of the software and compensate Customer X for her losses. However, to establish the vendor's liability, Customer X would have to show that the vendor had been dishonest about what the software could do, that is, the vendor had failed to fulfill a *role-responsibility*. Establishing that the vendor had been dishonest would entail that the vendor was *blameworthy*. Customer X would have to show that the vendor wasn't just ignorant about the software but knew the truth and withheld it. Moreover, Customer X would have to show that the vendor's lie was *causally responsible* for her losses. She would have to show that the disruption in her business was not caused by something else, such as employees that didn't know how to use the software or didn't pay attention to the instructions. So, in this case liability is dependent on the three other types of responsibility.

While legal liability is generally connected to the other types of responsibility as just described, there are situations when liability is *disconnected* from blameworthiness. *Strict liability is* liability "without fault." Strict liability is controversial because it goes counter to a common moral intuition that individuals shouldn't be held responsible for that which they can't prevent or control. Nevertheless, it is used in the law to encourage individuals to take precautions and make things safe. Where strict liability applies, the liable person (or company) is *responsible to* pay damages or compensation even though he or she did nothing wrong. Strict liability is an intriguing concept when it comes to computing because software is sometimes so complex that errors may slip through even though everyone involved did everything reasonable to test it and make it reliable. Strict liability will be further discussed in the next section.

BUYING AND SELLING SOFTWARE

Who is (or should be) responsible for what, when it comes to designing, producing, selling, and using computer software? A wide variety of accountability issues surround these activities. In very general terms it seems that designers and manufacturers should bear some responsibility for the safety and reliability of the software they produce. Software vendors[1] should bear some responsibility for what they sell and what they tell customers about products. Users, in turn, should bear some responsibility for reading instructions and knowing some general aspects of how to use software. This said, there are many questions about the types of responsibility at issue here and about the expanse and limits of duties and liabilities. How reliable must software producers make software? Who should be liable for what, when software causes harm? There will always be risks in computing, so how much risk is acceptable? How far can software companies go in disclaiming responsibility for their software? How much and what kinds of things should vendors tell customers about software? How much can the ordinary customer be expected to know when purchasing and using software? The list of questions having to do with responsibility and liability in the buying and selling of software is endless.

Some of these questions are already answered in the law, either in legislation or through precedents set in case law. Some of the relevant law existed prior to the invention of computers and some has been created since. In this chapter, we will look only briefly at the law. The aim is to review some of the more difficult accountability issues and, in particular, the conceptual puzzles that prevent a simple application or extension of existing law. Remember in Chapter 1, I suggested that it is not always easy to extend existing policies or even to create new policies because of conceptual muddles in thinking about computer and information technology. These conceptual muddles are especially challenging in sorting out accountability issues. It will be helpful to begin with the foundation of the buying and selling relationship.

The Categorical Imperative

At the heart of buying and selling is the relationship between the buyer and seller and this relationship is appropriately framed in terms of the categorical imperative. The categorical imperative entreats us never to treat a person merely as a means but always as an end in him- or herself. At first glance, this may seem to suggest that selling is immoral; the seller seems to be using the buyer as a means to making money, especially since sellers generally charge more than what it cost them to make or acquire the goods. Remember, however, that by selling something to another person, the seller may be helping the buyer. The seller provides something that the buyer needs or wants.

Remember also that the categorical imperative does not exactly prohibit us from using others as means to our ends; rather, it specifies that we never treat a person *merely* as a means. The merely means that we are constrained in

---

[1] I use the term *vendor* to refer to any person or unit that sells software. In reality, there are many different types of vendors—software manufacturers sell their software; distributors sell software to stores or catalogues; and, of course, stores, catalogues, and individuals sell software directly to users.

how we use others. We must always recognize the other as an end—a being with needs, desires, their own plans, and the ability to make their own decisions. There is, then, nothing wrong with selling something to someone, especially if they have freely chosen to buy it. To treat the buyer as an end, however, the seller must be honest about what he or she is selling and refrain from using coercion. If a salesperson gets a customer to buy something by deceiving the customer about what he or she is getting, or if the salesperson manipulates a customer into buying something the customer doesn't really want, then the salesperson has used the customer *merely* as a means to the salesperson's ends. If, on the other hand, the salesperson gives the customer accurate information—information the customer needs to decide whether or not to buy the product—and if the salesperson does not pressure the customer into buying, then the salesperson has respected the customer. The salesperson has treated the customer as a being with the capacity to decide for him- or herself whether to buy the goods or not.

So, there is nothing inherently wrong with selling computer software, or anything else for that matter. It all depends on how it is done. A salesperson has a duty both to be honest and not to coerce. (Duties also fall to the buyer, for example, to pay the amount promised, but we will not discuss these here.)

While this sounds simple enough, honesty and coercion are both complex notions. Take honesty. Yes, software salespeople shouldn't lie to their customers, but how much are they required to tell? It would be ridiculous to expect vendors to tell literally everything they know about the software they are selling. Most customers don't want to hear this and many could not understand it. Moreover, much of what a vendor knows is not relevant to the customer's decision. Most customers seek software for certain purposes and need only a subset of the information the vendor has. Generally, customers want to know what the software does and doesn't do, what features it does and doesn't have, how much it costs, what machines it will and won't work on, how fast it works, and so on. Hence, we might say that honesty in selling software is a matter of answering all customer questions and, of course, answering them accurately, to the best of the salesperson's ability. This means that salespersons should never lie, but it also seems to mean that salespersons need only give customers information they request.

This is consistent with the categorical imperative, but is it sufficient? What about customers who don't know the right questions to ask and, therefore, don't ask them? Is the software vendor being dishonest if he or she knows something about the software that is relevant to the customer's decision but doesn't say anything because he or she wants to make the sale? Computers and software have been around for several decades now, but in the early days of computing, customers had very little experience and frequently didn't know what questions to ask when purchasing software. While this is less true today, there are still plenty of customers who are new to computing or, at least, new to certain applications. When salespersonnel know much more about software than their customers, it would seem that they should inform their customers about aspects of the software that are likely to be relevant to the customer's interests—even if the customer doesn't yet realize it.

Recognizing the importance of customers being informed in the buying and selling of software, software vendors generally print much of the information relevant to the customer's decision on the outside packaging of software. Much of this information has to do with the licensing agreement established in the act of purchasing and this protects the software developer. Still, the visibility of this information is recognition of the contractual nature of the buying and selling relationship. Contractual relationships can be voided if a party to the contract is not informed about the nature of the agreement they are making. So, having information printed on the outside package of the software ensures that whoever the salesperson, all customers have access to basic information relevant to their decision to buy (or not to buy) the software.

Thus, being honest is complex, but it is of crucial importance to ethical selling. Salespersons should accurately and truthfully answer customer questions and they should provide customers with the kinds of information they need to make informed purchasing decisions. Fortunately for consumers of software, software is now sold in stores where a variety of products are available. In this context, the honesty issue is somewhat diffused because the salesperson is not as interested in selling a particular product as in making "a" sale. The salesperson may be most interested in establishing relationships with customers, relationships that will bring customers back to the store for future purchases. Customer satisfaction is more likely to be achieved when customers know exactly what they are getting and are not disappointed with or inconvenienced by the software they purchase. In other words, unlike manufacturers, software vendors have a built-in incentive to be forthcoming in comparing one software package with another.

Avoiding coercion is, like being honest, both complex and unquestionably an important part of the ethical character of buying and selling. To force someone to do something is to treat them as a thing, not a rational agent capable of choosing for themselves. To force someone to do something is to use the person as a means to your ends and to disregard their ends. As with honesty, it is easy to understand and avoid the extreme violations, but harder to understand the territory in between.

Though it is highly unlikely to happen, it would be coercive (and wrong) for a software vendor to hold a gun to a customer's head and make the customer buy the software. At the opposite extreme, while it wouldn't be immoral, it also wouldn't be helpful to customers if vendors were completely passive. Being completely passive might mean refraining from advertising or never using sales or special offers to encourage customers to buy. In between these two extremes, there are many possibilities for enticing customers to buy without crossing the line into exploitative practices. You might look at the activities of your local Better Business Bureau to see how it draws the line between fair and unfair sales practices. I will not go into any further detail here in part because coercive business practices have not been a special problem in the buying and selling of software. Moreover, this is not a matter that is special in the context of computing; rather unfair business practices are found in many contexts in which things are bought and sold.

Contractual Relationship

The buying-selling relationship is at its core a contractual relationship. One party agrees to do certain things, such as to provide a product or service, and the other party agrees to do something else in return, such as give money in exchange for the product or service. Often, especially when companies are buying and selling software, the relationship is formalized by means of a written contract that spells out all of the conditions of the relationship. In this situation, the seller can be sued for breach of contract (e.g., if a software system cannot effectively perform one of the functions specified in the contract).

While a contract seems a good way to clarify all the terms of a buying and selling arrangement, disputes do arise even after the details have been spelled out. As mentioned earlier, in the early days of computing, buyers were often ignorant about computers and computer software. Even though a contract was drawn up, buyers didn't know exactly what to specify in the contract. This happens less frequently today because buyers are more computer savvy and companies often hire computer consultants or lawyers to develop the specifications in the contract. Nevertheless, contractual issues involving software can and do end up in court. These disputes are worked out by appealing to a complex body of *case law* dealing with various disputes that have arisen in the buying and selling of all kinds of things, not just software.

Torts

In addition to the contract, the buying and selling of software may be covered by a category of law referred to as *torts*. Torts deal with any wrongful act other than a breach of contract for which a civil action may be brought. Just how this body of law applies to computer software depends on whether computer software is understood to be a product or a service. This is especially important since if software is a product, strict liability may be imposed, and if software is a service, the question of negligence may arise.

Software: Product or Service?

In many legal systems, including that of the United States, selling products is treated differently from the provision of services. When software first began to be sold, a fascinating conceptual puzzle arose as to whether it should be treated as a product or service. In Chapter 6, we saw how software challenged patent and copyright law because it was unclear whether it should be understood as a set of mental operations implemented by a computer or as algorithms or processes, and so on. A similar puzzle has challenged liability law. When a person or company designs software and then sells it to a customer, are they selling a product or are they selling the services of the software to accomplish certain tasks? If you consider that software is generally licensed, not bought outright, the case for calling it a service seems plausible.

Those unfamiliar with the law might equate product with things that are tangible and presume that since software isn't tangible, it can't be treated as a product. The machines, tapes, or disks on which software is stored are tangible but, as we saw in Chapter 6, the valuable part of the software is not tangible. The intangibility of software is not, however, the issue; product liability law does *not* view products as necessarily tangible. Such intangible things as leases and energy are treated as products. Hence, the intangibility of software does not determine whether it is a product or service.

How, then, can we determine whether software should be treated as a product or service? For a start, it is a good idea to let go of the idea that all software must be treated in the same way. An important strategy in the law is to focus on *how* things are bought and sold. Here the idea is not to focus on whether the vendor was honest or manipulative, but rather to look at the way the item was produced and sold. When it comes to software this means focusing on the difference between mass-marketed software and customized software.

This difference was recognized early on in addressing issues around software. For example, in a 1980 legal article, Prince distinguished three different ways that software can be sold to a customer (Prince, 1980). He made an analogy with buying a suit. A customer can buy a suit ready to wear ("off the rack"); no alterations will be made. Similarly, a customer can go to a computer store and buy a mass-marketed software package. The software is not supposed to be modified. It may be designed to give the user options, but the user is not expected or allowed to change the underlying code making the software do what it does.

A second way that a customer may buy a suit is to have a tailor make it specifically for the customer. Here the customer goes to the tailor, tells the tailor what he or she wants, and the tailor makes the suit as specified. Analogously, a person (or company) can hire a person (or company) to design and produce a computer system specifically for his or her use. The system will be designed and made to do precisely what the customer specifies, to meet the customer's special needs.

Finally, a customer can buy a suit "off the rack" and have it altered to fit his or her special measurements. In the same way, a person (or company) can buy a software system and hire someone (or a company) to modify it to fit his or her special needs and circumstances.

Prince suggested that we treat mass-marketed software as we do products, and treat customized software as we do provision of a service. The mixed case should then be treated as mixed. If there is a defect in the mass-marketed part, product law should be brought to bear; if an error is made in the process of modification, law dealing with services should be brought to bear.

This seems plausible, but why do it this way? Why focus on the manner in which the software is purchased and delivered? Prince provided an answer to this question by examining the rationale for strict liability. Remember that if software is treated as a product, then strict liability can be imposed, and that means liability without fault. In other words, software producers could be sued for errors or malfunctions in software even when they had no reasonable way of knowing about them or being able to prevent them. Prince argued that strict liability makes sense for canned software but not for customized software.

There are three factors that justify the imposition of strict liability. Each has to do with the role or position of the producer of a product. First, to fall within the scope of strict liability under the Unified Commercial Code (UCC), a thing must be placed in the stream of commerce. This leads to a justification of strict liability on several counts. First, since the producer has placed the thing in the stream of commerce in order to earn profit, he or she should be the one that bears the risk of loss or injury. Since the producer has placed the thing in the stream of commerce, the producer has invited the public to use the product and implicit in the invitation must be an assurance that the product is safe.

Second, the producer is in a better position than anyone else to anticipate and control the risks in the product. Because the producer is in the best position to control the risks, the imposition of strict liability can have a positive effect. Holding producers strictly liable gives them a powerful incentive to be careful about what they put into the stream of commerce. If their products are not reasonably safe, they will be held liable.

Finally, the producer is in the best position to spread the cost of injury over all buyers by building it into the cost of the product. If some products have inherent risks, then the cost of the risk can be distributed amount those who benefit from having the product on the market. In other words, we make the producer pay for injuries from use of the product, knowing that he or she will recover this cost in the price of the product. Instead of the burden being born by those who are injured, it is spread to all those who buy the product. When you pay for a product, you implicitly pay for some insurance. If you incur damages from using the product, you can sue the producer and, if you win the suit, the producer will be able to compensate you, using profits from the price of the product.

These three considerations demonstrate that strict liability makes good sense when it imposes liability on those who make products and put them in the stream of commerce. It makes sense because it imposes liability on those who are in the best position to minimize risk and distribute costs.

Notice that these considerations are utilitarian. They argue for placing liability where it will have a positive effect. Strict liability doesn't necessarily prevent the release of dangerous, faulty products, but it discourages their release. This is important to recognize because strict liability, as mentioned earlier, goes against a common moral intuition that individuals shouldn't be held responsible for what they can't foresee or prevent. Strict liability holds producers of products responsible regardless of whether they were at fault, but it does so in order to give them a strong incentive to make efforts to foresee and prevent bad things from happening.

With this understanding of strict liability, the question whether software should be treated as a product or service is clearer. Strict liability doesn't make sense for customized software because the producer of customized software doesn't exactly put the software into the stream of commerce. Rather, customized software is created and designed for a particular client at the client's request. Also, the producer of customized software may not be in the best position to determine the risks of the software or to distribute the costs of paying damages. The client may know more about the risks because the client knows more about the context in which the software will be used. Since the software is being sold to only one client, there is no way to distribute the cost of possible damages to anyone other than the client. For these reasons, strict liability should not be used in cases involving customized software, and hence, customized software should *not* be considered a product.

On the other hand, strict liability makes sense for mass-marketed software. The producer puts the software into the stream of commerce, inviting use, and hoping for profit. The producer is in the best position to anticipate risks. The producer is, also, in a position to distribute the costs of damage done by the software, by building it into the price of the software. Since strict liability makes sense in the case of mass-marketed software, it should be considered a product.

The mixed case can be treated as such. If mass-marketed software is purchased and modified, and if there is an error in the canned part of the software, then the consequent damage should be handled by product law. If, on the other hand, errors were introduced in the process of modifying (customizing) the software, then damage due to these errors should be treated as negligence in provision of a service. (More on this later.)

Prince's analysis provides valuable insight into strict liability law as well as helping to sort out whether software should be treated as a product or service. Among other things, his analysis illustrates the utilitarian character of attributions of legal liability. Holding individuals or companies strictly liable can have good effects; by threatening to make software developers pay damages when their software is faulty, we encourage them to take precautions and make their software reasonably safe and reliable before releasing it.

Lest my defense of strict liability be misunderstood, remember that this discussion has focused on civil, not criminal law. Quite a different analysis would be necessary to justify using strict liability in criminal cases. For example, were parents to be held strictly and criminally responsible for the behavior of their children, the justification would be more complicated. Sending individuals to jail if they produce and release faulty products would, no doubt, have a powerful effect on the production of products; however, it might also have the very negative effect of significantly reducing the number of people willing to put software into the stream of commerce.

So, mass-marketed software should be treated as a product and this means strict liability can be applied. What about customized software? What are the implications of treating the production of customized software as a service? Perhaps the most important implication is that those who produce customized software can be held accountable through the legal concept of negligence.

Negligence

In general, negligence can be understood to be a *failure* to do something that a reasonable and prudent person would have done. In common law, it is assumed that individuals who engage in certain activities owe a duty of care; negligence is a failure to fulfill that duty. If, for example, a security guard were knocked unconscious by a burglar, the guard would not be blameworthy for the robbery that took place while he or she was unconscious. However, if the guard had been drunk while on duty, making it easier for the burglar to break in and knock him or her out, then the guard would be considered to have been negligent in performance of his or her duties.

Negligence presumes a standard of behavior that can reasonably be expected of an individual engaged in a particular activity. Negligence is often used to describe the blameworthy behavior of members of professional groups. This is so because members of professional groups are understood to have role-responsibilities (duties) and members who fail to adequately perform one of those duties are considered derelict. Thus, software engineers, for example, have a responsibility to design software that doesn't crash under routine conditions of use. If a software engineer designs a database management system that repeatedly fails whenever files are merged or the database is sorted by an essential category, then the designer might be found to be negligent. The designer has failed to do what any competent database designer would have known to do.

When role-responsibilities are clear, it is easy to determine whether an individual has been negligent or not. The case of the security guard is simple because being drunk while on duty is unambiguously contrary to the guard's role-responsibility. On the other hand, when role-responsibilities are unclear or continuously changing, negligence is much harder to determine. In the field of computing, negligence can be complex and contentious because knowledge, technology, and techniques are continuously changing. For example, a software engineers might be considered negligent when he or she delivers customized software that has been tested to a standard that was adequate five years ago, but is deficient by current standards. This raises the complex and difficult question

of how up to date a software engineer must be to be considered competent, or—
the flip side—how far behind can a software engineer fall before he or she
should be considered not just out of date, but incompetent and negligent.

To prosecute computer professionals for negligence, prevailing standards
in the field must be identifiable such that a plaintiff or prosecutor can show
that the accused professional failed to do what any competent and responsible
professional would have done. Generally, other professionals are in the best
position to articulate those standards and distinguish between reasonable behavior and blatant incompetence. So typically, in court cases involving professionals accused of negligence, members of the professional group will be
called in to testify about standards in the field. As just explained, standards in
the field of computing are continuously changing.

The phenomenon of changing standards is not unique to computing.
There are many fields in which practice is based on scientific knowledge and
technology and these are continuously improving. Think, for example, about
the changing standards with regard to automobile safety or adequate health
care. What counts as a safe automobile? What counts as good medical care?
When is an automobile safe enough? When is a medical treatment extraordinary and when is it routine?

The parallels between standards for reliable software, automobile safety,
and adequate health care are interesting. In all three, it is often the case that the
experts know how to do things above and beyond the standard, but this knowledge is not put into use because of its cost or risk. In other words, experts are not
considered derelict when they opt *not* to do everything possible to make the
software reliable or not to make the automobile safer or the treatment more extensive. In all three cases, trade-offs can be made between reliability or safety or
adequacy of treatment *and* risks, costs, and other factors. Automobile designers
can do many things to make automobiles much safer than they are, but the additional measures of safety will increase the cost of the car, alter style, decrease
fuel economy, and so on. Similarly, doctors are often aware of treatments that
might improve the condition of a patient but they don't prescribe these treatments because they are considered unnecessary by insurance companies or considered too experimental by experts in the field.

Standards in software design are like this insofar as they balance a variety
of factors with reliability. What counts as adequate testing of customized soft
ware is, for example, a function of what is technically feasible, what is reasonable to demand or expect, what the costs will be of achieving a certain level of
reliability, and so on. This means that it is often not a small matter to determine when a software engineer has been negligent.

Negligence is an important concept for computing. Standards for computer professionals are continuously evolving because of the availability of new
knowledge and tools, changing client demands, and legal rulings. These standards are also being addressed as part of the discussion of licensing of software engineers mentioned in Chapter 3.

Y2K PROBLEM

The Y2K problem is described in Scenario 7.4. How could computer professionals make such a mistake? Who should pay for the enormous costs of upgrading computer systems and for the damage that resulted when systems failed? These questions frame the Y2K problem in terms of accountability. They frame it largely as an issue of blameworthiness, so, who exactly is blameworthy?

These are difficult questions to answer in part because of the number of actors involved and because of the role that time played. As for actors, is it the original inventors of computers who should be held accountable? Hardware and software manufacturers? Companies and agencies using computers? Individuals in charge of computing in businesses and government agencies? Computer professionals as a group? Perhaps as represented by ACM or IEEE? Or, perhaps, all of the above, since all made a causal contribution when they did nothing?

The time factor comes into play because the original inventors of computers don't seem to have done anything worthy of blame. At the time, they had no idea of the extent to which computers would come to be used. They were concerned with conserving space and their initial calculation seems reasonable. In other words, it would be hard to show that they were negligent in the decision they made.

On the other hand, fault and blame seem to lie with computer professionals who saw the problem but did nothing until it was getting quite late. Year after year, as space in computers became larger and larger, as cost became less and less of a factor, and as the use of computers became more and more prevalent, why wasn't a change made in the date field? The change was eventually made, but why did it take so long? If we say that computer professionals had a duty to speak out, at least, to pressure computer manufacturers to change the design of computers long before they did, then an interesting and difficult issue arises. On the one hand, we are saying that many computer professionals—those that were aware of the problem—were derelict in their duty; they were negligent. On the other hand, it is difficult to specify when they became derelict. When exactly did the situation switch from being one of reasonable calculation (and reasonable acceptance of the calculation) to one of dereliction of duty? At one point it was reasonable to accept a two-digit year field and at another point it wasn't reasonable. But when was the line crossed? There is no simple answer to this question.

Moreover, given that a catastrophe did not occur, it is plausible to suppose that most of the actors involved did do what they should have done. In hindsight, the Y2K problem may be looked at as a problem that was successfully solved because of responsible action on the part of many computer professionals.

In a provocative analysis of the Y2K problem, De George (1997–1998) argued that computer professionals are responsible for the Y2K problem and ought to be held legally liable for the harm that results. Writing before January 1, 2000, De George was concerned about what he called the Myth of

Amoral Computer Programming and Information Processing. This is the tendency to blame computers for problems that arise—"it's the computer's fault," "it's a computer error"—and, then, since computers don't or can't bear moral responsibility, to dismiss the problem. De George is quick to point out that computers don't make mistakes; the errors are the results of human mistakes in the writing of programs or entering of data.

De George takes time into account recognizing that there were changes in responsibility as time went on and the problem became clearer and clearer. The thrust of his analysis is that we should not allow the Myth of Amoral Computer Programming to reign. We should stop it by recognizing that computer programmers are responsible for the programs they produce and the harm that results when those programs are flawed. We can do this by holding them liable.

De George is concerned with *moral* responsibility and he recognizes that the courts may have difficulty implementing what he is proposing. From the perspective of moral responsibility, his claim is clear:

> [E]thically each company bears responsibility for its products and for the harm it does by failures due to its products. We can imagine scenarios with respect to the Y2K problem in which some people are not paid on time because of computer glitches. Simply pointing to computer glitches is no excuse for the harm done one's employees. The company ethically bears the burden of making good the harm by either instituting loans or paying interest on the late checks or making sure that employees' mortgages are not foreclosed or utilities disconnected because of its doings. Whether this is legally enforceable or not, and whether individual workers can afford the time and expense of suing is doubtful. Nonetheless the moral responsibility remains.

In this quotation, De George attributes responsibility to the companies using computer systems that fail. The company is, however, only one of many individuals and units that were typically involved in the development and ultimate use of systems with the Y2K problem. Even so, De George's concern with the Myth of Amoral Programming and Information Processing and his strategy of using liability to dissolve it can be extended to all the actors involved. All of those who are involved with the production, distribution, and use of computer technology should be understood to have role-responsibilities. Their actions should be understood to make a causal contribution to outcomes that affect human beings. The best strategy for minimizing the riskiness and unreliability of computing is (1) to make sure that role-responsibilities of all those involved are well articulated; (2) to make sure that all those involved understand the effects of their work on human beings; and, (3) to hold all those involved liable when they fail to live up to their role-responsibilities.

The Y2K problem is a salient example of what happens when businesses, government agencies, and individuals become dependent on computer and information technology. The more dependent we are, the higher the stakes when things go wrong; hence, the greater significance of working out the responsibilities of all those involved. The Y2K problem is just the tip of an iceberg of complex accountability issues in computing. Underneath the tip of the iceberg are a number of factors that lead to diffusion of accountability. I turn now to these broader factors.

DIFFUSION OF ACCOUNTABILITY

In situations in which computer and information technology is used, accountability is often unclear. This phenomenon occurs for a variety of reasons. We saw in an earlier section of this chapter that the newness of the technology was for a time a cause of uncertainty about who is responsible for what in the buying and selling of software. In the law, responsibilities depend on whether the thing being bought and sold is a product or service, and in the early days of computing that issue had not yet been worked out. There was a policy vacuum and the vacuum had to be filled before role-responsibilities became clear.

To some extent, the newness of computer and information technology persists because new applications are continuously being developed. Still, newness is a diminishing factor, especially when it comes to legal responsibility. Once the law has been clarified or specified, legal responsibility is clear. The situation is much more complex when it comes to moral responsibility. Here the most powerful factors contributing to diffusion of responsibility are (1) the scale and complexity of some computer systems, (2) the "many hands" involved in developing, distributing, and using them, and (3) the way in which computer systems sometimes mediate human decision making. Before delineating these, however, it will be helpful to clarify certain aspects of *moral responsibility*.

Moral responsibility is attributed to moral agents, and in Western philosophy that has exclusively meant human beings. This is best explained by referring back to Immanuel Kant and deontological theory, discussed in Chapter 2. Human beings can be held morally responsible for their actions because they have the capacity to control their behavior. To use Kant's terms, human beings have the capacity to act "in accordance with the conception of law." Rocks and trees and amoebas don't have this capacity. Human beings are responsible for their actions because they choose their actions. They have autonomy; they think and decide and then act.

This means that when it comes to moral responsibility in computing, role-responsibility, causal responsibility, blameworthiness, and liability all have to be traced back or assigned to human beings.[2] Only human beings bear moral responsibility and if we fail to hold human beings accountable, we slip into the Myth of Amoral Computer Programmers.

---

[2] I am not going to take up the issue of whether computers can be moral agents. There is a rich philosophical literature on this topic, a literature that illuminates the nature of morality and moral agency.

One of the most interesting problems that arises in attributing moral responsibility in computing has to do with the scale and complexity of computer systems. Computer systems are sometimes so large and complex—involving millions of lines of code—that no single individual can understand in detail what is going on in the system. How, then, can we hold an individual accountable for the harm that may result from use of such a system?

Integral with the complexity and scale of computer systems is another kind of complexity, the complexity of the number of individuals who might be involved in the development of a computer system. One or several individuals may design the general features of the system while others design various parts; others may code these designs; others may write the documentation; and yet others may advertise and market the system. Mistakes can be made (bugs introduced) in each of the parts as well as in the pulling together of all the parts into a single system. The design may be flawed; error may be introduced in the coding; the documentation may be in error; the advertising may misrepresent the system; and so on. Errors at any step can lead to harm when the system is used.

Nissenbaum (1995) refers to this aspect of computer software development as the phenomenon of "many hands" and she describes the effect that it has in obscuring accountability. She uses the case of the Therac-25, a computer-controlled radiation treatment machine to illustrate the diffusion of responsibility that occurs when many hands are involved in the development and use of a computer system. In the Therac-25 case, something went seriously wrong with the machine, and, as a result, several patients received massive overdoses of radiation. In at least three cases, patients died, and in other cases, the patients receiving radiation burns suffered irreversible injury. When an attempt was made to figure out what went wrong, the many hands involved made it difficult to identify the responsible agents:

> In sum, the Therac-25, a complex computer-controlled system, whose malfunction caused severe injury, provides an example of the way many hands can lead to an obscuring of accountability. Because no individual was both an obvious causal antecedent and decision maker, it was difficult, at least on the face of it, to identify who should have stepped forward and assumed responsibility. Collective action of this type provides excuses at all levels, from those low down in the hierarchy who are "only following orders," to top-ranking decision makers who are only distantly linked to the outcomes. (p. 531)

Not only do the many hands involved make it difficult in hindsight to identify who is accountable, they also may make it more difficult for individuals, during the process of development, to see themselves as accountable.

To be sure, we have legal mechanisms for addressing this problem. For example, the company that developed the Therac-25 would be held strictly liable and would carry liability insurance to cover the costs of compensating the victims. Strict liability has, as explained earlier, a utilitarian justification insofar as it keeps the pressure on software developers to thoroughly test the software and build in redundancy.

Still, strict liability justifies *legal* responsibility, not *moral* responsibility. Moral responsibility usually has a strong element of blameworthiness and this is precisely what is problematic in computing because of the scale and many hands involved in developing computer systems. Suppose a group of individuals in a software company does everything reasonable—everything they know how to do—to prevent the occurrence of dangerous flaws in their software, yet an unforeseen situation arises and a user is hurt. Utility justifies holding the company legally liable to pay for the harm done, but it doesn't justify the attribution of moral blameworthiness. The group may not be morally blameworthy.

To be sure, both kinds of situations are possible—those in which no one is morally blameworthy, and those in which someone did something wrong and is morally blameworthy. It is just that computing seems to have more of the former than might be the case with simpler and smaller scale technologies.

Yet another factor contributing to the diffusion of responsibility is illustrated in Scenario 7.2. Here the focus is not on responsibility for the development of a computer system; rather it is on responsibility in the use of a computer system. Kimiko Syun has to make a decision based on advice derived from an extremely complex computer model, yet she does not understand the model well enough to judge when to take the advice and when to disregard it. This scenario helps us to understand why some people fear that increasing use of computer systems will lead to a loss of human control and a de-skilling of human beings.

Kimiko Syun doesn't need to understand the model in order to use it, and there is pressure on her to use it. The pressure may not be explicit; that is, her superiors might never have said to her, "You must do what the model says." Nevertheless, consider that if she goes against the advice of the computer model and her decision has untoward consequences, the computer advice will be there as concrete evidence that her decision was bad. The advice the model gives could be considered the standard (or reasonable or competent) thing to do. On the other hand, if she takes the advice of the computer model and the decision has bad consequences, she can point to the advice given by the computer model as evidence that what she did was reasonable, prudent, and competent. Remember that computer models are typically designed using experts and are thought to embody the kind of reasoning that is standard in a field. So, computer models seem to have a self-promoting character. Once they are in use, there is a risk in disregarding them.

Computer models aside, we can characterize the situation in Scenario 7.2 as one in which a computer system mediates human decision making. Many work environments are now designed so that individuals must make decisions based on computer-mediated information. Think of air traffic controllers, doctors reading digital images, those who regulate the machines in automated factories, those who monitor Web traffic, and so on.

Van den Hoven (1994) argues that there are serious repercussions for individual autonomy and individual responsibility in many of these environments where individuals must act on mediated information. To act autonomously and as a moral agent, an individual must be able to form justified beliefs and make moral judgments. When individuals do not have control over the belief acquisition process, they do not have the conditions for moral agency. This is precisely the situation of Kimiko Syun in Scenario 7.2. She is responsible for the pension fund, and she must form beliefs, make judgments, and act on these by making decisions. Yet she is expected to believe the output from the computer model while not having information that is essential for evaluating the computer output. The fact that she does not have the conditions necessary for justified belief acquisition leads to another kind of diffusion of responsibility.

Consider van den Hoven's compelling military example:

> The users of the computerized Aegis combat system of the *USS Vincennes,* which shot down an Iranian airliner, were narrowly embedded. The human operators mis-identified it as "enemy aircraft," because of a design flaw in the human interface. They were unable to scrutinize the inside of the systems, they had to decide in split-seconds, on the basis of software that was so complex as to rule out mathematical proof of soundness, they could not question or quiz it, and they were unable to detect defeating information, except for the most obvious malfunctions, such as smoke coming out of the keyboard. And even if they would have had the expertise and opportunity, it would have been useless, because investigations showed no software errors, or hardware malfunction in this case.

Van den Hoven's analysis suggests that the operators using the Aegis combat system did not have the conditions essential for autonomous moral agency. To be morally autonomous, one must have the capacity to acquire justified beliefs and make judgments accordingly.

Were the operators who—using the Aegis combat system—pressed the button that shot down the airliner morally responsible for the loss of life that occurred? They are causally responsible for what happened, but their blameworthiness is questionable. To locate blameworthiness, we would have to identify what they did wrong and the only plausible candidate is that they didn't evaluate and disregard the data provided to them by the Aegis system. However, as already suggested, they were not given access to information necessary for doing this and they weren't given education for doing this.

This means that if fault is to be found, it is more likely to be found either in the design of the system or in the training specified for users of the system. To put this in another way, van den Hoven's analysis is not (necessarily) an argument against using computer systems. Rather it is an argument for a certain kind of training for those who use computer systems in decision making, and it is an argument for designing systems of this kind in ways that give users access to how the system works. The argument for these approaches to the development and use of computer-mediated environments is especially compelling when the systems are used in environments in which human beings can be harmed.

To return to an earlier point, the issue here is not one of legal liability or formal accountability. In the case of the Aegis system and the *Vincennes,* for example, the world community held the U.S. military, and ultimately the U.S. government, accountable for the deaths caused by the actions of the Aegis operators. The issue of concern has to do with moral responsibility and whether individuals can be held accountable for their actions in computer mediated decision-making environments. Van den Hoven seems to have identified an important way in which traditional standards for moral responsibility are being challenged by increasing use of computer systems

The analysis here has been only cursory, but it points to a variety of factors contributing to a diffusion of accountability around the development and use of computer and information technology. These factors include the newness of the technology, complexity in the size and scale of computer systems, and complexity in the many hands that are involved in its development and use. In addition, users of computer systems are often placed in environments in which the conditions for making decisions for which one could be held morally responsible are significantly diminished.

INTERNET ISSUES

So far none of the accountability issues discussed in this chapter have had to do with the Internet, and yet the Internet adds yet another layer of complexity in accountability issues. In Chapter 4, I described how anonymity makes it difficult to trace behavior and hold individuals accountable. I also pointed out that the Internet distances individuals from the effects of their actions, and this seems to weaken the sense of responsibility for actions. Because the Internet is still relatively new, these effects may be transitory, though for now, they are worthy of concern. Two areas of special interest when it comes to accountability and the Internet are the liability of Internet Service Providers and accountability in virtual environments. The first issue has already been addressed via legislation and tested in the courts; the second is just beginning to draw attention.

ISP LIABILITY

Internet Service Providers (ISPs) routinely make a wide variety of communication forums available to their customers. These forums—be they chatrooms, bulletin boards, listservers, or something else—allow individuals to communicate with one another quickly and easily. From the early days of computer-telecommunications networks, these forums have raised accountability issues. Scenario 7.3 illustrates the problem of online defamation, an abuse of free speech. In fact, it illustrates one meaning of the saying that "information is power" for it shows how information—true or false—sent to an electronic forum can have a powerful effect on the career of a journalist. Scenario 7.3 illustrates both the promise and the problem of electronic forums. On the one hand, they can be an enormously useful means of communication and a powerful source of information. They facilitate sharing of ideas, rapid communication across vast distances, bringing together like-minded people or people with different viewpoints who want to hear from each other. On the other hand, electronic forums can instantly spread false, damaging, and criminal information across the globe. They are extremely effective rumor mills and they can be used to manipulate opinions, deceive and defraud, among other harms.

An obvious way to minimize the negatives of electronic forums is to hold individuals accountable for what they say and do. However, this is not as easy as it may sound. One problem indicated earlier is that anonymity often makes it difficult to trace the culprit. Another problem is the enormous effort required to monitor the thousands and thousands of forums that exist. Perhaps more important, the effect such monitoring could have on free speech could be harmful. Of course, there still ought to be policies that encourage individuals to behave in responsible ways. Netiquette (discussed in Chapter 4) is just such an attempt, but the harm done is sometimes too serious to be treated merely as a matter of Netiquette.

Scenario 7.3 is an example of such a case. Simpson's professional reputation has been severely damaged and if the claims that have been made about him are false, they are defamatory and illegal. Defamation is publication of a false statement about another person that harms the person's reputation. If the claims made about Simpson in Scenario 7.3 are false, then Simpson has a legal right to recourse.

Because of the difficulty of tracking down those who behave in illegal ways in electronic networks, early in their history, bulletin board operators and, then, ISPs were picked out as possible targets for accountability, especially liability. Prodigy, AOL, CompuServe, and other ISPs were sued by individuals who had various complaints about the content of information in forums. In 1995 in *Stratton Oakmont, Inc. v. Prodigy Services Company,* a court imposed liability on Prodigy because Prodigy had advertised the editorial control that it held over its computer bulletin boards. The court found that such control made the ISP much like a newspaper and the court therefore applied a standard of liability used for original publishers (Kane, 1999).

While it would be difficult to make the case that ISPs are morally responsible for the behavior of their customers, it is not hard to see how from a utilitarian perspective holding ISPs liable pressures them to monitor and filter the content of their electronic forums. While this is a daunting task, ISPs have in many cases undertaken the effort. At the same time, many have argued vehemently against a policy of holding ISPs liable. ISPs have pushed to be understood as common carriers, like telephone companies, rather than as publishers. They provide the conduits for communication but not the content.

This issue continues to be bandied about in many countries. In the United States, it was clarified and settled to a large extent in the Communications Decency Act (CDA) of 1996. While the CDA was eventually struck down by the U.S. Supreme Court, Section 230 dealing with ISP liability still stands. Section 230 specifies that "No provider or user of an interactive computer service shall be treated as the publisher or speaker of any information provided by another information content provider." This policy has become known as the "Good Samaritan" immunity for ISPs. According to one legal scholar, Congress "recorded as its express purpose in enacting [Section] 230 the intent to overrule *Stratton v. Oakmont,* and to allow ISPs to exercise editorial discretion without fear of publisher liability" (Kane, 1999).

Thus, ISPs are encouraged to monitor and filter, but they are not liable for the content of electronic forums within their service domain. Section 230 has been tested several times in the courts and it has held up well. It was first tested in 1997 in *Zeran v. America Online, Inc.* In this case, an anonymous subscriber repeatedly posted allegedly defamatory statements about Zeran to an AOL bulletin board. The court held that Section 230 immunized AOL against liability. Later, in 1998 in *Blumenthal v. Drudge and America Online, Inc.,* a federal court dismissed a defamation case against AOL on grounds that AOL could not be liable for defamatory statements carried by AOL but written by gossip columnist Matt Drudge. Interestingly, the court found in favor of AOL despite the fact that AOL paid Drudge for the right to make his gossip column available to its subscribers.

So, ISPs are not liable for the contents of their electronic forums. It should also be noted, however, that this does not prevent ISPs from filtering and censoring forums. Customers as well as the courts have encouraged ISPs to do this.

VIRTUAL ACTION

The final issue to be taken up in this chapter is one of the most challenging conceptually. Scenario 7.1 describes a now famous case referred to as "a rape in cyberspace." On the one hand, since rape is one of the most serious crimes committed against human beings, it seems disingenuous to call what happened here "rape." Bungle did not have direct physical contact with another person. He simply moved his fingers over a keyboard, wrote and changed computer code, and manipulated graphic images. Legal authorities had no cause to arrest or prosecute Bungle for rape. On the other hand, Bungle did *something,* and what he did upset participants in LamdaMoo—so much so that many felt action should be taken against Bungle.

Bungle's behavior is representative of behavior in virtual environments and the puzzle that this behavior creates for moral analysis. What exactly did

Bungle do? Did he do anything wrong? How are we to think about moral responsibility in virtual environments?

What did Bungle do? And, what exactly did he do wrong? At first, it seems easier to explain what he didn't do—he didn't commit rape. Analogies are helpful here. We might think of behavior in virtual environments as comparable to writing or speaking words and/or making drawings, in other words as a form of expression. If Bungle's behavior—changing computer code and manipulating graphical images—is understood in this way, then we can draw on the earlier discussion of Scenario 7.2 where it became clear that written and spoken words can be harmful. In Scenario 7.2, Simpson's reputation was damaged by defamatory words. Bungle hasn't defamed anyone, but morally and legally we hold individuals accountable for exposing others to written, spoken, and visual obscenity, pornography, and violence, especially when the others are unwillingly exposed. Think here of the standards to which television and radio stations must adhere or how bookstores selling pornography are not allowed to advertise their goods. Imagine what would happen if an individual were to erect a roadside billboard displaying a picture of a nude couple having sex so that anyone driving by would see it! Bungle's behavior might, then, be understood as a somewhat new form of expression and he used this new form of expression to expose people to pornography and violence without their consent.

This makes sense, though it doesn't account for another problematic aspect of Bungle's behavior—he violated a rule of the MUD. MUDs are games; they are playful, entertaining environments. Imagine a group of people playing Monopoly. One of the players pulls a toy gun out of his pocket, aims it at another player, and asks for all of the player's money. The victim-player may or may not comply and the other players may or may not go along with the joke. It is possible to imagine that all the players might get upset because this player is disrupting the game. In Monopoly, one doesn't acquire money by robbery. To be sure, this rule isn't articulated at the beginning of the game and it isn't written in the formal rules of the game. Rather, the rule is implicit in the game and in general in playing board games.

Now, Bungle's behavior might be understood as comparable to the attempted robbery in Monopoly. When he took control of characters that were not his own, he violated an implicit rule of the game. The MUD was designed so individuals could create their own characters and control how their characters behave in the virtual environment. Bungle's behavior, thus, went contrary to the idea of the game.

These two analogies suggest that Bungle did two things wrong: He exposed participants to pornography and violence without giving them a chance to avoid it, and he violated an implicit rule of the game.

This much seems clear, but it is worth pushing a little further. Monopoly is, in some sense, a simulation game. It simulates how capitalism works. One buys and sells property, accumulates wealth, tries to use one's money to make more money, and luck plays an important role. Most players recognize that the game is a very simplified model of capitalism. The game captures certain elements of the real world and leaves out many others. Many virtual environments are just like this. Individuals are placed in environments that simulate a real-life situation. Think of educational video games such as Symcity, or flight simulators used for training pilots, or simulation models of global climate change. These computer-created environments can have a variety of purposes ranging from entertainment to education to support for real-world decision making.

At first glance, it would seem that individuals acting in these simulated environments are not accountable for their behavior, at least not in the ordinary sense. If I intentionally, and even maliciously, kill a figure in a video game, I am not accountable for murder. If I crash the plane I am flying in the flight simulator, I have not done any real damage to myself or an airplane. If the climate change I simulate in the computer model creates a devastating hurricane, no houses are blown away, no real people are killed, and so on. Because virtual environments are "virtual" and not real, an intuitive response to them seems to be that there need be no accountability for what goes on in such environments. Thus, it may be tempting to think that Bungle's behavior wasn't real. It was merely ephemeral, just a game.

While this response might be appropriate for some virtual environments, it is dangerous and deceptive for others. The telling part of the Bungle incident is the effect that Bungle's behavior had on people. Behavior in virtual environments is real in the sense that it has consequences for the actor and for others who are affected by the actor's behavior. Of course, behavior in virtual environments is different from behavior in nonvirtual environments. Both are real though they are real in different ways. The primary difference is the technology that mediates. Behavior in virtual environments is mediated by computer software that designs the environment so that individuals can and can't do various things by this or that behavior. In nonvirtual environments, the natural world provides an environment in which individuals can and can't do various things with this or that behavior. Of course, in many nonvirtual environments, technology also plays a big role. Electricity, automobiles, and buildings structure the spaces through which we move. They allow and disallow, facilitate and constrain the things we do. As I explained in Chapter 1, technology instruments human action, but it's still human action.

It is false to say that when individuals act in virtual environments, there are no "real" effects. Rather, the effect that one has depends on the software and hardware through which one is acting. The effect that one has is mediated by technology. When I crash an airplane in a flight simulator, there is no explosion. No material, three-dimensional airplane that cost millions of dollars is destroyed. On the other hand, the crash is real in the sense that I have made decisions about which buttons to press and which levers to pull. If I am studying to be a pilot and my behavior in the flight simulator is being monitored for my preparedness, then the crashing of the virtual airplane may have a very real effect on when or whether I ever get to fly a real airplane. While the nature of the effects on children of playing violent video games is disputed, if there is a negative effect, this is another example of how behavior in virtual environments can have real effects.

Virtual environments are not morally neutral environments (Brey, 1999). The effects of behavior in virtual environments are real; accountability for your behavior cannot be entirely deflected. What you are accountable for in a virtual environment is complex, as illustrated by Bungle in LamdaMoo. Bungle was not guilty of rape; he was blameworthy for breaking a rule and unwittingly exposing others to pornography and violence.

From the perspective of accountability, acting in virtual environments is acting, and one is accountable for one's actions. The kinds of responsibility discussed at the beginning of this chapter apply in virtual environments, though in different ways than they apply in nonvirtual environments. Insofar as Bungle violated informal rules of the game, he could be understood to have violated his *role-responsibility* as a participant. His behavior was *causally responsible* for participants witnessing pornography and violence that they didn't chose to witness. Admittedly, his *blameworthiness* is complex, but he seems blameworthy for violating the rules and for not seeking the consent of participants in raising the level of violence in the game. The issue of his *liability* is also complex, but clearly applicable since participants in LamdaMoo took this matter up when they debated what should be done to Bungle.

While progress has been made in understanding the so-called rape in cyberspace, this analysis cannot easily be extended to other virtual environments. That is, how different types of responsibility will apply to other virtual environments is likely to be a function of the particularities of the virtual environment. Bungle acted in an entertainment environment, and virtual environments are used for a variety of purposes, including for education and training as in the pilots' training case. In yet other cases, virtual environments are interfaces for doing real things: consider virtual businesses (businesses that operate on the Web) or telemedicine (e.g., when doctors perform surgery via remote access) or the Aegis combat system described earlier. Each of these environments has to be analyzed in its own terms, and each is likely to have some special ethical issues.

It is unfortunate that the term *virtual* has been used for these environments because virtual suggests almost but not completely real. This understanding of what one is doing in a virtual environment contributes to the diffusion of responsibility discussed earlier. It suggests that one is not doing anything real; yet nothing could be farther from the truth. Individuals are doing real things in virtual environments, it's just that what they are doing is instrumented with software and hardware. The technology instruments so that particular physical movements of our bodies have particular outcomes,

outcomes we couldn't produce without the technology. The instrumentation of technology allows us to do some things we couldn't do without the technology, but it is still *us* doing. It is still real human beings performing real actions.

CONCLUSION

The accountability issues surrounding computer and information technology are complex, numerous, and, in many ways, daunting. In this chapter, I have reviewed a subset of the issues and tried to illustrate their character and complexity as well as to suggest how they are or can be handled in law and in ordinary morality.

STUDY QUESTIONS

1. Identify and describe the four different meanings of responsibility.
2. Does the categorical imperative prohibit the selling of software? Explain.
3. Give examples (hypothetical or real) of dishonesty in selling software.
4. Give examples (hypothetical or real) of coercive practices in selling software.
5. Explain Prince's argument for treating mass-market software as a product and the sale of customized software as provision of service.
6. How is the use of strict liability ever justified?
7. What is negligence? Why is it difficult to show that a software producer has been negligent?
8. How did time come into play in responsibility for the Y2K problem?
9. What is the Myth of Amoral Computer Programming and Information Processing?
10. How do computers diffuse accountability?
11. What is the legal liability of an ISP according to recent court decisions?
12. What did Bungle do wrong (in Scenario 7.1) according to the author?

SUGGESTED FURTHER READING

Chapter 6, "Responsibility, Liability, and Professional Codes" in *Computers, Ethics, and Social Values,* eds. Deborah G. Johnson and Helen Nissenbaum (Englewood Cliffs, NJ: Prentice-Hall, 1995), pp. 470–605.
Chapter 10, "Compensating for Private Harms," in *Readings in Philosophy of Law* (2nd ed.), eds. John Arthur and William Shaw (Englewood Cliffs, NJ: Prentice-Hall, 1993), pp. 405–464.

CHAPTER 8

Ethics and the Internet II: Social Implications and Social Values

Computer and information technology and the Internet are said to be *the* most significant technological developments of the twentieth century. Many of our most fundamental social institutions and values are being transformed as we translate them into the new medium and move more and more activities onto the Internet—business, work, sociality, entertainment, government, education, and so on. The changes taking place are more than worthy of our consideration for while it is clear that the character and quality of human lives is being transformed, it is not clear that all of these changes are for the good. We need both to understand and to evaluate what is happening. Moreover, some of the changes taking place seem to be out of human control, or at least out of the control of the individuals being affected. So it is also important to understand what is driving this change and how it might be shaped. How does computer and information technology cause social change and what causes technological development?

The task of identifying and evaluating the changes taking place as a result of computer and information technology is daunting. Even if we focus just on the Internet, as I will do in this chapter, the task is daunting because the change is so broad (i.e., so many aspects of life are being affected). The Internet is changing the fundamental shape of the economic and political order of the entire globe. It is changing how individuals see themselves, how we think about what it means to be a human being, and how we work, learn, and play. The breadth of the social change makes the task unwieldy.

Even if we cannot understand all of the changes taking place, it is important to try. It is important to identify factors and forces that shape technological development and in turn lead to social change. Among other things, understanding gives us the opportunity to influence if not steer the change for the good.

It is tempting to ask very big questions: Is computer and information technology making human lives better? Is it enhancing or eroding important social values? Is the Internet impeding or facilitating democracy? Does this technology increase safety or increase risk? Is the technology making some of us better off at the expense of others? Are human beings losing control of their lives as technology takes over decision making? These are very big questions. They are unwieldy in the sense that they are too broad to be answered with a simple "yes" or "no." Computer and information technology, and the Internet are, like most technologies, a mix. Human lives are improved in some ways, diminished in others. Some values are enhanced while others are eroded. There are benefits and drawbacks. Some problems are solved while others are created.

I begin this chapter with a general discussion of technology and social change. I, then, turn to an analysis of the Internet focused primarily on its implications for democracy and democratic values. The starting place for this analysis is the Kantian conception of human beings as ends in themselves. This conception of human beings underpins the value of individual autonomy and the value of democracy. That is, the idea that human beings should be respected as ends in themselves necessitates a form of government that gives individuals freedom to pursue their own plans for their lives and that gives them a say in the governance of public institutions that directly and indirectly shape their lives. In other words, the Kantian conception of human beings as ends in themselves provides the moral justification for democracy and democratic values. Of all the possible social effects of the Internet, it seems especially important to ask about its implications for democracy, democratic values, and democratic institutions.

A just society is one in which freedoms and constraints and benefits and burdens are fairly distributed. If the rules systematically skew things to the advantage of certain groups and to the disadvantage of others, then justice does not prevail. Computer and information technology and especially the Internet have been implicated in the widening gap between haves and have-nots within countries and among countries of the world. This issue is often referred to as "the digital divide." After examining the digital divide with an eye to understanding what exactly is at stake, I briefly discuss the value of freedom of expression and the Internet. I conclude this chapter by pointing to three issues that will be particularly important to watch in the future.

TECHNOLOGY AND SOCIAL CHANGE

To lay the groundwork for discussion of democracy and access, it will be helpful to briefly explore the relationship between technology and social change in broad perspective. Discussions of the social impact of computer and information technology often make assumptions that get in the way of fruitful discussion unless the assumptions are made explicit and confronted. An example illustrates this point.

Consider what computer and information technology has done to the banking industry. Not only can individuals perform banking transactions remotely and electronically, but when money moves from one place to another, the movement is essentially a matter of electronic activity. It is tempting to say, then, that money and banking have been "radically" and "fundamentally" transformed by computer and information technology. The very meaning of "money" has changed in the sense that "money" no longer means coins and paper. Money now is, at base, electronic configurations.

On the other hand, consider that it is equally plausible to argue that banking has not fundamentally changed in the sense that the purposes and the functions of banks and the banking industry are what they have always been. Individuals want to store and accumulate wealth (*value* in abstract terms). They want to move their wealth around in various ways to achieve their ends (i.e., to buy things or pay debts or invest and increase their wealth). Banks and the banking industry facilitate these transactions. This is essentially what banks did before computers and information technology, and probably what they will always do. Whether the wealth that is moved around is represented by coins and paper or by electronic impulses seems, from this perspective, insignificant. Banking hasn't changed fundamentally; only the tools that are used.

Now, you might pursue this debate further and try to figure out which side is right. Has the banking industry been radically transformed or is it fundamentally the same? Rather than doing this, however, it is enlightening to step back and reflect on the dispute. Assumptions are made on both sides about what counts as "radical" or "fundamental" change. On the one side, the assumption seems to be that a mere change in tools is not significant; significant change occurs when there is a change in aims and purposes. On the other side, the assumption seems to be that a change in the material basis of an activity or industry is significant and transformative. In some sense, the opposing sides miss each other entirely; they have different ideas about what counts as fundamental or significant change. The disagreement would be more fruitful if each side were forced to articulate and defend the criteria they are using for "radical" or "fundamental" change. In some sense, the important thing is not the conclusion about whether the banking industry has been radically transformed or not; rather, the important thing is identifying what has and has not changed.

Notice also that proponents on each side of the dispute make assumptions about the state of the world before the technological change. These assumptions may not, however, be accurate or, at least, may be interpretative and contentious. For example, it could be argued that money has never been based on just coins and paper. Yes, there is the gold standard, but coins and paper have always been representations of other things and some of those things have always been somewhat ephemeral—promises to pay, contracts, or incorporated entities. So, the claim that banking has changed because electronic impulses have replaced coins and paper as the basis for money is an enormously complicated and somewhat contentious claim.

The point is that below the surface of discussions of the social change being wrought by computers and information technology are usually a set of assumptions that need to be made explicit and critically examined. Three issues of this kind are worth keeping in mind as you engage in discussions of the social impact of computer and information technology and especially the Internet.

(1) What Counts as a "Social Revolution"?

The social changes taking place today that are attributed to computers and information technology and the Internet are often compared to the Industrial Revolution or to other times in history when very comprehensive and fundamental changes occurred. Social and technological change continuously occurs, so the big question is what counts as ordinary, evolving change and what counts as revolutionary change? Is it the comprehensiveness of the change, the speed, or the type of change? For many, social revolution means a change in political structure or a change in the distribution of power. For others, social revolution means a change in how individuals think about themselves (e.g., what it means to be a human being). Yet for others, it has to do with the economic base of a society. Many have argued, for example, that a social revolution has taken place in the United States because of the shift from manufacturing to information services as the largest portion of the U.S. economy. The important thing is to understand what is being claimed and what is happening and what can be said for the significance of the change.

One error to be avoided is confusing technological change with social change. A change in technology does not necessarily mean a social change. Another error is to suppose that all technological change leads to social change. There are many cases that you might consider here as you reflect upon the connection between technological change and social change. Popular examples of significant change include the shift from horse and buggy to automobiles and the changes that occurred with the invention of the telephone and the television. However, you should also consider cases in which technological change did not lead to such dramatic social change. For example, the change from ink pens to ballpoint pens and the change from electronic to microwave ovens. You should also consider cases in which there has been resistance to technological change (e.g., public transportation in some big cities, solar and nuclear power to some extent). The nonstandard cases are sometimes quite revealing in terms of understanding the intertwining of technological and social change.

(2) Is There Change or Entrenchment of the Status Quo?

A second issue worth keeping in mind is when and to what extent technological change entrenches social patterns that already exist rather than causing social change. This issue is related to the question of revolutionary versus ordinary change in pushing us to identify and make explicit what is and isn't changing. You should be alert to the possibility that technological change sometimes reinforces and entrenches social patterns and hierarchies, especially relationships of power and authority that already exist. This is precisely what is at issue with the digital divide, a concern that access to computer and information technology and the Internet will further entrench patterns of wealth and power that already prevail.

In his seminal book, *Computer Power and Human Reason,* Joseph Weizenbaum (1976) suggested that computers might, in a certain sense, prevent social change and entrench social arrangements. He gives two very powerful cases from the period just after World War II in the United States. The two cases are the stock exchange and the military bureaucracy in Washington, DC. According to Weizenbaum, both institutions were under enormous pressure for change. Both institutions had a centralized organizational structure and both had grown so large in the first half of the twentieth century that the centralized structure was difficult to maintain. In the case of the New York Stock Exchange, the number of transactions occurring daily was becoming difficult to transact. In the case of the military bureaucracy, the number of troops, the amount of equipment, and the size of the budget were making it difficult for centralized control. Weizenbaum's point is that the invention of computer technology came along just in time to allow these institutions to continue as they had been. Computer technology allowed them to handle the large volume of transactions and to keep track of equipment and manpower with a centralized structure. If computer technology had not come along when it did, both of these institutions would have been forced to make some very fundamental changes.

Now, whatever you think of Weizenbaum's analysis, his suggestion that the technology may facilitate old patterns in continuing is worth keeping in mind. With a careful eye, you will be able to find as many examples of computer and information technology reproducing old patterns of power and access (social hierarchies) as of the technology causing fundamental change. Here, for example, you may find the literature on the impact of computer and information technology on work especially interesting. While there is no doubt that the character of work has changed in many work environments because of computer and information technology, it can also be argued that computer and information technology has entrenched the preexisting employer-employee relationship. Employers have more power than ever to monitor and control workers, even when it appears that workers have more autonomy.

(3) Is Technology Good or Bad?

A third issue that is likely to arise in discussions of the social changes being wrought by computer and information technology is whether technology is good or bad. Technology may be seen by some to be the panacea, the solution to all of our problems, while others are more distrustful of technology. Discussions of this kind are generally not very fruitful; they tend to be overly simplistic. Whether technology is good or bad depends on which technology you are referring to and which of usually multiple effects. Many technologies are a mix of benefits and costs. Moreover, technologies tend to affect individuals differently. They affect different socioeconomic classes differently. Technologies differentially affect men and women, racial groups, age groups, occupational groups, regions within a country, and across the world, to name just a few. Hence, it is a mistake to assume technology is all good or all bad.

Individuals who are planning careers in engineering and computer science sometimes feel threatened by criticisms of technology. This is unfortunate because critical discussions of technology can be and should be seen as a means of improving technology. Technologies have often been improved because of criticism. Consider, for example, that automobiles and many manufacturing processes are safer and better for the environment today because of individuals who were willing to look at the drawbacks as well as the benefits. The ideal here is that the designers of technologies (engineers and computer professionals) hear the criticisms and/or do the critique themselves while they are in the process of designing rather than "after the fact."

EMBEDDED VALUES, ENHANCED AND IMPEDED VALUES

Discussions of technology and social change often lead to disputes about whether technology is value-neutral or value-laden. Up until twenty to thirty years ago, the literature on science, technology, and society was filled with claims about the value-neutrality of both science and technology. Many scholars believed that technologies did not embody values, and they emphasized that values come into play, if at all, only when technologies are used. Perhaps the most memorable example of this was the claim about guns. "Guns," it was said, "don't kill, people do," as if a gun were a neutral tool. Computers, as well, were thought to be neutral tools that acquire values only when used for particular purposes and in particular contexts.

The claim that technology is value-neutral has rested in part on the alliance between science and technology and with several ideas about science being carried over to technology. The presumption about science was that it is objective and that it progresses in a natural sequence of development. The unfolding of our knowledge, it was claimed, is determined by nature, not by society. New discoveries were thought to proceed and progress in a natural sequence. The same was then said about technology. It was understood to have a natural sequence of development somewhat independent of social forces, though to a lesser extent than in science.

These presumptions have now been rejected, or at least substantially modified and qualified, by scholars in the field of science and technology studies (STS). It is now well accepted among STS scholars that technology and science are both value-laden. For example, when it comes to the topics on which scientists choose to do research, an array of social factors influence their choices. Think, for example, of how government funding impacts the directions of science. Similarly, the direction of the development of technology is pushed and pulled in various ways by social factors—investors, market demand, government funding, and regulation. These all influence what technologies are developed, when, how, and by whom.

Two tenets now form the foundation of STS: that technology shapes society and that technology is shaped by its social context. These are broad claims and a variety of accounts have been given of each tenet. STS is a multidisciplinary field with many theoretical perspectives. Whatever the account, social values are present in the social construction of technology. Hence, the two tenets could also be understood as: Technology shapes social values, and social values shape technology.

It is easy to understand why someone might believe that technology is neutral. We can, in our minds, separate human activity and material objects. The material objects exist independent of human beings. They don't disappear when humans aren't looking at them. Thus, material objects seem to be like facts in the sense that they just "are," while human activities embody values in the sense that the human actors have desires, intentions, preferences, and purposes. Human beings value things.

Nevertheless, while it is possible to engage in this mental exercise of separating material objects and human activity, the exercise hides more than it reveals. For one thing, it asks us to imagine *human-made* material objects without human purposes. This seems odd. Human-made objects are made by humans who have intentions and purposes. Humans make computers and software and the Internet to do things that they want to do.

It is true that often we find that technologies created for one purpose, can do more or can do something different, but even so, when we find these other capabilities, it is human purposes—human values—that lead us to recognize the additional capabilities of the technology. Humans create material objects for human purposes, be it objects for symbolic and spiritual purposes or for assisting transportation and communication or making fire and catching animals. In this respect, human-made objects are far from value-neutral.

When it comes to computer and information systems, embedded values are not all that difficult to see. Software engineers intentionally design systems to do certain jobs. The tasks that the software accomplishes are valued, and the way the software does the job will also contain values. The system designer may, for example, seek an efficient or elegant or user-friendly design. Efficiency, elegance, and user-friendliness are values. For other examples, an inventory control system identifies stores in which the inventory of certain products has dropped below a certain level, and then it responds in certain ways. In other words, the system values keeping inventory above those levels. A computer system that assists in the evaluation of applicants for college admission incorporates SAT scores, high school grade point average, extra curriculum activity, and job experience. Each element is considered valuable in the evaluation of applicants; hence, each element is a value in the system.

Not only do computer professionals recognize this, they build on it when they ask their clients for input on the design of software or hardware-software packages. They recognize that the client's values should be built into the software.

At the heart of this issue of values in computer and information technology is the question whether computers, by their very nature, carry or favor certain values. You might concede that there are values designed into software but still insist that computer technology is itself neutral. You could argue that the technology's neutrality is related to its malleability. Because computer and information technology is malleable, values—any values—can be designed in, but the technology itself (i.e., the hardware) is neutral in that it does not predetermine or preclude any values being designed into the software.

In the very early days of computers, an argument against this position was made. Computers, it was argued, are value-laden in the sense that they favor the quantitative. This is an interesting argument. Even if you don't like the term "quantitative," it seems that tasks and information have to be understood and formulated in a certain way to be handled by computers.

To see this, consider first an example. Suppose a politician wants to find out what her constituency thinks about an issue before she votes on it. She has her staff design a questionnaire and distribute it to citizens in her district. The questionnaire contains a list of questions and for each question, there is a list of possible responses, a, b, c, and d. Those who fill out the questionnaire simply check the box indicating the response that is closest to what they think. Of course, the questionnaire could be available online as well as on paper. Either way, using information technology, the politician's staff is able to process thousands and thousands of questionnaires and to make a thorough report on the results of the questionnaire.

The problem is that the questionnaire gave individuals a very limited range of choices in responding to questions. Individual opinions are extremely complex and the questionnaire only gets at a portion of this. In a sense, the questionnaire forces an individual to give her or his view in summary form and to pick a response that comes closest but may not be all that close. It doesn't seem accurate to say that the information derived from the questionnaire is merely quantitative for when an individual chooses a, b, c, or d, she or he gives substantive information. Moreover, the survey could be redesigned to get more refined information by asking more questions or asking the questions in different ways. Even conceding all of this, however, it seems that designing the questionnaire so that it can be processed by computer shapes and limits the type of information obtained.

We can compare the results of the survey at issue with alternatives. Instead of the survey just described, the politician could use an open-ended survey allowing constituents to describe their views in whatever way they choose and not be confined to an a, b, c, or d choice of response. This would provide *qualitative* data. The politician could also go out and talk to her constituents or she could use e-mail and a chat room. Notice that any of these more direct and qualitative forms of contact with constituents take an enormous amount of the politician's time. Even doing the open-ended survey is time intensive if the politician is to read the responses one by one. Notice also that if, instead of reading or hearing the responses herself, the politician has her staff do this for her—they read the open-ended survey or they communicate with constituents in a chat room or via e-mail, then they have to report the results to her. The staff would have to distill the constituent opinions into a summary similar to the summary report made from the original a, b, c, d survey. The distilled qualitative surveys may be better than the distilled a, b, c, d surveys, but in both cases, the politician receives "processed" information, not direct contact.

There seems to be a trade-off here. Partly it's a trade-off between quantity and quality. The politician is able to have access to the thoughts of *many more people* though the *type of information* she gets access to is limited. Still, this characterization doesn't seem quite accurate because computer and information technology can facilitate the qualitative as well. The point is rather that computer and information technology facilitates a mediated form of information. The information is mediated by the technology. This doesn't make it bad, it just makes it different.

As to the politician, one way out of the trade-offs between direct contact and mediated, quantitative data is to say that the politician should use both or all available kinds of information. She should talk to some of her constituents directly and have contact with some through e-mails and in chat rooms and she should have her staff administer surveys. All of these provide valuable, albeit different kinds of, information. This is reasonable, though remember that the point of the example was to show that the kind of information provided by computer and information technology is value-laden. The *kind* of information one gets is very much a function of the technology.

Computer and information systems are now an important part of the decision-making process in many public and private sectors. Think, for example, of the complex computer models used in financial markets, national health insurance, air traffic control, and law enforcement. These systems may incorporate thousands of factors, modeling the interactions of these factors, so as to predict what will happen if there is a change in the real world, a change in interest rates, or a change in the weather, and so on. The question about whether the technology limits the kind of information that can be obtained leads to the question about whether computer models adequately take into account important human values such as the value of human life, aesthetic value, the importance of leisure time, or national pride.

Sometimes such models must assign a dollar value to things for which it seems inappropriate. For example, in the computer models used to plan for our national forests, use of land for recreational purposes is assigned a dollar value so that this use can be compared to using the land for logging. There are also computer models that evaluate the risks of certain undertakings by putting a dollar value on the incidence of human maladies so that these can be balanced against the benefits of a project. For example, a model may be used to help make the decision to build a hazardous waste disposal facility in a neighborhood and the model may trade off the economic benefits in terms of job creation and tax revenues against increased risk of cancer to the population.

The point here is not to argue against the use of computer models in decision making. As with the politician's survey, the information provided is useful and important. The point is only that computer and information technology do limit the kind of information that can be created. These limitations should be kept in mind when the information is used in decision making. To return to our starting place, the limitations of technology-generated information are sometimes made invisible when computer and information technology are seen as value-neutral.

DEMOCRATIC VALUES IN THE INTERNET

Reflections and predictions concerning the social implications of the Internet frequently connect the Internet to democracy and/or democratic values, though the connection is made in a wide variety of ways. Some claim that the Internet is "a democratic technology," suggesting that it is inherently democratic. Others claim that the Internet can facilitate and enhance democracy— in organizations, national, state, and local government, as well as on a global scale. Yet others claim that democratic values are at stake in the policies we adopt to shape and regulate the Internet; they claim that the Internet should be developed along democratic principles (Ess, 1996).

Democracy is both a simple and complex idea. It is closer to a cluster of ideas, values, and arguments than it is a fixed or well-defined term. The core idea is, perhaps, best expressed as the idea that political power should reside in the citizens of a nation, rather than in a single person (a monarch or dictator) or small group of persons (an oligarchy or aristocracy). In a democracy, citizens are the ultimate authority, and government is accountable to those citizens. But, this idea has been interpreted in a variety of ways, and has been reinterpreted and modified over time; it has been expressed and realized in somewhat different ways at different times and in different places (Dahl, 1989; Arblaster, 1987). Abramson, Arterton, and Orren (1988), for example, suggest that three competing understandings of democracy vie for supremacy in American politics: plebiscitary democracy, communitarian democracy, and pluralist democracy.

The moral idea underlying democracy is the idea that individuals are sovereign over themselves and to be recognized as such they must have some say in the governments by which they are ruled. It follows from this moral basis that not only should citizens have a vote, but also a high degree of freedom.

In its more modern expression, in large scale, representative nation-states, democracy has meant that citizens have a right to elect representatives to the government. The size of nation-states has been a persistent and daunting challenge to the idea of democracy, diluting the power of citizens to influence government. Some see the Internet as having the potential to facilitate democracy on the scale of nation-states or even on a global scale.

Indeed, the literature on Internet democracy associates the Internet with a variety of elements connected to the simple idea. If one searches the Web under the topic of Internet democracy, for example, depending on which search engine one uses, the first listings provided are likely to have something to do with free speech. On- and offline, the popular and scholarly literature on the Internet and democracy refer to the following: voting and elections, participation, town meetings, political campaigns, tolerance, equal access, privacy, grass roots organizations, decentralization.

Yet, before the Internet and even today, technology has not been regarded as an important factor in political organization, at least not by mainstream political scientists and political theorists.[1] As mentioned earlier, in the past, technology was regarded by many to be value-neutral.[2] So, why all this attention to the Internet and democracy? What are we to make of these claims about the Internet being democratic or facilitating democracy or promoting/diminishing democratic values?[3]

The Internet can be understood as a value-laden technology in a number of different ways but the literature on democracy and the Internet seems primarily centered on the idea that there is something in the design of the Internet that makes it democratic. As mentioned in Chapter 4, the fact that the Internet connects many individuals to many other individuals is one of the features that makes the Internet special and many see this as a democratic characteristic. The web of telecommunication lines connecting people is seen as inherently democratic because it is not hierarchical.

There are several related arguments that seem to be at work in the claim that the Internet is democratic. My strategy here will be to articulate these arguments, and give them the best possible hearing, before I take issue with them.

Unmediated, Many to Many Interaction (Argument #1)

The core idea in many discussions of the democratic character of the Internet is an idea, just mentioned, that the Internet differs from other forms of communication insofar as it facilitates many-to-many communication. According to

---

[1] Recent literature in science and technology studies takes issue with the idea. Of particular importance in explaining the connection between political organization and technology is the work of Langdon Winner (1986) and Richard Sclove (1995).

[2] To be sure, technology has been the subject of public policy but not as a factor shaping political organization. It has not, for example, been recognized that technology is a form of legislation.

[3] Now and then technologies such as the automobile, the telephone, and television have been called democratic, though this seems to have meant that they could be made available to many.

this argument, the novelty and power of the Internet is that any individual (who has access) can, in principle, talk directly to any and every other individual (who has access). What is new and unusual here is that the power to communicate to many (hundreds and thousands across the earth) is now in the hands of many.[4] In the past, the power to communicate to many was only available to television and radio stations or, more importantly, to the few who could afford to take advantage of those technologies, namely large companies using the technology for advertising. (Ham radio is closer to the Internet in facilitating many-to-many communication, but its reach has been limited in part by the small number of users and perhaps because of its inconvenience.)

From the point of view of democracy, what is important here is that the many-to-many communication is unfiltered, unmediated, and relatively uninstitutionalized. What the many say to one another is not filtered by the news media or shaped by a political process that sets an agenda for discussion. Individuals can talk directly to one another and interpret what they hear, rather than listening to media interpretations of polls, first person interpretations of discussions with others, press releases issued by interested parties, and so on. These institutionalized forms of power (for that is what mass media and press conferences and magazines are) are bypassed when individuals can get information directly from primary sources.

The examples that are often given here to support the democratic character of many-to-many communication are revealing. Nation-states may try to control information flow in and out of their country so as to shape attitudes toward various events in their own or other countries (e.g., Tiannamin Square, the Kosovo war) or about proposed legislation. Yet because of the Internet, individuals have access to information independent of what their country might prefer (e.g., information from those who may be close to the event or information from sources with radically different interpretations).

It is important to remember that the Internet facilitates the distribution of institutionalized information as well. So, some argue that the Internet is democratic in the sense that it facilitates access to many more (even if filtered and mediated) sources of information. If you are American, you no longer need to rely exclusively on American news sources. On the Web, you can find international news sources, as well as news from a wide variety of perspectives.

Another important aspect of unmediated, many-to-many communication is that it allows new associations to form. The best illustration here is the groups that have formed online due to a common interest, such as a medical illness, a minority political position, a special fetish, or unpopular idea. A wide variety of special interest associations have been and will continue to form offline. The difference with the Internet is that associations can form and there can be frequent and intense interaction *independent of geography*. When those who have

---

[4] Notice that I say "many" and not "all"; it is important to note that the Internet is not now and may never be available to everyone in the world, though from a technical point of view, universal access is possible.

a common interest are geographically dispersed in such a way that they may not even be able to identify one another, their ability (power) to take action collectively remains fragmented; they have no means of working together, keeping each other informed, making joint decisions, and so on. Separately such individuals or groups are ineffective minorities. The Internet facilitates the joining of some otherwise fragmented groups. It makes it easier to have frequent contact with individuals who are geographically distant but share an interest. Some such associations remain informal; others become institutionalized. The point here is that new kinds of associations can form whereas in the past there were geographic barriers to association.

To summarize this argument, it claims that the Internet is democratic because (1) it allows many-to-many communication; (2) the communication can be unmediated by institutionalized forms of communication; (3) even when the Internet is used to gain access to institutionalized information, it facilitates access to a diversity of sources; and (4) it allows the formation of new associations independent of geographic location, especially associations around issues that would, otherwise, have been minority issues.

Information Is Power (Argument #2)

Before evaluating the unmediated many-to-many argument, it will be useful to articulate a second, somewhat overlapping argument with a different emphasis. The emphasis in the second argument is on the idea that information is power. Again the argument plays on the idea of power moving to the many, but here the Internet is seen as democratic because it gives power to the many.[5]

The argument goes as follows: (1) Democracy means power in the hands of individuals (the many); (2) information is power; (3) the Internet makes vast quantities of information available to individuals; (4) therefore, the Internet is democratic (Johnson, 1997). In this argument, the important thing about the Internet is that it provides information to individuals, be it direct access to other individuals or access to the World Wide Web, be it mediated or unmediated information. The kingpin of the argument is that information is power and this idea needs unpacking.

Information is power only if it is accurate information and relevant information. Mis-information is not empowering nor is such a glut of information that one drowns in it. There is nothing inherent to the Internet that guarantees accurate or useful knowledge. It seems clear that the Internet can facilitate the spread of mis-information as well as information. Whether it provides information or mis-information depends on the filtering and authenticating systems that are available.

---

[5] This argument is related to the debate about information technology causing centralization and decentralization of power. See Deborah G. Johnson and Helen Nissenbaum, *Computers, Ethics and Social Values* (1995).

Moreover, there are two parts to the claim that information is power. The argument for the democratic nature of the Internet works by playing on both. On the one hand, the argument suggests that information goes to individuals and those individuals who receive information acquire power. If information is going to the many than, presumably, the many are being empowered. The more one knows, the more power one has. Again, this is only partially true depending on the quality of the information, its relevance to one's life, and so on.

On the other hand, the idea that information is power suggests that the sender of the information has power—namely the power to shape attitudes and behavior by influencing people to see something their way. Television and radio stations are powerful because they convey ideas and influence individuals both in their buying habits and in their political and cultural attitudes. According to this interpretation of "information is power," each of us acquires power when we can send information. We can set up a Web page, send e-mail, participate in chat groups, make postings on bulletin boards, and so on. If the many have the power to send to the many then, in theory, the many have been empowered.

The reality is a bit more complicated than this in that the many do not, by any means, acquire the power of a television or radio station, and one's power depends to some extent on one's resources. Nevertheless, there is, at least, some degree of empowerment.

So, in the second argument, the Internet is democratic because information is power and the Internet both gives individuals access to information and allows individuals to be senders or providers of information. Since the Internet gives this power to the many, it would seem the Internet facilitates democracy.

More Power to the Less Powerful (Argument #3)

The first and second arguments are combined in some sense in what might be characterized either as a variation of argument #1 or #2 or as a third argument. According to this argument, the Internet is democratic because it gives power to the less powerful and takes power away from the more powerful. The Internet empowers the dis-empowered and dis-empowers the powerful. Here again, special interest groups who were not able to find each other before or form effective associations, can now find each other online and by combination gain power. Their lack of power before had to do with their geographic fragmentation or their lack of identity when interspersed in majority groups. The Internet eliminates the barriers to association that existed before and in this way gives power to the otherwise less powerful.

This argument is connected to the second argument in the sense that members of Internet-empowered groups are both senders and receivers of information. The Internet has allowed them to find an audience of like-interested others and allows them to become informed by other members about their common interest. The Internet assists a newly formed group in recruiting other members, and in their acting as a group despite their geographic distance. It assists them as well in contacting political representatives, informing the public, and so on.

SUMMARY OF THE THREE ARGUMENTS

Taken together, these three arguments claim that the Internet is democratic because: It facilitates many-to-many communication; it facilitates unmediated communication; it provides access to a diversity of mediated information resources; it facilitates the formation of new associations independent of geography; it gives power to the many to be both receivers and senders of information; and it gives power to the less powerful. What, now, are we to make of these arguments? Are they right? And, if they are right, what will it mean for democracy? Will the Internet naturally lead to more democracy?

IS THE INTERNET A DEMOCRATIC TECHNOLOGY?

To their credit, these arguments in support of the Internet's democratic character do identify patterns of behavior that are facilitated by the Internet. That is, the Internet does make it possible for many individuals to communicate with one another, to have access to a diversity of information sources, to form associations, to send and receive information, and so on. Not only does the Internet make this type of behavior *possible*, many individuals actually use the Internet in the patterns described. The arguments are problematic but not because they are false.

The arguments are problematic because of what they fail to acknowledge (not in what they affirm). While the Internet facilitates the patterns of behavior described in the arguments, it also facilitates other patterns of behavior. Some of these other patterns of behavior are neutral to democracy and yet others are undemocratic. Remember the malleability of this technology. It is closer to the truth to say that the Internet *can*, though not necessarily does, facilitate democracy (democratic values, relationships, or institutions). As well, it *can*, though not necessarily *does*, facilitate just the opposite. By just the opposite, I mean here that the Internet can facilitate hierarchical relationships, can increase the power of the already powerful, and can control and enslave rather than liberate individuals.

Consider the following counters to the three arguments in support of the Internet's democratic character. First, it is questionable whether the characteristics attributed to the Internet in the three pro-democracy arguments are, in themselves, democratic. Many-to-many communication, unmediated communication, and access to a diversity of information resources can each be undemocratic depending on the structure that surrounds or frames the activity. For example, many-to-many, unmediated communication often simply means chaos. When everyone speaks to everyone in whatever order they choose and there is no clear agenda or purpose or rules of order, little may get done. Individuals are not facilitated in having a say in implementing their ideas. Indeed, in anarchy there is no guarantee that everyone will have a say. In fact, often in such environments (offline as well as on), the loudest and most aggressive individuals come to dominate the conversation. Many of those who use the Internet for decision making have already learned this lesson and have developed tools to facilitate decision making. The point is that the tools determine whether and in what ways the decision-making processes are democratic or not.

Similarly, when each of us has access to a wide variety of information resources, those who want our attention (i.e., want to provide us with information) must compete for our attention. When they compete for our attention, whether they get it will depend on the resources they have. Can they afford to be on the Web? Can they afford to pay for, or do they have the skill themselves, to design the most attention grabbing Web page? Can they pay to be listed in various search engines? Or can they pay to be linked to service providers such as America Online? When it comes to sending information or getting attention, those with the most resources to begin with have much more power than those with fewer resources. The point here is that democracy is not created simply when every person is connected to every other person.

It would seem more accurate to say that the Internet creates the *possibility* of democratic processes and/or democracy enhancement, but to make the possibility a reality something more is required—rules of order, agenda setting rules, rules for membership, and so on. To be democratic or democracy-enhancing, the Internet must be structured in ways that support democratic processes and institutions.

The Internet is malleable and so while it facilitates many-to-many communication, it also facilitates one-to-many communication and one-to-one communication. While it facilitates the formation of new associations, it also facilitates the consolidation of old associations. While it gives power to the less powerful, it also gives new power to the already powerful. So while many individuals have acquired the power to send and receive information, it is also true that large newspaper conglomerates and television networks use the Internet to enhance their power to send and receive information. The Internet supports tendencies in many directions and there is nothing inherent to the Internet that favors democratic relationships. There are good reasons for predicting that the Internet will do at least as much, and probably more, to facilitate the consolidation of old power relationships than to create new power.

The Internet makes possible actions and interactions (information exchanges) that far exceed the capabilities of human beings. When we consider the capabilities of individuals for absorption and use of information, it becomes clear that despite what the Internet makes possible, human beings need help in figuring out what information to look at and with whom to form associations. Individuals are likely to, and currently do, use a variety of methods to find the information they want. They use search engines; they subscribe to listservers; they access familiar sources; and so on. Yes, the Internet puts information at the fingertips of many, and it makes it easy to review many more sources of information. Yes, the Internet has facilitated the entry of many new players into the game of filtering and providing information.

Nevertheless, because of the limited capacity of human beings for information, we need institutionalized filtering, selecting, and routing of information. Search engines are one example of a new form of institutionalized selection. The designers of search engines have decided how to structure knowledge and order information. Whether or not such tools as search engines are democratic is a subtle question involving how information is selected and ordered. There is no reason to believe that search engines are inherently democratic. In fact, if information is ordered on the basis of how much the source is willing to pay, there is good reason to believe that search engines are not democratic, but rather are tools which the wealthy and powerful will use to become more wealthy and powerful (Nissenbaum and Introna, 1998).

Again, this is not to deny that the Internet facilitates unmediated, many-to-many communication, that it facilitates the formation of new associations, and so on; nor is it to deny that individuals will avail themselves of these opportunities. Rather, the point is that the Internet makes possible a wide variety of patterns of interaction and information access and exchange. It is far from clear whether it will facilitate democratic patterns more than undemocratic patterns of activity.

Even the idea of unmediated, many-to-many communication is somewhat of a misnomer, since communication on the Internet is always mediated; it is mediated by computers and information technology. Information technology shapes the nature of communication in a multitude of ways, for example, by favoring text, favoring those who have access, favoring those who have the best equipment, and so on. And this is not to mention the way software packages and service providers mediate interactions with others and with information.

Too much emphasis on the idea that the Internet facilitates many-to-many communication skews our understanding of the Internet. It suggests a picture of wires connecting every individual to every other individual. The more accurate picture is one of information flowing from individuals to nodes and then from nodes to other individuals. The nodes are, in a sense, points of control or power. However, the picture is even more complicated than this. The Internet was designed as a decentralized system capable of functioning even when parts of the system are attacked and destroyed.[6] That is, information moving through the Internet can be immediately re-routed to avoid damaged or dysfunctional nodes. Nodes are control sites in the sense that information flow

---

[6] Here is where the Internet's military roots show their face.

can be stopped at nodes in order to control access to information. The world has witnessed this in several cases where a country wanted to stop Internet traffic in or out of its borders. So, while the Internet has a very decentralized and fluid design, it does have the potential for a high degree of social control of information. Another aspect of the potential for social control is the Internet's surveillance capacity, which will be discussed shortly.

Even if the picture of lines connecting everyone to everyone did give us a democratic situation, it would be important to note that it is not an accurate picture of the Internet. Information does not flow to and from every individual in the world or every individual within a nation-state. Within each country and globally, there are billions of people who do not, and never will, have access to the Internet.

As I have already mentioned, we must always keep in mind the malleability of computer and information technology. The danger in thinking that the Internet is inherently democratic is in presuming that nothing need be done and the Internet will naturally bring about and enhance democracy. Nothing could be farther from the truth. The Internet lends itself to undemocratic as well as democratic arrangements. There is no guarantee even that the Internet's current characteristics will persist. Conscious efforts will have to be made to retain its democracy-enhancing potential.

Indeed, there are several tendencies in the evolving development of the Internet that seem to threaten democracy. The first is the surveillance capabilities of the Internet and the second is management of the Internet's global scale.

As described in Chapters 4 and 5, one of the seemingly built-in features of computer and information technology is its reproducibility. The level of privacy we have as we communicate, navigate, and perform transactions online is very limited. Everything we do on the Internet endures. Traffic patterns as well as content are available to service providers (and hackers) and law enforcement with a warrant. Private marketing agencies also want this information as evidenced by the creation of cookies. I pointed out in Chapter 5 that people behave differently when they know they are being watched. The Internet's reproducibility could have a dampening effect on individual freedom.

In an attempt to counter the powerful forces interested in information about Internet use, technologists have been working on a wide variety of privacy-enhancing tools (e.g., PGP and other cryptographic techniques). We are likely to see ongoing development of privacy enhancing technologies and they will have enormous significance for the democratic character of the Internet.

The second undemocratic tendency of the Internet is its global scale. This is, perhaps, an ironic claim to make since the global scale of the Internet is also one of its most powerful features. The Internet brings people closer together and makes geographic location less relevant. However, our notions of democracy are based on the implicit assumption of shared geographic space. The idea of democracy arose in the Greek city-state consisting of people who bumped up against each other, so to speak, physically. Political theory is, in a sense, about this physical bumping up against one another. How are individuals to live together and achieve justice in their interactions in the same space? And international relations are largely about space—conflicting claims of ownership, borders, the natural resources inside borders, and so on.

The fact that the Internet has a global scale and facilitates communication, action, and interaction among individuals across the globe is often taken to be another sign of its democratic character. The global interaction is taken to be a means of promoting tolerance and/or helping the spread of democracy throughout the world. Pressures in the other direction may be seen but are generally not seen as undemocratic.

The pressure in the other direction has to do with national sovereignty. At the level of international politics, democracy and democratic relationships might be understood as recognizing the autonomy and sovereignty of individual nations. Yet, that is precisely what is threatened by the Internet. The Internet facilitates many-to-many communication and many-to-many communication bypasses national sovereignty. The Internet facilitates information flow across the globe. It facilitates the formation of global associations and alliances.

At the moment, an extremely complex and powerful issue is taking shape around the Internet. The Internet makes possible or at least suggests the possibility of an intensely intertwined global economy and all that goes with a global economy. A global economy leads to other kinds of cultural, social, and political intertwining. The Internet suggests the possibility of global democracy, but who are the citizens of a global democracy? Are the citizens of a global democracy individuals (all the people in the world) or nation-states?

While the Internet facilitates tendencies in many directions, as I have already indicated, its capacity for undermining national autonomy should not be underestimated. Two tendencies in this direction are becoming apparent. One is the significance of weakening control of information flow and the other is the effect of more intense competition.

It is precisely the unmediated character of Internet communication that conflicts with national sovereignty. It undermines the power of nation-states by making it difficult to control the flow of information to and from citizens as well as making it difficult to control a wide variety of unlawful behavior. This is democratic in the sense that citizens have freedom of access to information but it can, at the same time, undermine democratic processes. This was demonstrated by the Homolka case in Canada in 1993. A Canadian judge prohibited the Canadian press from temporarily publishing information on a trial in order to ensure that a second accused would get a fair trial. Information went out of Canada and then came back in through the Internet. Of course, information could have been taken out of the country "by foot" or by telephone, but the point is that nations do sometimes have legitimate reasons for wanting to control information flow in and out of their borders. In this case, the Canadian judge had a good reason for wanting to control the press. While he could stop publication of the story in the Canadian press and this would slow the stories flow out of Canada, the Internet facilitated a very speedy flow of information out of the country and back into the country. It raises the question whether a country can maintain some degree of control of activities inside its borders when it is part of a global communication system.

The global reach of the Internet is also threatening to nation-states because a global economy compels nations to harmonize their policies with other countries and, hence, to give up or compromise values which they might otherwise choose. This tendency can be observed in any number of domains including privacy, property rights, crime, and liability. As the world economy becomes more intensely intertwined, there seems to be a need for uniform laws from one place to the next. In other words, when people and information and business activity become increasingly global, moving rapidly from one country to another, it is disruptive for the rules to change dramatically from one place to the next.

There is much more that could be said about globalization. The arguments concerning the democratic character of the Internet are both fascinating and contentious. In the end, they give a mixed picture of the Internet as a democratic technology. It seems most accurate to say that the Internet has the potential to change, and already has changed, patterns of communication among individuals across the globe. Whether or not the changes enhance democracy and democratic values depends on an array of complex issues including how we understand democracy and which trends we emphasize. The Internet could greatly enhance the power of individuals to access information, form associations, and interact with one another or it could become a powerful force against democracy if it becomes a web of total surveillance or if it becomes a tool of manipulation by the already powerful.

The discussion of the Internet as a democratic technology has been useful for teasing out and getting a handle on the social changes that are taking place as a result of the Internet. Other patterns of change and other social values must now be discussed.

ACCESS AND THE DIGITAL DIVIDE

In Chapter 2, I introduced the Kantian idea that individuals should be treated as ends in themselves. Democracy is a form of government that recognizes individuals as ends in themselves insofar as it gives individuals a significant degree of freedom and control over their own lives. Moreover, it gives individuals a say (even if indirect) in decisions that lead to laws and public institutions that affect their lives. In the preceding section, I explored the connection between the Internet and democracy. In the remainder of this chapter, I explore two other ways to think about the connection between democracy and computer and information technology and the Internet: access and freedom of expression.

Unequal access poses a serious threat to democracy. Indeed, a good deal of concern has been expressed in recent years about computer and information technology and the Internet widening the gap between haves and have-nots within the United States and among countries of the world. The phrase "the digital divide" is now used to refer to this issue. The divide that receives the most attention is the gap between rich and poor, but there is also concern about differential access and use among racial groups, men and women, and the disabled. The issues here are complex and I will only scratch the surface. My aim is to get to the heart of the matter by explicating the moral arguments and making clear the values that are at stake.

The widening gap between haves and have-nots arises from inequities in access to computer and information technology in general, not just to the Internet. In other words, this issue is as much about access to machines and software and knowledge of and experience with the technology as it is about the Internet. Hence, my focus is not exclusively on the Internet; often I refer simply to access to the technology.

In 1999, the National Telecommunications and Information Administration (NTIA), an agency of the U.S. Department of Commerce, using data from the Census Bureau, reported the following:

> The good news is that Americans are more connected than ever before. Access to computers and the Internet has soared for people in all demographic groups and geographic locations. At the end of 1998, over 40 percent of American households owned computers, and one-quarter of all households had Internet access. . . . Accompanying this good news, however, is the persistence of the digital divide between the information rich (such as Whites, Asians/Pacific Islanders, those with higher incomes, those more educated, and dual-parent households) and the information poor (such as those who are younger, those with lower incomes and education levels, certain minorities, and those in rural areas or central cities). The 1998 data reveal significant disparities, including the following:
>
> Households with incomes of $75,000 and higher are more than twenty times more likely to have access to the Internet than those at the lowest income levels, and more than nine times as likely to have a computer at home.
>
> Whites are more likely to have access to the Internet from home than Blacks or Hispanics have from any location.
>
> Black and Hispanic households are approximately one-third as likely to have home Internet access as households of Asian/Pacific Islander descent, and roughly two-fifths as likely as White households.
>
> Regardless of income level, Americans living in rural areas are lagging behind in Internet access. Indeed, at the lowest income levels, those in urban areas are more than twice as likely to have Internet access than those earning the same income in rural areas. (www.ntia.doc.gov/ntiahome/fttn99/)

The starting place for understanding the access issue is recognizing that computer and information technology and the Internet are resources, powerful resources for achieving a variety of individual, group, organizational, community, and national/international purposes. Democratic societies are committed to the idea that every citizen is equal with respect to the state and the law; that is, democratic societies are committed to *political equality*. However, political equality cannot be entirely separated from social and economic equality. That is, social and economic *in*equality can lead to political *in*equality. Hence, democratic societies have to be concerned about social and economic inequality.

Unequal access to a powerful resource such as computer and information technology can skew social and economic opportunities. Unequal access to a powerful resource can give some individuals much more power than others, so much so that democracy is threatened. Because computer and information technology and the Internet are such powerful resources, democratic societies have to ask how these powerful resources are being distributed. How are they affecting individual opportunities?

It is important to keep in mind here that computer and information technology and the Internet are means, not ends. They are tools—resources as I said above—that assist individuals and organizations in acquiring goods and achieving goals. For this reason, the access issue is always about something else in addition to access, something that access leads to, something that can be achieved with, or can be better achieved with, access.

The most fundamental and important question is, then, why access to computer and information technology is so important? To what is this technology a means? If access is not equal or at least broad, exactly what kind of harm is done? That's the first and most important question.

If the answer to this question is that something very important is at stake— so important that we should not ignore a pattern of unequal distribution, then a second question arises. Should universal, or at least very broad, access be made an explicit social goal?[7] Should access be given the status, for example, of a right? Should it be a right for all American citizens? Should it be a right for all citizens of the world? Yet a third question arises if the answer to the second question is that universal or very broad access should be an explicit social goal. The third question is: What is the best way to achieve this goal? Should we use government regulation to ensure universal access? Or should we avoid government mandates and let the market determine access? Can the market achieve universal access or something close to it? Or do we need some sort of combination of government regulation and market competition?

It is helpful to keep these questions separate. It is one thing to say that access is important, another to say that a nation or the United Nations should do something about unequal access, and yet another to claim that the market or a government mandate is the best way to achieve broad access. The first question is the most important because it lays the ground for the other two. A good answer to the question why access is important provides the justification for being concerned about access and for doing something to ensure access. Hence, I focus primarily on this question.

Why is access so important? What is at stake? Let's begin with a cynical, negative argument. You might not think we should be worried about access to

---

[7] I say "at least very broad" access rather than universal because if some individuals choose not to have access, then universal access is not necessary. At least, it would take an additional argument to show that all individuals must have access regardless of their choice.

computer and information technology. You might think there is nothing new or special here. You may believe that the distribution of computer and information technology is like everything else. The wealthy and powerful are always the first to get access. Those who don't already have resources are always the last to get new resources. For example, the wealthy are usually the first to get access to new medical technology because they can pay for it; the poor may never get access or may get access later. Children in wealthy neighborhoods generally get access to the newest textbooks as well as the best teachers. Large, established companies are able to benefit from efficiencies of scale in production and this gives them a competitive edge. Industrialized countries use their wealth and knowledge in a variety of ways to protect and promote their interests around the world. There is nothing new or unique about computer and information technology or the Internet. They are simply the newest, powerful resource to come on the scene and get distributed.

Notice that this argument is largely descriptive. It points to how things often get distributed. If one is looking to describe what seems to be happening or to predict what distribution will look like in the next decades, the argument seems plausible, albeit oversimplified. The cynicism of the argument lies in the presumption that distribution in the future will be like the past and that things can't be otherwise.

From a moral perspective, there are two counters to this cynical argument. First, while it may accurately describe how resources often do get distributed, it says nothing about how resources *ought* to be distributed. The argument doesn't recognize the distinction made in Chapter 2 between descriptive and normative claims. In addressing ethical issues, we are concerned with how access should be distributed, not just with how it is being distributed. The second counter to the cynical argument incorporates the first but goes a step further. The second counter suggests that there is something special about computer and information technology and the Internet. While there may not be good, normative arguments for broad access to all new technologies, there is a special case to be made for broad, even universal access, to computer and information technology.

This second counter is interesting and especially promising for making the case for broad access. Why is computer and information technology different? Why should we worry about the pattern of its distribution more than other technologies?

The literature on the digital divide is quite diverse and a wide variety of goods are seen to be at stake. Education and job skills/opportunities are, perhaps, mentioned most often. That is, access to computer and information technology is seen as a means to equality of educational opportunity and a means to equalizing job opportunities.

Education

The argument here is that in a democratic society, education is the mechanism that is most powerful in promoting equal opportunity. We can't have equal opportunity with regard to jobs and positions of authority unless there is equality of opportunity in becoming qualified for those jobs and positions. If access to education is unequal, there is inequality of opportunity. Sometimes the argument is cast in terms of equal access to a decent education; other times, it is cast in terms of equal access to the same quality of education.

In this context, computer and information technology is seen in two different ways. First, it is seen as a powerful resource that affects and enhances the quality of education. Hence, it is important that poor schools as well as rich schools have access. Otherwise, the better schools will be able to provide an even better quality of education while poorer schools fall even further behind in the quality of education they provide.

Second, in a somewhat different way, computer and information technology are seen as the technology that can equalize education. Using the Internet in particular, the best teachers and the best materials can be delivered to thousands of schools across the country. The argument here is different in the sense that computer and information technology and the Internet are seen not just as any old resource that might be distributed unequally; rather they are seen as special insofar as they can be the means to equal educational opportunity. The technology makes it possible to distribute the same expertise and materials to all.

Both arguments are important though I want to draw attention to aspects of these arguments about which you should be cautious. To adequately evaluate these arguments, we would have to discuss education in much greater detail. We would have to explore what the goals of education are and how children learn. We would have to explore what deficiencies exist in schools where children do not seem to receive a high quality education. And then we would have to match our understanding of education with an exploration of the capacities of computer and information technology and the Internet. In other words, we have to understand what is needed in education and what computer and information technology can provide. The technology can serve some aspects of education, but not others. Our best hope for improving education and educational opportunity is by keeping an eye on what is *needed* rather than simply following what the technology can do.

Jobs and Job Skills

One thread of the argument about education takes us to jobs and job skills. If nothing else, those who are concerned about inequities in access to computers and information technology in education are concerned about the job opportunities of the future. It appears likely that the jobs of the future will either be in computer and information industries or will make use of computer and information technology in other fields. The fear is, then, that if computer and information technology is unequally distributed among educational institutions, the pattern of unequal distribution is likely to result in an unequal pattern of employment in the future. Students who are exposed to the technology at school (and at home) become comfortable with it, understand it, and know how to use it will be much better prepared for the jobs of the future. Those who are not exposed, don't learn how to use it, and don't become comfortable with it will be much less prepared.

It is interesting to note here that in some sense the technology is moving in the other direction. Computer and information technology continues to become more and more user friendly so that individuals need less and less skill to use it. It is possible that many of the jobs of the future will not require a very sophisticated understanding of the technology. This is a trend to watch, not an argument for setting aside concern about the distribution of skills and experience with computer and information technology.

The Capacity to Send/Receive Information and Form Associations

In addition to education and job skills, the discussion of the Internet in the previous section points to at least two other goods at stake. The Internet gives individuals the capacity to receive and send information and it gives individuals the capacity to form associations with others (independent of geographic location). These capacities are particularly important for political equality because political decisions are influenced by information flow between government and citizens. Those who are able to send information can influence both their political representatives and other citizens; those who receive information know more about the issues and know more about their representatives. Moreover, political decisions are often shaped by interest groups and insofar as the Internet facilitates group formation, those who have access are in a much better position to combine forces and have an influence.

Remember also that the Internet can give power to those who already have power as well as to those who had little power in the past. If access goes primarily to those who already have power or if they get access first, then the interests of the already powerful are more likely to be served.

The same goes for the argument focused on association. If the wealthy and powerful have access first, then they will have a greater ability to form associations around their interests and further them. The pattern of interactions on the Internet will be skewed in this direction.

The Comprehensive Argument

Each of the arguments just mentioned is important. Together they suggest an overarching argument, an argument that returns us to the idea that there is something special about computer and information technology: *Computer and information technology seems to be special because of its comprehensive usefulness.* This is related to its malleability but the point here is that the technology affects so many different aspects of live. It is used in so many different contexts, to achieve so many different ends. The comprehensiveness of its use provides an argument for its broad distribution. Unlike any other technology that was developed in the twentieth century, computer and information technology is transforming so many domains of life that its distribution will affect the distribution of opportunity and power in the future. Hence, unlike any other technology, broad or even universal access to computer and information technology and the Internet is essential for democracy.

Other Inequities: Gender, Race, the Disabled

If we think of the digital divide only as an issue affecting the gap between haves and have-nots, we may miss an important part of the problem. There are some signs that the digital divide is not merely an economic divide. There are some signs that gender and race are at work here independent of economic differences. The NTIA report cited earlier suggests some racial differences in access that may or may not be economic. As well, there are some studies that suggest that women and men use the Internet in different ways and to different extents. Yet another inequity in access has to do with the disabled. Here there are two concerns. On the upside, computer and information technology hold great promise for enabling the disabled. Again malleability is relevant here; it is the malleability of the technology that gives it this promise. On the other hand, concern arises because the potential of the technology to help the disabled may not be pursued to the extent that it could be (Weil, 2000).

Evidence of the role of gender in attitudes toward, and use of, computer and information technology (especially the Internet) has been growing in the past decade (Cooper et al., 1990; Huff et al., 1992; Winter and Huff, 1996). Yet from an ethical perspective, the issue is difficult to frame because it does not appear to be a simple case of discrimination. Women and minorities, it appears, choose not to (1) use computers, (2) major in computing in college, (3) take jobs in computing, or (4) leave the field despite what sometimes seem to be sincere attempts to bring them in and keep them. Thus, if there is discrimination or injustice, it is subtle rather than blatant.

The discrimination may have something to do with the design of the technology, the design of the workplace, the public depiction of computing (Turner, 1998), and many other factors that are difficult to control and change. Yet the importance of eliminating gender and racial imbalance seems crucial for a democratic world in which computer and information technology are so integral.

In summary, the arguments for recognizing the digital divide as a serious social problem—a threat to democracy, seem compelling. I have only sketched the arguments here. I leave it to you to further explore and evaluate these arguments. While inequities in education, job opportunities, the capacity to send and receive information, and the capacity to form associations existed prior to the development of computer and information technology, differential access may broaden those inequities. On the other hand, computer and information technology and the Internet could be part of the solution. They could even be used to counteract prior inequities. I did not address the strategy question but there seems reason to be concerned that if little is done to ensure broad access, the cynical argument may accurately predict what will happen.

FREE EXPRESSION

Though there are many democratic values affected by the Internet, one that has received a good deal of public attention in the United States is freedom of speech. Free speech is a fundamental precept of American democracy and many fear that any control of speech (expression) on the Internet will not only make the Internet undemocratic but will interfere with democracy offline. The event that sparked this debate in the United States was the successful attempt of several senators to pass the Communications Decency Act (CDA) in the U.S. Congress. The CDA would have limited certain kinds of speech on the Internet; that is, it would have made it a crime to use telecommunications devices and interactive computer services to disseminate "indecent or patently offensive sexually explicit material" to children under 18 years of age. The U.S. Supreme Court later ruled that the Act was unconstitutional, but its initial passage in the U.S. Congress made clear the very real potential for a dampening of free expression on the Internet. [This event further illustrates the point that the Internet will not of its own accord (naturally) lead to democracy.]

Since the CDA was targeted at the protection of children, the debate is far from simple. It brings the value of free speech in tension with the protection of children and it does so because of the Internet's accessibility. Freedom of speech goes to the heart of the Internet-democracy connection because freedom of speech is (in American democracy, at least) essential for government accountability and citizenship. When government has the power to censor information, it has the power to shield its own activities from public scrutiny. Instead of being accountable, the government then has the power to manipulate the public. Moreover, in order for citizens to vote intelligently for their own best interests and the interests of the country, it is essential that information is readily available and that citizens have opportunities to discuss issues and form opinions. This can only happen when freedom of speech is protected. In other words, freedom of speech is essential for the protection of democratic accountability and democratic citizenship.

In a utilitarian framework, democracy is justified on grounds that it is much more likely to lead to social progress and individual development. When individuals are free to develop their own ideas, to vigorously debate, and to choose how to live their lives, they will develop their active capacities and social progress will take place. Each individual becomes in effect an experiment in living. Individuals will try different things and out of these multiple experiments, the best ways of living will emerge. John Stuart Mill makes an argument of this kind as well as an argument to the effect that true ideas can only be understood in an environment in which ideas are freely and forcefully debated. When suppression and censorship take place, false ideas can be kept alive. Moreover, true ideas may be held as "dead dogma"; that is, individuals affirm true ideas but have no idea why they are true. In an open society, false ideas are shown to be false, and true ideas are shown to be true.

So, there are strong and compelling arguments for freedom of speech on the Internet. On the other hand, as mentioned before, the issue is not simple. It is complicated because of the ease of access that children can have. Adult bookstores on geographic streets can control access by observing who is walking in the door. On the Internet, one's age is difficult to detect (and easy to lie about). Those who believe in free speech often acknowledge the importance of restricting children's access. The problem in the case of the Internet is that it is difficult to restrict access by children without at the same time restricting access by adults.

Another compounding factor for freedom of speech on the Internet is the Internet's global scope. National policies limiting access to certain kinds of expression are difficult to enforce. Once individuals in one country get access to the Internet, it is difficult to stop them from accessing information made available in other countries.

The threat to privacy on the Internet was discussed in Chapter 5; nevertheless, it is important to mention it again in relation to free speech. Most of the attention given to free speech focuses on the threat of censorship. Yet freedom of expression can be significantly dampened as a result of surveillance. Individuals do not feel free to express themselves when they know that everything they are saying is being recorded. As mentioned before, technologist are trying to develop new tools to protect personal privacy, but at the same time, law enforcement and commercial interests make powerful claims for monitoring traffic patterns as well as the content of Internet communication and browsing. The surveillance capabilities of the Internet are indirectly in conflict with free speech.

OVERARCHING AND FUTURE ISSUES

Another approach to the Internet-democracy connection is to ask whether the Internet is being developed through democratic processes. While I will not have time to address this issue, it is important to watch the development of Internet governance closely and ask the hard questions: How should the Internet be governed? How should the autonomy of nations (states or local communities) be recognized in policy decisions regarding the Internet? How can we avoid economic interests undermining the Internet's potential for serving public interests? How should freedom of expression be protected? How should privacy on the Internet be protected?

The issues discussed in this chapter are the broadest and the most unwieldy. On the one hand, the discussion has provided a good deal of food for thought; on the other hand, there seems to be a good deal of uncertainty about how computer and information technology and the Internet will, in fact, change the shape of the world. Nevertheless, there are some important lessons to be learned from this chapter, lessons to keep in mind as you try to make sense of the social changes taking place in the twenty-first century. Perhaps the most important is to remember that technology *is* value-laden. It is created and shaped by human interests and social values, and when it is used, it affects social relations and social values. In this chapter, I have used democracy as the lens through which to view social changes taking place as a result of the Internet. Democracy is an important human value that should continue to be used in evaluating social change, though there are other values that also might be used such as community, identity, and autonomy. Increasing use of the Internet affects each of these and it is worth considering just *how* they are being affected.

What are the most important areas of change to keep an eye on in the coming decades? Three areas to watch are jurisdiction, systems of trust, and insularity.

Jurisdiction

The importance of jurisdiction should now be clear. Since the Internet makes geographic location less relevant, issues of jurisdiction have already arisen and are likely to continue to arise. Whose laws apply to what activity and who has the authority to enforce the laws? Within the United States the most prominent jurisdictional issues have been those surrounding where (in which state if any) taxes should be paid on Internet commerce and those surrounding local statutes on obscenity. Does one violate the obscenity laws of Memphis, Tennessee, when one sits in front of a computer screen in Memphis and accesses material that resides on a server in California when the material violates Memphis law but does not violate the local law in California?

The international jurisdiction issues are equally challenging and apply to many activities including property rights, data privacy standards, criminal jurisdiction, and so on. Which country has jurisdiction? Under what circumstances are a country's laws violated? Resolutions to these issues may change the fundamental character of the world by changing the nature of the units that constitute the world. Many believe, for example, that nation states, at least as we now know them, cannot survive the existence of an intensely intertwined global communication system and economy. It is difficult to maintain national borders when it is so easy to cross them. So, jurisdictional borders are likely to change and the changes are likely to have very powerful implications for the character of nation states and/or for the creation of new units of political, economic, and social power.

Systems of Trust

The role of trust in Internet communication was discussed in Chapter 4. As more and more activity takes place on the Internet, individuals are likely to become more and more dependent on Internet institutions. Whether it be institutions for delivering news or performing service transactions such as consuming or banking or just chatting with others, individuals will want and need some guarantees. They will want some level of trust in those with whom they are interacting. Trust can be achieved by social, political, and legal arrangements that assure reliability, confidentiality, and security. Hence, we are likely to witness the creation of a variety of systems of trust and accountability. This will no doubt consist of laws and law enforcement mechanisms, but it will also include other technical and social systems for authenticating and insuring individuals and institutions in various ways. One way to think about this is to identify the systems of trust that we currently rely on and then to imagine the creation of comparable systems on the Internet. For example, we currently rely on insurance companies; private institutions like the Better Business Bureau and credit bureaus; a variety of public institutions that license professionals such as doctors, lawyers, engineers, and architects and accredit educational institutions. We rely on visual identifiers for personal identity, and we rely on courts when these other institutions of trust fail. Watching the development of comparable systems on the Internet will be important to understanding the kind of world that is being created.

Insularity

Most Internet observers are aware of and focused on the diversity of information, products, and choices available on the Internet. Yet, there is an interesting trend in the other direction, a trend that is largely ignored. Computer and information technology and the Internet also facilitate what might be called, for lack of a better term, individual insulation. There are a variety of types of insulation. In Chapter 4 we saw how individuals can be insulated from the effects of their behavior on others. Another powerful form of insulation arises from the customization of services made possible by computer and information technology and the Internet.

Perhaps the best illustrations of this have to do with marketing information and news delivery. Before the Internet and the customization of marketing, advertisers placed adds in newspapers, magazines, and on television and hoped that among all the readers and viewers, some would be interested in what was advertised. Similarly, newspapers reporting news knew that they had a diverse audience and reported a variety of news pieces knowing that various topics would be of more and less interest to different readers. In both cases, readers and viewers were exposed to a variety of advertisements and news stories that they would not have asked for and in which they were not particularly interested.

Enter computer and information technology and especially the Internet. Advertising and news can be targeted to those who are most interested and most likely to respond. One can have news customized so that you only get stories you know are of interest to you and you can get the news with the bias you want. From a market perspective, this is much more efficient.

The problem is that this means that individuals are not exposed to anything outside their already-formed scope of interest. Your choice of news and news sources is likely to feed the interests, attitudes, and biases you already have. Marketers will watch your buying patterns or your reading patterns and offer you more of what you apparently want. The problem is that individuals are facilitated in becoming more and more what they already are. Individuals may become more and more insulated from what is different and challenging. Moreover, individuals may come to have less and less in common with a diversity of individuals and spend more and more time with individuals like themselves; they may not learn about others who are different from themselves.

Shared information seems to be important for binding individuals together. For example, citizens of a community share an experience and an understanding when they read the same local newspaper. The Internet and computer and information technology seem to push in the other direction, against what binds people together. It seems to insulate (or at least make it easy for individuals to become insulated) from ideas, information, and people who are different from themselves.

The point here is not to denigrate the capacity of the Internet for customizing services. The Internet's potential for this is enormous. Moreover, as pointed out earlier in this chapter, the Internet can facilitate exposure to a diversity of sources of information. The point is only that computer and information technology and the Internet can facilitate both, exposure and insulation. We should keep an eye on tendencies in both directions.

CONCLUSION

Computer and information technology and especially the Internet offer great riches for the future, but they also pose threats. I end with a caution that this technology, like all technologies, will not miraculously and of its own accord lead to riches and avoid danger. Technology needs human vigilance in shaping and steering it. The idea of this book is to bring some light to the darkness into which our boat is headed.

STUDY QUESTIONS

1. How does a Kantian conception of the value of human beings lead to a focus on autonomy and access?

2. Identify and explain at least three broad issues about technology and social change that often underlie discussions of the social implications of computer and information technology.

3. Give examples of how computer and information technology seems to be causing a revolution. Give examples of how computer and information technology seems to reinforce the status quo.

4. Give examples of values embedded in technology. Give examples of values embedded in particular applications of computer software.

5. Describe the three arguments that support the claim that the Internet is a democratic technology.

6. Explain why the author is reluctant to accept these arguments.

7. Why is access to the Internet important for democracy?

8. Why do computers affect the relationship between haves and have-nots? Explain.

9. What does the author see as important broad issues to monitor in the evolving development of the Internet?

10. What do you think will be the important ethical issues in the future of the Internet?

11. Why aren't computer systems likely to be developed for the have-nots unless some deliberate social efforts are made?

12. Explain how computer systems may be value-laden versus their being biased?

SUGGESTED FURTHER READINGS

CAMP, TRACEY, "The Incredible Shrinking Pipeline," *Communications of the ACM*, vol. 40, no. 10 (1997), pp. 103–110. Available: www.talus.Mines.EDU/fs—home/tcamp/cacm/paper.html

DUTTON, WILLIAM H., *Society On the Line: Information Politics in the Digital Age* (Oxford, England: Oxford University Press, 1999).

HAGUE, BARRY N., and BRIAN D. LOADER, eds., *Digital Democracy: Discourse and Decision Making in the Information Age* (London: Routledge, 1999).

KAHIN, BRIAN, and CHARLES NESSON, eds., *Borders in Cyberspace: Information Policy and the Global Information Infrastructure Project* (Cambridge, MA: MIT Press, 1997).

SCHILLER, HERBERT I., *Information Inequality* (New York: Routledge, 1996).

WALTON, ANTHONY, "Technology Versus African-Americans," *The Atlantic Monthly* (January 1999), pp. 14–18.

References

Abramson, Jeffrey B., F. Christopher Arterton, Gary R. Orren, *The Electronic Commonwealth: The Impact of New Media Technology on Democratic Politics* (New York: Basic Books, 1988).

"Against Software Patents," League for Programming Freedom (October 24, 1990) (LPF, 1 Kendall Square #143, P.O. Box 9171, Cambridge, MA 02139).

Alpern, Kenneth, "Moral Responsibility for Engineers," *Business & Professional Ethics*, vol. 2, no. 2 (1983), pp. 39–56.

Anderson, Robert M., Robert Perrucci, Dan E. Schendel, and Leon E. Trachtman, *Divided Loyalties: Whistle-Blowing at BART* (West Lafayette, IN: Purdue University, 1980).

Anthes, G. H., "Better Equipped Yet Shortchanged," in *Computers in Society*. 8th ed., ed. Kathryn Schellenberg (Guilford, CT: Dishkin/McGraw-Hill, 2000).

Apple v. Franklin 714 F.2d 1240 (3rd Cir 1983).

Arblaster, Anthony, *Democracy* (Minneapolis: University of Minnesota Press, 1987).

Baron, Marcia, *The Moral Status of Loyalty* (Dubuque, IA: Kendall/Hunt, 1984).

Bayles, Michael, *Professional Ethics* (Belmont, CA: Wadsworth, 1981).

Becker, Lawrence C., and Charlotte B. Becker, *Encyclopedia of Ethics,* Vol. 1 and 2 (New York: Garland, 1992).

Bentham, Jeremy, "Panopticon, 1787," in *Jeremy Bentham: The Panopticon Writings*, ed. Miran Bozovic (London: Verso, 1995).

Bozovic, Miran, *Jeremy Bentham: The Panopticon Writings* (London: Verso, 1995).

Brey, Philip, "The Ethics of Representation and Action in Virtual Reality," *Ethics and Information Technology*, vol. 1, no. 1 (1999), pp. 5–14.

Browning, Daniel, "Setting the Record Straight on Patents," ACM Forum *Communications of the ACM*, vol. 36 (1993), pp. 17–19.

Burk, Dan L., "Transborder Intellectual Property Issues on the Electronic Frontier," *Stanford Law & Policy Review*, vol. 6, no. 1 (1994), pp. 9–16.

Bynum, Terrell Ward, and James H. Moor, *The Digital Phoenix: How Computers are Changing Philosophy* (Oxford, England: Blackwell Publishers, 1998).

Cooper, Joel, Joan Hall, and Charles Huff, "Situational Stress as a Consequence of Sex-Stereotyped Software," *Personality and Social Psychology Bulletin*, vol. 16, no. 3 (1990), pp. 419–429.

Dahl, Robert, *Democracy and Its Critics* (New Haven, CT: Yale University Press, 1989).

Davis, Michael, "Thinking Like an Engineer: The Place of a Code of Ethics in the Practice of a Profession," *Philosophy and Public Affairs*, vol. 20, no. 2 (1992), pp. 150–167.

Davis, Randall, Pamela Samuelson, Mitchell Kapor, and Jerome Reichman, "A New View of Intellectual Property and Software," *Communications of the ACM*, vol. 39, no. 3 (1996), pp. 21–30.

De George, Richard, "Computers, Ethics, and Business," *Philosophic Exchange* (1997–1998), pp. 45–55.

de Jager, Peter, "Y2K: So Many Bugs . . . So Little Time," *Scientific American* (January 1999), pp. 88–93.

Diamond v. Diehr, 101 S. Ct. 1048 (1981).

Edwards, Paul, ed., *The Encyclopedia of Philosophy* (New York, Macmillan Publishing, 1967).

Ess, Charles, "The Political Computer: Democracy, CMC, and Habermas," in *Philosophical Perspectives on Computer-Mediated Communication,* ed. Charles Ess (Albany, NY: State University of New York Press, 1996).

Forester, Tom, and Perry Morrison, *Computer Ethics: Cautionary Tales and Ethical Dilemmas in Computing* (Cambridge, MA: MIT Press, 1990).

Franklin Computer Corp. v. Apple Computer, Inc., No. 83–704. Supreme Court of the United States, 464 U.S. 1033; 104 S. Ct. 690; U.S. (LEXIS 477) (1984); 79 L. Ed. 2d 158 (January 4, 1984).

Fried, Charles, "Privacy," *Yale Law Journal*, vol. 77 (1968), p. 477.

Fried, Charles, *Right and Wrong* (Cambridge, MA: Harvard University Press, 1978).

Gemignani, Michael C., "Legal Protection for Computer Software: The View from '79," *Journal of Computers, Technology, and Law*, vol. 7 (1980), p. 272.

Goldman, Alan, *The Moral Foundations of Professional Ethics* (Totowa, NJ: Rowan and Littlefield, 1980).

Huff, Charles, and Joel Cooper, "Sex Bias in Educational Software: The Effect of Designers' Stereotypes on the Software They Design," *Journal of Applied Social Psychology*, vol. 17 (1987), pp. 519–532.

Huff, Charles W., John H. Fleming, and Joel Cooper, "The Social Basis of Gender Differences in Human Computer Interaction," in *In Search of Gender-free Paradigms for Computer Science Education*, ed. C.D. Martin (Eugence, OR: ISTE Research Monograph, 1992), pp. 19–32.

Johnson, Deborah G., "Do Engineers Have Social Responsibilities?" *Journal of Applied Philosophy*, vol. 9, no. 1 (1992), pp. 21–34.

Johnson, Deborah G., "Is the Global Information Infrastructure a Democratic Technology?" *Computers & Society*, vol. 27, no. 3 (1997), pp. 20–26.

Johnson, Deborah G., and Helen Nissenbaum, eds., *Computers, Ethics and Social Values* (Upper Saddle River, NJ: Prentice-Hall, 1995).

Kane, Michelle J., "Internet Service Provider Liability: *Blumenthal v. Drudge*," *Berkeley Technology Law Journal*, vol. 14 (1999), p. 483

Kennard, William E., "Internet: The American Experience." An Address to the Conference on "Internet & Telecommunications: The Stakes" (Paris, January 28, 2000).

Layton, Edwin, *The Revolt of the Engineers: Social Responsibility and the American Engineering Profession* (Baltimore: John Hopkins University Press, 1971, 1986).

Lessig, Lawrence, *Code and Other Laws of Cyberspace* (New York: Basic Books, 2000).

Maner, Walter, "Unique Ethical Problems in Information Technology," *Science and Engineering Ethics*, vol. 2, no. 2 (1996), pp. 137–154.

Marx, Gary, "Privacy and Technology," *Whole Earth Review* (winter 1991), pp. 91–95.

Moor, James H., "Are There Decisions Computers Should Never Make?" *Nature and System*, vol. 1 (1979), pp. 217–229.

Moor, James H., "What Is Computer Ethics?" *Metaphilosophy*, vol. 16, no. 4 (October 1985), pp. 266–275.

Mowshowitz, Abbe, *The Conquest of Will Information Processing in Human Affairs*. (Redding, MA: Addison-Wesley, 1976).

Nissenbaum, Helen, "Computing and Accountability," *Communications of the ACM*, vol. 37, no. 1 (1994), pp. 73–80.

Nissenbaum, Helen, "Computing and Accountability," in *Computers, Ethics, and Social Values*, eds. Deborah G. Johnson and Helen Nissenbaum (Upper Saddle River, NJ: Prentice-Hall, 1995).

Nissenbaum, Helen, "Should I Copy My Neighbor's Software?" in *Computers, Ethics and Social Values*, eds. Deborah G. Johnson and Helen Nissenbaum (Upper Saddle River, NJ: Prentice Hall, 1995).

Nissenbaum, Helen and Lucas Introna, "Notes on the Politics of Search Engines." Presented at Computer Ethics, Philosophical Enquiry, London School of Economics (London, December 15, 1998).

Nozick, Robert, *Anarchy, State, and Utopia* (New York: Basic Books, 1974).

NUA Internet Surveys, Nua. Available: www.nua.ie/surveys/how_any_online/index.html

O.P. Solutions, Inc. v. Intellectula Property Network, Ltd., 1999 U.S. Dist. LEXIS 979.

Orwell, George, *1984* (New York: Harcourt, Brace & World, 1949).

Parnas, David, "Professional Responsibility to Blow the Whistle on SDI," *Abacus*, vol. 4, no. 2 (1987), pp. 46–52.

Personal Privacy in an Information Society, Privacy Protection Study Commission (Washington, DC: U.S. Government Printing Office, 1977).

Prince, Jim, "Negligence: Liability for Defective Software," *Oklahoma Law Review*, vol. 33 (1980), pp. 848–855.

Rachels, James, "Why Privacy Is Important," *Philosophy and Public Affairs*, vol. 4 (summer, 1975), pp. 323–333.

Rawls, John, *A Theory of Justice* (Cambridge, MA: Harvard University Press, 1971).

Regan, Priscilla M., *Legislating Privacy, Technology, Social Values, and Public Policy* (Chapel Hill, NC: University of North Carolina Press, 1995).

Reiman, Jeffrey H., "Driving to the Panopticon: A Philosophical Exploration of the Risks to Privacy Posed by the Highway Technology of the Future," *Computer and High Technology Law Journal*, vol. 11 (1995), pp. 27–44.

Rosenberg, Richard.

Samuelson, Pamela, "Benson Revisited: The Case Against Patent Protection for Algorithms and Other Computer Program-Related Inventions," *Emory Law Journal*, vol. 39 (1990), pp. 1025–1154.

Shattuck, John, "Computer Matching Is a Serious Threat to Individual Rights," *Communications of the ACM*, vol. 27, no. 6 (1984), pp. 538–541.

Scolve, Richard, *Democracy and Technology* (New York: The Guilford Press, 1995).

Spafford, Eugene H., "Are Computer Hacker Break-Ins Ethical?" *The Journal of Systems and Software*, vol. 17, no. 1 (1992), pp. 41–47.

Stallman, Richard, "Why Software Should Be Free," in *Computers, Ethics, and Social Values*, eds. Deborah G. Johnson and Helen Nissenbaum (Englewood Cliffs, NJ: Prentice-Hall, 1995), pp. 190–199.

Turner, Eva, "Advertising Ethics: The Role of Women and Minorities in Advertising Computing," *AISB Quarterly*, vol. 100 (1998) pp. 37–52.

U.S. Congress, Office of Technology Assessment, *Finding a Balance: Computer Software, Intellectual Property, and the Challenge of Technological Change*, OTA-TCT-527 (Washington, DC: U.S. Government Printing Office, May 1992).

U.S. Congress, Office of Technology Assessment, *Federal Government Information Technology: Electronic Record Systems and Individual Privacy*, OTA-CIT-296 (Washington, DC: U.S. Government Printing Office, May 1986).

van den Hoven, M.J., "Towards Ethical Principles for Designing Political-Administrative Information Systems," *Informatization and the Public Sector*, vol. 3 (1994), pp. 353–373.

Wall Street Journal, "Popular Software for Computer Cursors Logs: Web Visits, Raising Privacy Issues" (November 30, 1999).

Wallace, Kathleen A., "Anonymity," *Ethics and Information Technology*, vol. 1, no. 1 (1999), pp. 21–31.

Weil, N., "Computers Open the Doors for Disabled," in *Computers in Society*. 8th ed., ed. Kathryn Schellenberg (Guilford, CT: Dushkin/McGraw-Hill, 2000).

Weizenbaum, Joseph, *Computer Power and Human Reason: From Judgment to Calculation* (San Francisco: W.H. Freeman, 1976).

Whelan Assocs., Inc. v. Jaslow Dental Laboratory, Inc., 609 F. Supp. 1307 (E.D.Pa. 1985), aff'd, 797 F.2n 1222 (3d Cir. 1986), cert. denied, 479 U.S. 1031 (1987).

Winner, Langdon, *The Whale and the Reactor: A Search for Limits in an Age of High Technology* (Chicago: University of Chicago Press, 1986).

Winter, Debra, and Chuck Huff, "Adapting the Internet: Comments from a Women-Only Electronic Forum," *The American Sociologist* (winter 1996), pp. 30–54.

Zamyatin, Y., *We* (Harmonsworth, England: Penguin Books, 1972). Originally published in Russia, 1920.

INDEX